SLURRED SAGA

An Erotic Sea Story About Naval Aviation Flight School, Marine Helicopter Combat in Vietnam and Sexual Revolution in the Sixties

Robert K. Pincer

Copyright © 2016 by Robert K. Pincer.

All rights reserved. No part of this book may be reproduced or transmitted in any form or by any means, electronic or mechanical, including photocopying, recording, or by any information storage and retrieval system, without permission in writing from the copyright owner.

This is a work of fiction. Names, characters, places and incidents either are the product of the author's imagination or are used fictitiously, and any resemblance to any actual persons, living or dead, events, or locales is entirely coincidental.

CONTENTS

Prologue vii
Foreword—June 1963 ix

Okie Joe's 1
The First Love Story 7
The End Of Forever 31
Temporary Insanity 37
Pensacola Found 87
Sudden Shift 135
The Weekender 145
Third Time's A Charm 171
Helicopter Transition 187
Embarkation 199
Transpac 205
Debarkation 211
Qui Nhon 219
Rest And Recuperation 225
Night Medevac 235
Paladin 243
The Princeton Again 249
Routine Mission 255
Happy Hour 265
Extension To Duty 271

Epilogue 275

Many, many thanks to the several "beta" readers and editors and workshop classmates who contributed to this work. Special gratitude is due my favorite Bible Belt English professors whose advice and friendship are exceptional and irreplaceable. Finally, to my loyal coheart for her remarkable endurance and tolerance during this seemingly endless task.

Dedicated to my cherished wife, who always believed in, trusted and supported me, no matter what. God bless your soul. Rest in peace, my love.

Prologue

Do you know the difference between a *sea story* and a *fairy tale?* ... No?

Well, a fairy tale starts out, "Once upon a time," and a sea story starts out, "This is no shit!" A fairy tale is also politically correct fiction told in a language suitable for children. A sea story is for adults and is usually an actual event, the telling of which may be colorfully enhanced with coarse language and erotic visions, including nudity and sex, and it can go downhill from there. Otherwise, the two are pretty much the same.

What you are about to read may not have any similarity to usual perceptions of truth or reality, but as I recall, everything revealed in this story actually happened, although it may have happened to different people than are portrayed here—or at different times than are depicted here. However, if I've learned anything at all, it is that personal "truth" and particularly theological "Truth," may be as unique as the individual. Reality it seems, like beauty, can be viewed as if seen through a prism, presenting as many colors as exist in the life experiences of every individual participant.

I started writing in school, and it was one of the few tasks I enjoyed and at which I was any good. I won a prize in an essay contest in high school, and English was the only course in college, besides ROTC, in which I managed to get any above-average grades. I tried to write fiction in the past, but if I didn't write every day, I forgot where I was and had to start all over. So while this story is not intended to be autobiographical, nonfiction or historically accurate, it is derived from and built upon the skeleton of my life experiences. I have, of course, changed the names of all the living characters, including my own.

Ultimately, this is just my story, the way I remember it and the way I've chosen to tell it, and the *brain committee approves.*

Foreword—June 1963

"Jesus, this place smells worse than a cow barn," Dutch lamented. His dark, close-set eyes were barely open as they searched in the dim light to identify my body among the others.

I didn't bother answering with more than a grunt. I was disgusted not only with the place and the situation but with myself. How many times do I have to do something stupid and wind up in trouble? Again. *Some graduation celebration this turned out to be.* Some members of my brain committee were disgruntled.

The drunk tank in the Juarez jail is dark gray, with deeper shadows behind the inanimate bodies sprawled on the concrete floor. The Monday morning light came into the cell only through a small barred window in the steel door that led directly to the outdoor asphalt courtyard. The cell is formed with concrete in a rectangular shape about 40 feet long and 20 feet wide. A single water hydrant, on the opposite end from the door, leaks constantly and runs into an open hole about ten feet away in the middle of the floor, which also serves as a toilet. Mixed odors of urine, sweat, booze, vomit and dysentery hang heavily in the air. The floors and lower half of the concrete walls are covered with years of grime from the fluids of hundreds of unintentional visitors, such as ourselves. The water is foul tasting and smells as if it is somehow tainted by the disgusting aroma.

Some of the prisoners are still drunk from the night before, but most were just hungover. Many of them are American gringos, but a few seem to be locals.

Stories about Mexican jails are abundant. I try to remember a song we used to sing about them, but my head hurts too much to think. Maybe it was about Tijuana? I was dizzy, nauseated and miserable.

The brain committee pondered, *Would the locals get out before we would, or would their justice system be tougher on them? Would this be one of those trips you hear about where you would never get out and you just rot in jail until everyone forgets you exist?* The committee was disgusted with each other and churned the rotten air with meaningless arguments.

Dutch went back to sleep, oblivious to the situation and the smelly kettle of drunken fools. He didn't have a job. He didn't have a wife anymore and had not yet found a steady girlfriend since the divorce. I wondered if he even cared when we would get out or if we would get out. His personality had gone flat, and his ambition disappeared. He was more alive during this weekend celebration than he'd been since he left to go try out for the 49ers. Reflecting on past successes, getting drunk and lamenting failures seemed to be the only way he could relate to his continued existence. At this point in our lives, we both seemed to be near the bottom of a deep pit of depression.

How did we get into this awful situation? Could it get any worse? The brain committee was confused, and the ensuing foggy and irrational discussion included a lot of finger-pointing among the members.

Okie Joe's

We were at the bar on Friday for happy hour, where I worked. I started as the bouncer a couple of years earlier and then bartended for a while until the owners decided to semiretire and promoted me to night manager.

Ruthie, a worn but still very attractive former beauty of about 45 years, moved from day-bartender to night-bartender when I was promoted, and we hired a new girl for the day shift. I usually let Ruthie go home early if there weren't many customers, and I would tend the bar myself later in the evening, but occasionally she would offer to stay and play. So at nearly 20 years my senior, she became the oldest woman I'd been with at the time. It was a busy happy hour early on a Friday evening, and not only was Ruthie there but one of the owners was working the bar as well.

It was a sleazy college bar and pretty much known around the campus as the local "toilet." We tried to keep it freshly painted and clean, but since we didn't get exactly what you would call the tea-sipping, upper-class drinkers, it was mostly a losing battle. Almost every weekend something would get broken in a fight, and the writing on the restroom walls would reappear over the new paint. The Albuquerque Police knew Okie Joe's and me very well, from those bar-bouncing days.

After the owners promoted me to manager, they didn't mind if I shot bumper pool with the customers. In fact, they liked it, as long as I took care of the package store at the same time, because it also increased business. I was an okay singles player, and many of the local hustlers would come in to challenge me and spend their bucks on the table and at the bar. We never hired a bouncer replacement, so checking the age of customers and bouncing drunks, when they got too rowdy, remained an additional duty. A funny thing though, the pay continued at $1.25 per hour. I was in the package store when Dutch came in.

"Hey, Pisser, let's shoot some pool."

Dutch and I played bumper pool against each other about even, but as partners we were nearly unbeatable on our home table at Okie Joe's. There were other players who were better at singles, and they could beat me most of the time, and Dutch on rare occasions, but they and their lesser partner usually could not beat Dutch and me when we were together as partners. Bumper pool, booze and women were the steady curriculum for my last year in college, although the latter didn't come into play until the second semester. The booze seemed to help me remember the good times and forget the bad times. Bumper pool was our entertainment and usually a source of a little extra income, and we both felt like we had some catching up to do in the female department.

"Not now, Dutch, I gotta catch up on the inventory but if a team comes in I'll join you for some doubles. Okay?"

"Sure great," he nodded. I'll just practice a little until someone shows up. Ruthie, you gorgeous creature, gimme a beer and some quarters for the table please," he called out as he passed by the bar on the way to the table.

"One Coors draft on the bar when I saw you comin', handsome." She flashed him a huge smile and a little jiggle of her best assets showing along the lines of her low-cut blouse.

By the spring of 1963, Dutch had already dropped out of school, tried out for the San Francisco 49ers—didn't make it—returned to Albuquerque and was divorced. We had the divorce in common and more.

"You know I went to college, mostly to play football, so dropping out didn't mean much, but not making it in the pros and losing the marriage are eating me up," Dutch confessed.

He was a typical fullback type, a little under six feet tall and about 240 pounds. He wasn't fast, but he was quick and strong. All his achievements before, as a Golden Gloves Heavyweight Champion and as an All-American fullback in junior college, led him to believe he could be successful at whatever he wanted.

Dutch was as strong and tough in the boxing ring as he was on the football field, but the experience had left him a little punchy. If he got hit, it was an automatic reaction to hit back. Suddenly, a successful career in sports was not in the cards for him, and he had not planned for any other future.

I literally ran into Dutch during tackling drills at football practice in the spring of 1960. It was not a pleasant experience. Hitting him was like running into a raging bull. We were both "new guy" junior college transfers trying to make the team, and we were both married at the time we were recruited. Dutch was from New Mexico but played JC ball at Ft. Lewis Junior College in Durango, Colorado. It was natural for us to run around together, but we really didn't get to know each other well until we got into a fight. Thank God he was on my side!

I'd just started as the bouncer at Okie Joe's Lounge in the spring of 1960 when Dutch came in looking for a bumper pool game.

We didn't drink or smoke in those days because we knew it would interfere with our athletic condition, not to mention cause the loss of our scholarships if we got caught. I was in great shape at six feet two inches tall and 205 pounds.

The owners were also on the scene working as bartender and manager. I wasn't allowed to play pool in those early days of my employment and sat on a stool by the door. My job was to check IDs, watch for kids trying to steal pitchers or beer glasses and keep an eye on the crowd to try to prevent trouble before it could start.

It was mostly quiet during the happy hour portion of the evening, but all of a sudden three or four college boys from different fraternities started mixing it up. It was hard to tell who was on which side, so it became necessary for me to jump in the middle and try to break it up. I was holding my own pretty well, but just as I heard Dutch yell, "Look out," someone hit me behind the neck with a pool cue. I was down on my knees, so stunned I couldn't move, but I didn't have to do much after Dutch joined the fray. By the time I was able to get up, Dutch had laid out two of them on the floor and the others were scrambling out the door as quickly as they could go.

We cuffed the ones on the ground, and I thought it was all over, but the owners had called the cops, so I had my initial introduction to the Albuquerque Police. I didn't get arrested, but they didn't know me, so it took a while to convince them I actually worked there and had been trying to stop the fight. Finally, they got the story straight, cited the frat boys and went on their way.

Dutch instantly became my best friend. During our two years of eligibility, we won most of our ball games but didn't win the conference in the 1960 or '61 seasons. We were homecoming and bowl game cocaptains in our senior season and won both of those games. The Aviation Bowl, which was the only bowl game in which UNM had participated in recent years, had occurred on December 9, 1961, in Dayton, Ohio. It was very cold, and the field actually underwent snow removal just before the game so the sidelines and yardage lines could be visible. We beat Western Michigan 28 to 12 in a storm that dropped several inches of snow during the game. Attendance at the game was limited by icy and snowbound roads, and we attracted only about 3,500 people. After that, the Aviation Bowl was declared a financial disaster and was never played again.

After our eligibility ran out, Dutch and I helped coach in the spring and fall of 1962. We won both freshman games, and the varsity won the conference.

Dutch and his wife were separated for a long time before his divorce became final, but I was suddenly hit with final divorce papers that had been cooking on the back burner for nearly a year without my knowledge. Bonnie filed for divorce the year before, when we were separated for a few months, but we got back together during the summer. There hadn't been any talk of divorce since the reconciliation. I thought it was simply a thing of the past, a bump in the road of a lifetime together, but there it was, in my face, suddenly final on December 7, 1962. Pearl Harbor Day Anniversary no less, and she was leaving again, this time for good.

She stood by the dresser in the tiny bedroom of our tiny apartment and said flatly, "Here, sign this. Our divorce is final."

Instant rage and some kind of uncontrollable reflex caused me to snap, and I slapped her. I had never hit a woman before. "Oh God, I'm sorry!" I sputtered. I knew it was terrible, and I was immediately ashamed, sorry and humiliated all at the same time—ashamed and sorry I'd lost control and humiliated to realize I was naive or stupid enough to think everything was okay, when it wasn't.

The brain committee was outraged. *How could she have been so conniving? She was the one who had called and asked for reconciliation. Wasn't she? We had made up and started over. Hadn't we? Obviously not!*

She didn't yelp or cry or say a word, but the look of surprise in her eyes turned quickly to hatred, which cut into my gut like a hari-kari slash.

She threw the papers on the bed and walked out. The institution of marriage seemed suddenly like a farce in a very bad script. Love, hope, future, faith and marriage all were like empty buckets. I felt as if all the blood in my body had suddenly been sucked out. My body went limp, and I could barely lift my arms. The pain in my gut was so intense I bent over and wrapped my arms around my waist to try to stop it.

Eventually, I signed the papers, put them neatly on the dresser, went to work in a daze and got drunk on the free booze. Sometime during the night, the pain finally subsided, but when I awoke the next day, all the memories, all the happy times and all the regrets were still there racing in and out of my thoughts. The aching pain and anguish were back with a blistering vengeance, accompanied by a hangover and a driving headache.

How could this happen? *Only a Bloody Mary can fix this.* The brain committee was as confused as ever. *Fuck it! Let's go get drunk!*

The First Love Story

Bonnie and I almost went out on a date in high school. On the way to lunch one Friday during the football season of our senior year, she sent one of her cheerleader teammates, Susie, to ask, "What do you think about going out with Bonnie after the game tonight, Bobby?"

Surprised, I quickly responded, "Sure, Susie. Why not? That would be great!" A freckle-faced, blue-eyed bubble of red-topped energy, she was off in a flash, almost skipping away, with a twisting wink over her disappearing shoulder. What great fun Susie had always been, wherever she happened to be. Unlike the other cheerleaders, she was an ardent supporter of the wrestling team. I guess it was partially because her brother was a wrestler, but she also seemed to show a genuine interest in this most grueling of individual sports combined into a team endeavor.

Less than five minutes later while I was still standing in the cafeteria line, Bonnie came to stand in front of me, looking up anxiously with a big toothy smile and sparkling blue eyes surrounded by short blonde curls. "I hear you have something you want to ask me?"

I couldn't help matching her smile as we stood there staring at each other like two awkward cretins. Finally, I managed to blurt, "Yes, I would like to go out after the game tonight but I'll have to ask my mom for the car and let you know."

"No need," she said emphatically, very much in control. "I have my mom's car. I'll wait for you in the parking lot outside the gym."

She went away as quickly as she arrived, but I watched her all the way back to where the rest of the cheerleaders were sitting in a group. They wore their uniforms on game day, and the cluster of laughing, chattering faces, hands flailing and bodies flouncing, transformed them into something like baby birds jumping and pecking at seeds.

"Hey, Bobby, you seem chipper and in a good mood, considering the circumstances," said my best friend. He played center on offense and linebacker on defense, on our very successful football team.

"Considering what circumstances?" The door closed behind me as I observed the unexpectedly empty locker room.

"The game's been cancelled."

"No! What the hell? You're kidding?"

"I wouldn't kid about it. Our coach and principal got together with the other team's coach and principal and decided the potential for lightning and tornados is too great to tempt fate. So the game will be played tomorrow night instead."

"I can't believe it!" Never in my seven-year football life had one of our games been cancelled because of bad weather, and Oklahoma was an area known for almost constant bad weather. Baseball games had been canceled, sure. But never football! We played in rain, snow, sleet and whatever windy, cold or hot temperature you could imagine. What the devil was going on? "Lightning? Tornados?"

"Well, they did it, Bobby, so you better believe it," he reiterated emphatically.

It had already started to drizzle when I came out of the gymnasium, and I had to walk home before I could call Bonnie.

"Hi, Bonnie, you're not gonna believe it but the game's been cancelled."

"I do believe it. Mom was still working at school when the decision was made and she told me when she got home."

"Just my bad luck, I guess." *Bad luck for sure*, the brain committee lamented. *Just when we thought the dream date was about to happen—poof, gone.*

"We could go out tonight anyway if you want," she suggested.

Maybe she could hear the disappointment in my voice? "I can't. Well, I couldn't go for very long anyway. It's almost seven and tonight has now become the night before a game and the team is under curfew. Our rules are 'in the house by nine' and 'in bed by ten,' so it's probably best to skip it."

There was a short pause. "Well, I guess we have to wait for another time then, Bobby." She sounded resolute, if a little let down.

"We can go out tomorrow night after the game?" I offered.

"No. Sorry, Bobby. I already have a date for tomorrow night"

"Don't you have to cheerlead at the game?" Incredible! It became instantly obvious that she wasn't particularly interested in me. She just didn't have a Friday night date after the game. *How could she be so cavalier? How could I be so naive?* The brain committee was incensed.

"My Saturday night date was originally for dinner and a movie but he knew I would have to be at the postponed game so he already called and reset the date for afterward," she answered.

How did he already know the game had been cancelled? Maybe he was one of the other players? She didn't offer to identify him, and I didn't ask. Maybe it was on the radio already. "OK, Bonnie. We'll do it some other time then. You take care and God bless."

"Bye. Bless you too. Good luck in the game."

We continued to run into each other at church on Sundays and occasionally at youth group meetings on Wednesday nights, but the opportunity to date didn't arise again during our senior year. In fact, during a Friday night youth fellowship dance, her date showed up early and ripped the pocket off my shirt because I was dancing with her.

I was so stunned at the assault I couldn't say anything at first. Awkwardly then, I snapped, "Thanks, asshole. This is the only good white shirt I have."

He just smirked, laughed, and then said sarcastically, "I'm sure it is."

"I felt bad," she said later. *Not bad enough to break the date with him though*. The brain committee was still upset.

As fate would have it, at the end of the year, we walked down the aisle together and sat next to each other for the graduation ceremony. Ready for the usual answer I asked again. "D'ya wanna go for a bite after rehearsal?"

"Oh, Bobby, I wish I could, but I have a date." *She always does.*

She sounded sincere, so I ventured further, "How about tomorrow after graduation?"

"Similar story," she said apologetically. "Busy, but not a date. My family is planning a dinner afterward."

"It's okay." *Don't let the disappointment show.* "When are you leaving for college?" We were both headed for Oklahoma University at Norman.

"Right after Labor Day weekend. How 'bout you?"

"I'm not sure exactly, but some time before the middle of August. I wanna get there as soon as they open the athlete's dorm so I can find my way around and work out some before two-a-day practice officially starts on the fifteenth."

"What're you doing 'til then?"

"I'll be working most of the time, traveling, on the road, in sales." I was reluctant to tell her I was selling magazines. "I've saved enough already to pay my tuition, books and fees for the first two semesters but I need some extra for clothes and spending money."

We didn't see each other the summer of '57 or at college in the fall, even to say hello. But back in the city for the high school homecoming game in early October, she was already in the stands by herself on Friday night when I arrived. "Oh, you brought a blanket," she exclaimed. "It is cold!"

"Yep, never been in the stands for football before but figured it would be cold or, if not, I could always use it as a cushion. I remember how hard these concrete seats used to get when we came here to the stadium for the car races in the summer."

"Me too. I was always moving and jumping with the cheerleaders during the games and didn't realize it would be so cold sitting up here on the concrete."

"Well, here, let's share this one." It was an old green Marine Corps blanket Dad brought home after World War II over a decade ago. "How are things going at school?"

"Okay, I suppose," she said pensively. "I'm kinda bored actually."

The small talk continued as we watched the game, and eventually, I found the nerve to ask once again, "Are you busy after the game?"

"No," she said softly as she smiled, tipping her head down and rolling her beautiful blues my way. "What do you have in mind, Bobby?"

I didn't have any idea what I had in mind. I didn't expect the answer to be favorable. The committee pondered, *We've loved you, it seems, ever since we've known you, and whatever WE do is okay, as long as WE do it together.*

I was caught off guard but said, trying not to show my excitement, "Whatever you want, Bonnie."

"There's a homecoming dance at the gym after the game. We could do the dance, meet and greet whoever is there and go to Sussey's on the way home if you want to stop for pizza?"

"Sure, sounds great!"

The game continued though I don't have any memory of who won or even what team we played but that night we started dating, which was the only thing that mattered to me.

We met occasionally for lunch between classes and sometimes in the evening for a movie or a play or just to walk around the campus holding hands. We kissed and petted and talked about our future. I told her of my dreams of being a pilot and an engineer, maybe an aeronautical engineer and test pilot if I turned out to be any good at either one. She talked about having kids and a home and family.

During Thanksgiving break, the night I lost my virginity, we stood in her parents' living room afterward, kissing good night, and she asked, "Don't you have something you want to give me?" She leaned back with her hands clasped behind my neck, pressing her lower body into mine, smiling, teasing and twisting her hips a little.

I could see my hands clasped around her waist, in the mirror over the fireplace behind her, and slid them down and pulled her now more familiar, tight little cheerleader body firmly into mine. "Yes," I said, as I returned her smile. She could tell I was starting to swell again.

She smiled and looked up directly into my eyes. "That's not what I meant, Bobby, and besides, you'll have to get some condoms before you get any more of that action, honey."

"I'd offer a fraternity pin if I had one, sweetheart." Being pinned would be a sign of dating exclusively and the nearest thing to being engaged. We'd been dating since the chance meeting at homecoming, but I didn't know if she'd been dating anyone else at the same time. I hadn't. I didn't ask about her.

"Your class ring will do and will mean the same thing for us independents." She smiled and stretched up to kiss me again. I slid the high school class ring off and slipped it into her hand while still kissing. At the same time, I made a mental note to buy a stash of condoms, and the brain committee approved.

My folks had picked us up for the weeklong Thanksgiving break, and her parents picked us up for the two-week Christmas vacation. These short but wondrous times at home were filled with movies and dinners, or any other excuse to go out, followed by long nights parked alone in a secluded area by a lake. Soft music, moonlight, love, future, family and sharing what we wanted out of life were the usual subjects, and sex was usually the eventual conclusion. Sometimes we would go directly to our favorite secluded spot on the lake for immediate sex followed by heavy petting and more sex.

Whenever she came near me, an erection was sure to follow shortly, if not immediately. I never seemed to get so much I didn't want more. I was so infatuated with her beauty and so much in love, it seemed irrational. It was definitely overwhelming. I felt my behavior ludicrous and considered the possibility I might be insane. Studying became a problem because my mind wandered, and I couldn't remember what I'd read. How could anyone be so enamored as to be completely submerged in mind and thought to the point of intellectual deadening and judgmental impairment?

After Christmas break we were still going steady but not seeing as much of each other. Neither of us had a car at school, and I didn't have much money, so dating just meant walking to a free sporting event or a free play at the university theater or walking around campus looking for a deserted spot to neck. There were no places secure enough to take the chance of having sex on campus, but the petting was so intense, we both went home with wet pants most of the time.

We spent less time together than I wanted, but even so, my grades suffered during the spring semester. "Bonnie, honey, you know I want to see you as much as possible but spring football practice and time to study leave little time for anything else."

"Maybe we shouldn't be dating," she said softly.

It felt like I'd been pounded in the stomach with a sledgehammer. "Oh my God! How can you say such a thing?"

"Because, maybe it's just not the right time for us."

It was amazing and unbelievable to me that she could say such a thing. It was mind-boggling and so painful I was suddenly bewildered. We were in a clearing on campus where a large statue decorated the grounds, and I swung around the cold stone base, out of her sight, and slumped over, weak-kneed and sweating. Overwhelmed with pain and embarrassment, I sobbed and couldn't catch my breath.

She followed me around. "Don't Bobby," she whispered. "I didn't mean to hurt you. It'll be okay."

We didn't break up, but we began to see less of each other. I ached inside all the time, like I had a fever, and realized just how much I missed spending time with her.

A future college education depended on a scholarship, and while I was told I had tested at an above-average level of intelligence, I was not the studious type. My grades were good enough to get into college but not for an academic scholarship. My only real talent was for football, and the Oklahoma University freshman coach, Port Robertson, promised, "If you make the top 33 in spring training, you will earn a full ride."

There was no way to make enough money in one summer to pay for a whole year or even one semester for that matter. It had taken three summers to save enough to pay for one year.

"We're moving you to end, Pincer. You're not big enough to play tackle in Double-A ball."

"Okay, Coach." As far as I was concerned, it was a promotion from interior lineman to a *skill* position. In any case, at six feet, two inches tall and 165 pounds, I knew I was too small to be a Double-A college tackle.

In the first game of the two we played as freshman my left shoulder was injured. It was impossible to catch the ball with an arm I could not raise above my head so I was not allowed to suit up for the second freshman game. However, the shoulder healed well and in time to get in shape by spring practice. I hit hard and worked every drill to the limit. I caught every ball thrown anywhere near and when the ball was in my hands I cut quickly and hit hard for good yardage after the catch. On defense I successfully brought all my skill as a tackle to bear on sealing up the edge of the formation. I did everything I could, and finally, for the last five days of practice, I was the 1958 varsity, third string tight end, on the second best football team in the country. We were still number two in the national ratings, even though the same varsity team, minus the seniors, lost to Notre Dame 0-7 in the previous fall of 1957, ending a 53-game winning streak.

I went in to see Coach Robertson as soon as we turned in our equipment at the end of spring practice. "Hi, Coach." I tried to sound positive and at ease, but I was so anxious I was shaking inside. I hoped it didn't show on the outside. "I came to see about the scholarship."

"I know, Pincer, but we don't have any."

I thought he must be kidding, so I sort of half chuckled. "Whaddaya mean we don't have any, Coach? I met my part of the deal—I made third string just like you said."

"Yeah, you did, Pincer, but we don't have any scholarships to give this year. Usually, someone flunks out or quits but this year it didn't happen. You made the team because two people at your position were injured."

"Yeah, I know, Coach. I hit one of them so hard he was dizzy and turned himself into the infirmary. I also beat out one other guy at my position who was on scholarship."

"Well, he was also injured, and injured players are still on scholarship. We can't take a scholarship away from an injured player, even if he never plays again, and all of those players are likely to be back healthy next year anyway."

The brain committee was stunned. I'd done my part. *Against all odds, I'd beaten out two guys who were on scholarship. I'd won. I was due.*

"I'm sorry, Pincer. There's nothing I can do. The NCAA has been watching our scholarship program because we had such a winning streak going and we're limited by the rules. We would like to have you back next year if you can afford it and I'll honor the deal if a scholarship opens up."

"Can I redshirt on a freshman scholarship?"

"I already checked on it. I wish you could but you played in the game against Oklahoma State, so you're not eligible."

It was over. I was done. There wasn't even enough smoke left of my grandiose plans to make the smallest puff on a Cherokee peace pipe. Gone the way of a wistful dreamer, fishing in other people's ponds. I wasn't going to be an engineer or a pilot. Hell, I wasn't even going to be a college football player.

I didn't even want to see Bonnie, but she knew I was going to get the news that day, so I reluctantly met her after dinner. I felt very out of place, walking across the familiar campus, knowing it would only be a few weeks before I would be gone for good.

We walked our usual path around the campus and talked about what happened. She seemed to take it all very calmly. Like maybe she never expected it to happen anyway. "It'll be okay," she tried to console. "You can go home and get a job and you'll be okay. Maybe it's just not meant to be. Or maybe you can go to night school and still be an engineer, someday. Maybe you can take flying lessons and still be a pilot, someday."

I knew she meant well. "Yeah, I know," was all I could say to her suggestions, and she knew my halfhearted responses were coming from a broken spirit. I resolved to finish the semester with at least some acceptable grades so, if I were ever able to continue, I would have a better place to start from than zero.

The month of May 1958 was the darkest of my short life. I felt the depths of depression so intensely my wounded guts flamed and my body ached all over. Fever and chills fought for control and clung to me like sweaty steam or cold moss on the north side of a tree. I couldn't shake it.

I entombed myself in my room and hid in the books that were mostly ignored during the earlier spring training part of the semester. The late spring heat and humidity smothered the small room even though a light breeze entered the open window, but there was more space since my roommate had dropped out. Too bad he wasn't a scholarship football player instead of baseball. I was so engrossed I didn't notice someone standing in my open door.

"Pincer?"

I was hot, sweaty, depressed and in no mood to be friendly or gracious. Without even looking up I responded, "Yeah, who wants to know?"

"Coach Montgomery from Cameron. I'm wondering if you'd be interested in coming to play ball with me next fall?"

My head snapped toward the voice like a door with a suddenly broken spring.

He was tall, well-built and well-dressed but casual, in a short-sleeve shirt and khaki trousers. No rippling muscles but hardy looking, like a strong lean baseball player or a big quarterback. His reddish blond hair was curly and unkempt, and his youthful, bright blue eyes shone out of a freckled, ruddy face on which a big smile slanted toward a wad of tobacco in his cheek.

Fall? Ball! I jumped out of my chair and leapt across the room, leading with my hand out to shake. "Yes . . . uh . . . sir . . . uh . . . Coach?"

He laughed out loud as he stuck out his hand. "I've never had quite this kind of reaction before," he said chuckling still. "I was talking to Port and he said you were a pretty good player with a lotta potential but he didn't have a ticket for you."

"Right, Coach. I made varsity third string as a freshman just like he said I should, but the way it turned out, there are no scholarships available this year . . . At least, that's what he said."

"Well, it's true, as far as I can tell. He told me he would book you if he could because you did all he asked. Anyway, my deal is a full ride with books, tuition, room and board, and 50 bucks a month for laundry and expenses. Sound all right to you?"

"Yes sir, Coach!"

"Okay then, be there before the fifteenth of August for two-a-days and be in shape. We're in a tough conference and we're startin' with two tough games in Texas." He was gone like gully fog on a crisp fall morning. As if he wasn't even there, but his presence lingered like dew on the grass.

I ran to the pay phone to call home. Dad answered. Thank God, he was home! "Hello?"

"Collect call from Bob Pincer. Will you accept the charges?"

"Yes, I will." He sounded a little wary because he figured maybe something is wrong if I'm calling home collect.

"Dad! Where and what is Cameron?"

"Hi, son." I could tell he was happy now but trying to slow me down a bit. "Cameron is a junior college in Lawton. Why?"

"I've just been handed a scholarship. A full ride plus a little money. Port Robertson recommended me to the coach and he was just here and made the offer! I was so excited I couldn't even think, but I didn't want him to know I'd never heard of him, or Cameron, so I just said yes."

"And just like that, your world is turned around!"

Dad was one of the most positive people I'd ever known. When I told him about not getting the scholarship, he said, "Keep an open mind, son. Stay in shape and be ready."

"You think it's okay, Dad? Have you ever heard of Cameron? Are they any good?"

"Sure I have. They're in the Pioneer Conference and play mostly Texas teams. They've been in the Junior College Rose Bowl out in California a couple of times and have played some California JC teams also. You tell Bonnie yet?"

"No, Dad, I haven't. I wanted to find out about it before I talk to her so I can explain. I'll go see her now since I've got the scoop."

"Okay, son. You have a birthday coming up in a couple of weeks, don't you? Will you be home in time?"

"I'll be home if you come and get me." I laughed. "I'll be all done with finals by then!"

"I thought you might be riding with Bonnie's folks."

"No, they're coming to pick her up but she has so much stuff there's no way she can get it all in her mom's car and have room for me and my stuff."

"Okay, Mom and I will work it out to come and get you. How much stuff do you have?"

"Dad, you know how much stuff I have," I chided. "It all fits in one small suitcase that goes along with a little box of books and my portable typewriter."

He chuckled. "Yeah, I do and I will pick you up!"

"Thanks, Dad. See ya soon—I love ya!"

"Bonnie honey, you're not gonna believe it! I got a scholarship to Cameron! It's a junior college in Lawton!"

"Wow, Lawton?" she exclaimed. "Lawton's an army town, isn't it?" She obviously knew more about it than I did.

"I don't know, sweetheart. All I know is, I got a full ride plus 50 bucks a month."

The summer of '58 was one of near bliss. The flowers couldn't have been more colorful; the breezes could not have been more comforting. Even the muggy rain seemed to be fresher than usual. No bad tornados. No floods. No disasters of any kind. I worked selling magazines again, which actually went even better than in the past.

Because of the poor reputation of other magazine salesmen, collecting money, pocketing it, and never giving the subscription to the magazine publisher, the company I worked for offered a pay-as-you-go plan. "*Good Housekeeping* and your choice of any three others on the list for only twenty-nine cents a week. All four, for only a dollar and a quarter a month, just like your newspaper. If you don't get 'um, you don't pay for 'um." We knocked on doors to make our pitch from nine to noon in the morning and from four to seven in the evening.

Push-ups and sit-ups were the afternoon regimen between sales shifts along with running several miles every day in the muggy heat of the afternoon. I was bound and determined to be in the best shape of my life by the middle of August.

I made enough money in two and a half months to take Bonnie out every weekend to the movies, the zoo or the amusement park and buy flowers and candy and still save enough to buy a car just before heading to Cameron—a red 1949 Ford Coupe. Certainly not fancy, like the new ones they gave to extraordinary players at OU, but practical. It was my first car. I was proud of it and spent hours waxing and polishing the faded paint to make it look as good it could. Certainly a lot less work than unsuccessfully gathering parts to put together the junkers I bought and worked on in high school but never drove.

I reported for two-a-day football practice at Cameron 30 pounds heavier than I was the year before, and it was all in my chest, shoulders, neck and arms. I was in the best shape of my life. It was two weeks before the fall semester classes would start on Tuesday after Labor Day and three weeks before our first football game on the Friday night after Labor Day.

Coach Montgomery was there to meet me when I drove up to the gym. His red hair shined in the sun, and the wad of tobacco in his cheek skewed his broad smile to one side. "Looks like you put on some weight, Pincer, and in the right places."

"Yep, I put on about 30 pounds since last year, Coach."

"That's good 'cause we think you're gonna be a great tackle."

"Tackle, Coach? I was an end at OU." He could hear the disappointment in my voice. I had begun to think of myself as a specialty position player with the opportunity to catch the winning touchdown instead of as a middle-of-the-line workhorse.

"Yeah, I know but I looked you up and you were also an All-Conference and All-City tackle in high school. I like you better at tackle, especially with the extra weight and strength. What are you weighing, Pincer?"

"I'm 195, Coach, but I think some of those awards were Honorable Mentions."

"Good." He looked me up and down like a rancher buying a horse. "Good," he said again, while ignoring my disclaimer. "You're gonna be the dorm monitor and have a room to yourself but you're gonna also be Donny Green's English tutor."

"Donny Green?"

"He's a colored boy who got turned down at the universities for low grades. He's a hell of a halfback and he's only here with us 'cause I promised him a tutor who would help him stay eligible and graduate."

"Well, Coach, I'll do what I can but I don't know how much good it will be."

"You'll do fine, Pincer. You think I didn't check you out? You want to major in engineering but your best subjects were English and German in high school and English in college. Which isn't sayin' much 'cause the only As you got at OU were in ROTC."

He had me pegged, of course, but I wondered if he knew how I felt about black people, and if he knew, how would he know? Although I am generally very proud of my home state and the patriotic, upstanding character of the people, I am thoroughly ashamed of the way some of our fellow Okies have treated black people. "Separate but equal" was not the right thing to do, but it was still the state law in public facilities and schools up through high school in 1957, when I graduated, but many of the colleges and universities had been quietly integrated for several years.

Clara Luper, a black activist, had earned her master of arts degree in history at Oklahoma University in 1951 after receiving her bachelor of science in mathematics at the all-black Langston University in Langston, Oklahoma.

Most restaurants, cafes and soda fountains in Oklahoma—and, for that matter, anywhere in the South—did not serve black people in 1958. They could order food to take out and sometimes pick it up at the cash register but usually at the back door. When Clara and her young black friends started their sit-in demonstrations in Oklahoma City in the summer of 1958, employees tormented and ignored them and customers yelled and cussed at them—and even poured drinks on them. Disgustingly ignorant and detestable behavior!

I met Donny Green, from Hugo, Oklahoma, the same week Clara Luper and her students started demonstrating at Katz Drug Store in downtown Oklahoma City. "I'm sorry about the way things are and the way they treat your people, Donny," I said, as I shook his strong hand. "It's not how I feel and I'm ashamed of the way some people are acting. I think they're just plain stupid and obnoxious!"

"Not your problem, Bobby." He smiled ruefully. "Those people will have to answer to their own conscience sooner or later. It's just the way it's always been for us, at least as far as I know, but maybe things are startin' to change now."

"Yeah, Donny. I feel, and I think most people feel, it should never have been done, the 'segregation, separate-but-equal-way,' in the first place ... Prentice Gautt was a sophomore at OU last year, ya know?"

"Yeah, I know. I tried to follow him there this year but I didn't have the grades to get a scholarship."

"Yeah, I heard. You're built a lot like him, Donny. What are you—about six feet and 200 pounds? Are you as fast?"

He turned in a sort of half-running pose and gave me a big toothy grin. "Not quite 200 and not quite as fast as he is but I'm a little bigger and stronger in the shoulders. I wish I had his brains. He's a top student too, ya know."

"Yeah, I know but you do your stuff on the field and we'll work together on your grades so you can follow him there when you graduate from here. Okay?"

"Yeah, 'at's what Coach said." He flashed his gleaming, straight white teeth against his handsome dark face as we shook hands again.

Lawton is located only 75 miles southeast of Oklahoma City, but it's an hour-long drive on narrow, winding, tree-lined, two-lane roads and then clear across the sprawling city to the Village, a township area of northern Oklahoma City, where home was located. My folks were always happy to have me home for a weekend break, although they knew my tight practice schedule wouldn't allow for a long visit, and they realized it was impractical, if not impossible.

The fall schedule changed to practice four days in the afternoon and games on Friday night, which also left little time or energy for homework and tutoring, much less the opportunity to take off for a drive to the city.

I talked often on the phone with Bonnie, but when she showed up at my dorm one Sunday afternoon in early October, I was surprised and excited. She was pretty bold walking through the men's athletic dorm and right into my open room.

Her plain white blouse buttoned down the front from just below the collar and tucked into a full, pleated black skirt. A black velvet ribbon choker around her neck matched a small silver watch with a black velvet band on her wrist. Sheer hose and shiny black pumps finished off the outfit. It looked like something she might have worn to church earlier that day.

We hugged and kissed hello in the room, but there was no privacy with the door open and other athletes wandering around in the hall.

"Let's go for a ride and get something to eat," she suggested. "I have gas and money," she offered with a clever smile.

"Sounds great to me," I offered. "Do you want to eat first or drive first?"

She drove her mother's light blue '53 Chevy out to a mountainside park, where the Easter story is presented every year, as an outdoor pageant. It was familiar because we had been there for the show and sunrise service when we were seniors in high school. It was a church youth group event, not a date, because, coincidentally, we wound up going as part of the church group. We sat together on the bus and during the service.

It was almost like a date. Wasn't it?

She pulled off the road into the park near the top of the hill, pointing downward, so we could see anyone coming up the winding road. Setting the hand brake, she turned toward me. I was sitting on the passenger side of the bench seat, so she scooted over and leaned in, but not close enough to kiss. Her beautiful bright blue eyes locked on mine. She stared a long time without moving or saying anything and, without moving her eyes from mine, slid her body closer to me, lifted her left leg across my lap and placed her knees on each side.

She sat up there, in my lap, looking down at me like she did that first time, a year ago, when I lost my virginity. "How am I supposed to see if anyone is coming up the hill with you in front of me?" I grinned.

"Never mind." She breathed hotly into my mouth, and I greedily sucked the hot air to fill my lungs. I wanted to possess all of her. Her small body was not heavy, but she was hot, and I was already hard just being next to her. It was uncomfortable. I adjusted my jeans to relieve the pressure.

"I don't have a condom, honey," I said quietly. It was important to us. She didn't want to get pregnant, and I didn't want to get married before I finished college.

"I do." She smiled . . . "I've missed you, Bobby." Leaning in and kissing me again, long and deep, she left enough room between us to untuck and unbutton her blouse, which she accomplished slowly, almost rhythmically. She deftly unsnapped the hook in the middle of the bra between her breasts and let the cups hang to the sides on the shoulder straps.

The pinkish white skin of her breasts was a slightly lighter color than the rest of her chest and stomach. Her delicate small pink areolas surrounded stubby little nipples, hard with excitement. She rose to her knees and bent her head down and to the side to clear the headliner so she could bring her breasts up to my mouth. My hands cupped, massaged and squeezed her breasts, and my tongue found her nipples. First one and then the other and back again while she rubbed my erection through my jeans with her pelvic arch.

When she was ready, she rolled off to the side and took off her panties while I rolled my jeans and underwear down to below my knees. She smoothly cloaked me in a condom and rolled back on top to guide me in with her hand as she slowly sat down. When she had done this the first time, I hadn't expected how hot she would be inside, and I exploded immediately. I didn't have a condom on then and needed to pull out, so I pushed her up and off into the headliner so quickly, it banged her head hard on the car top. Now, a year later, and with a little experience under my belt, I vowed it would not be so quick, even though it had been a long time since we'd been together. The heat of her settling over me, and the tight, smooth squeeze was nearly more than I could handle, but I was able to hold off until she was ready. *Good work!* The brain committee cheered

Later, while still sitting on my lap, she said flatly, "Bobby, we need to get married or start seeing each other more often—or start dating other people."

I was taken aback with the manner in which the proposal was put. Did she mean now or never? Would she start looking for a more immediate marriage candidate? Or did she just need more company? More sex? I didn't want to lose her. She was my first love and first lover—the only woman I had ever known intimately.

I had loved her, in a way, ever since we first met, as friends in the church youth group and at school, but when she gave herself to me, I fell deeply in love.

We'd been going steady since the first time we made love and often talked about marriage, but I had said several times and thought it was understood between us, no marriage plans until I graduate from college. We were not engaged. I'd never asked her, but now, the thought of losing her caused fear and immediate anxiety in my guts.

I conceded, "Well . . . if the coach can help both of us get jobs, I suppose, between the two of us, we could afford it. He recruited a player last year who was already married and found jobs for both of them."

She lurched and nearly hit the car top with her head. Her eyes popped open wide and sparkled with excitement as her still moist pelvic arch swept involuntarily over my crotch. "Really, Bobby? When do ya think we could do it?"

"I'll be in the city for Thanksgiving break and we can finalize plans for a wedding during Christmas vacation if you want?"

"Whaddaya mean, if I want? Of course I want, you fool!"

I chuckled and chimed in, "I'm starved. Can we get something to eat now?" She swiftly removed herself from my lap and put on her panties. She drove back to town and went to a drive-in restaurant so we could continue to make plans in the privacy of the car.

She went home to finalize the plans, and since the football season was over, I got a job selling Kirby vacuum cleaners. My commission was $75 per sale, and I sold enough in a month and a half to buy a cheap string of pearls for a wedding present, make a down payment on a small wedding ring and pay for a motel room for the "honeymoon."

We were married in December, in the winter of '58, between Christmas and the New Year, in the same church where she had gone all her life and where I attended during high school. It was finality for me. It was a union blessed by God and everyone involved, I thought. Although Bonnie's father was less than enthusiastic, he accepted and endorsed the inevitable as he had done forever with everything concerning his only daughter. But he was not especially keen about the prospects for my future. He worked for an insurance company and had been with the same company for so many years Bonnie couldn't remember when he started, and they had lived in the same house ever since she could remember as a little child.

My father, on the other hand, had a few jobs before and many jobs after WWII, which caused us to move all over Oklahoma. Each job was better than the last, from the standpoint of income and opportunity, but Bonnie's father just saw us as a kind of gypsy family without stability. He was right, in a sense, but Dad would eventually be very successful with his own nutritional supplement manufacturing and distribution company, headquartered in California, and serving over 500 health and natural food stores in the southwestern states.

Nearly a year later, the rest of the life plan seemed to come together as I casually walked between classes. A marine sergeant was standing in the hallway at Cameron next to a dramatic marine recruiting poster with helicopters and jets flying around bursting bombs, burning buildings and tracers screaming across the sky.

"I didn't know the Marine Corps had helicopters and airplanes. What's the deal here, Sergeant?"

"Yes, sir, the Marine Corps has hundreds of helicopters and fixed wing aircraft and we're here looking for volunteers who want to become Marine Corps pilots."

"Wow, how does it work? What are the qualifications?"

"Sir, a candidate would have to be single, a junior college graduate, be aviation qualified physically and pass an aviation aptitude test. The candidate would report to flight school after graduation and complete a Marine Officer Candidate School while attending aviation ground school. Flight School takes about 18 months to complete. The candidate gets his wings and is commissioned a second lieutenant upon graduation and then serves four years of active duty as an aviator."

"Well, all of that sounds almost perfect, Sergeant, but I'm married and I want to complete my college education first."

"Very good, sir. We have another program that I think might be even better for you. It's called the Platoon Leaders Course for Aviation. The candidate is required to complete twelve weeks of school at Quantico, Virginia, during the summer while in college and upon graduation with a bachelor degree is commissioned a second lieutenant. The lieutenant then proceeds directly to flight school. It's pretty much the same as for JC graduates but the candidate goes to officer training during the summers while he's in college and goes through flight school as an officer instead of as an enlisted candidate."

"What happens if you sign up and don't graduate?"

"Well, if a student were single, we could drop him back to the JC candidate status and proceed along those lines but if he's married, he would have to go to boot camp and serve three years of obligatory service as an enlisted man."

"Wow, that's a big penalty."

"Yes, sir, it is. It behooves one to graduate once you're in the program."

"Well, I promised myself I would be the first one in my family to ever graduate from college and I'm very intent on fulfilling the pledge." I studied the poster intently as I tried to think of the drawbacks. "So how do I find out if I'm aviation qualified?"

"When can you be in Oklahoma City to take the physical and the aviation aptitude test?" He looked me directly in the eye, perhaps to see if he could tell how serious I was.

"We'll be going home to the city for Thanksgiving so I could do that over the holidays if the tests are available?"

"The Marine Corps is open 24 hours a day, seven days a week, sir. Let me take your name, address, and draft card number and we'll make an appointment for you."

I found Bonnie in the kitchen as I came in the back door and grabbed her around the waist. "The Marine Corps recruiter is visiting school this week, honey, and what a deal they have," I wanted to broach the subject carefully but couldn't help blurting it out. "He's traveling around to the colleges looking for candidates from junior colleges and officer candidates working toward their bachelors. The officers program provides for a commission, as an officer, in the Marine Corps and also guarantees flight school training upon graduation from college, if you're qualified.

"How do you qualify?" she asked with a little caution.

"Well, you have to pass a written aviation aptitude test and a physical test. The physical test is primarily an eye test because you have to have 20/20 vision."

"Then what?"

"I would have to attend Officer Candidate School in Quantico, Virginia. The school is 12 weeks long but I could split it into two summer vacations or do all 12 weeks at once, as long as it's completed before I graduate. When I finish flight school, I'll have to serve four years as a pilot in the Marine Corps."

"What happens if you don't graduate?"

It seemed to me she had very little faith that I would ever graduate. I played it down. "I would have to serve three years of active duty as an enlisted marine but I don't think that scenario is gonna happen."

"What happens if you don't finish flight school?"

"Then I'd have to serve four years of active duty as an officer." I picked up our little white kitten named Bum, held him in my arms, scratched casually behind his ears and smiled at Bonnie, wondering if she could feel any of the excitement the discovery of the day had created in me. "Whaddaya think, sweetheart?"

"Well, Bobby, it sounds like it gets you everything you want." It was not a question or a confirmation. Maybe it was more resigned. Like she didn't have an opinion or didn't want to share her opinion, if she had one.

Monumental decisions and events were occurring in November and December. Last year we were officially engaged during the Thanksgiving holidays in November and married in December just after Christmas. This year I would take the exams and sign up for the Marine Corps and flight school during the Thanksgiving holidays and graduate from junior college in December.

Meanwhile, football at Cameron was outstanding. The Pioneer Conference junior colleges offered great opponents and high visibility. Coach Montgomery and Assistant Coach Charlie Dean were serious, hard-nosed, no-crap, knowledgeable competitors. The specialty coach, who was also the head basketball and head baseball coach, was smart and a very good teacher. We won the conference in the '59 season, and Coach Montgomery was named the All-American Junior College Coach of the Year. Three other teammates and I were named Junior College All-Americans, and scholarship offers were now plentiful but complicated.

Oklahoma University wanted me to come back, but they could only offer a one-year scholarship. I had played freshman football at OU, and the Big Eight Conference rules counted the one game in which I played as a year of eligibility and junior college as two years, and therefore, only one year of eligibility remained for any school in the conference. I didn't even suit up for the second game because of a shoulder injury. The freshman coach, Port Robertson, who had been there when I was a freshman, tried to get my freshman year exempted because of the injury but was unable to. The Oklahoma State recruiters tried the same gambit, thinking they might have a better chance, since I had not played at their school before, but were also unsuccessful.

After those attempts, I told other interested schools in the conference, Kansas and Nebraska, they were sure to have the same problem, and they agreed. However, there were several schools outside the conference with offers for two-year scholarships—Baylor, Rice, University of Denver, Colorado State and Wyoming, as well as several smaller state schools like Oklahoma Central State Teacher's College and Southeastern Oklahoma University. I was relieved because I knew I would be able to go somewhere and finish up with a degree. I considered them all but did not make a decision prior to the Junior

College All-American game in Albuquerque at the old stadium on campus at the University of New Mexico.

At an arranged meeting with the head coach, Marv Levy, in his office at UNM, he asked, "Is it okay if I pull your records from Cameron and OU so I can check with our counselors on how long it would take for you to graduate?"

"No, Coach, of course it's okay, I don't mind."

"What's your major, Pincer?"

"Engineering, Coach. I will have a degree in civil engineering from Cameron when I graduate at midterm."

"Good, we'll get right on it and maybe have an answer before you leave town. What's your schedule?"

"The JUCO committee arranged for our commercial plane tickets and I think we are scheduled for sometime Sunday afternoon, Coach."

"Okay, I'll give you a call at your hotel not later than Sunday morning. Good luck in the game." He stood up behind his desk and reached out his hand to shake. "Nice meeting you, Bobby—I hope we can get together on this."

Later, Coach Levy found me on the field after the game. "Nice game, Pincer!" He was smiling broadly and stuck out his hand to shake.

"Thanks, Coach." I returned his smile.

"How do you feel about playing end for us instead of tackle?"

"It's okay with me, Coach. I played end at OU and I liked the position."

"Well, no one seemed to be able to figure out how long it would take you to graduate because of the differences in the curriculum at OU and at Cameron. So the scholarship I can offer is, continuation in school with a full scholarship until you graduate, as long as you carry at least 12 hours per semester, and maintain a 2.0 average." He looked at me, then down at his watch.

I wasn't really hesitating, but there was a little pause before he started again. "I'll get your wife a good full-time job and I'll get you a good summer job." He raised his head to look me squarely in the eye again.

"But, Coach, I have to go to Marine Corps Officer Candidate School in the summers—6 weeks over two summers or 12 weeks in one summer."

"No problem—as long as you're here by the middle of August for two-a-days." He began to walk away before finishing his sentence. *A busy guy*, the brain committee offered.

Somehow all of the complicated issues suddenly dissolved into one easy decision.

The End Of Forever

My wife, my life, my love, my sweetheart, with whom I'd committed to spend my life, did not seem to enjoy sex as much after we were married as she did before. She no longer initiated sex, as she had always done before, and would only occasionally, reluctantly it seemed, resign herself to the task.

I didn't know the first thing about being a good lover. I'd been a virgin up to when we started dating steadily, when she was my first. I think the early times in our relationship were good for her, because of the lengthy time between sessions and the long, intense kissing and petting.

Recently, and probably the majority of time in our married life, there had not been much time for foreplay. She worked all day, while I was in class, and she was home alone at night, while I worked from six in the evening until the bar closed at two in the morning. She began to hide her fair-skinned, taut cheerleader body like it was a sanctuary. She went from parading in sheer "baby dolls" to flannel pajamas under a heavy robe. She was always tired, and it seemed such a chore for her, I felt guilty just for trying.

Is our relationship normal? the brain committee pondered. *Is this why our society allows prostitutes and why other cultures have developed systems that include mistresses, multiple wives or harems? Do other men, who can't afford a prostitute or mistress, masturbate to ease the pain of unrelieved erections?*

How she ever got pregnant in such an environment is beyond my comprehension. She used the diaphragm religiously during our increasingly rare encounters since she "didn't want to have children, yet," any more than I did. But it happened.

She was tense and said nervously, "I wish I didn't have to tell you this Bobby, but we're going to have a baby." It was late spring, after spring football practice, during the third semester we were at UNM. We'd been married a little less than two and a half years, and I'd made only fair progress toward graduating since there were lost credits due to transfers from OU to Cameron to UNM. It would take another three semesters to complete the degree, which might not be feasible with a baby.

She cried. I held her close and tried to console her. "It'll be okay, honey. We'll figure it out. We're gonna have a baby!" I tried to sound positive, but it was obvious I was not successful. For me to quit college and get a job, something she already said she wanted, pregnant or not, was not an available option. The contract with the Marine Corps could not be cancelled, which she apparently did not understand.

So since the pregnancy was upon us, I took the first opportunity to sneak out to talk to the local recruiting sergeant. "Sergeant, my wife is pregnant and I may have to quit school. Can you tell me exactly what happens to me regarding the program if I have to drop out? And when?"

"It's pretty simple. You get orders to boot camp in San Diego as soon as you are officially no longer in school."

"Yes, I know. That much is all in the contract I signed but what is 'official' and how do I handle my wife and a baby on the way? And what's my pay gonna be? I'm a corporal in the reserve, you know."

"I know. We're familiar with your record, including the extra stripe you got for finishing Jump School, but you don't get to wear your stripes or get corporal pay in boot camp. Pay wise, you get private's pay while you're in boot camp but the difference is accrued and you'll get it in a lump sum when you finish."

"What about my wife and the baby on the way?"

"After boot camp, she can join you at the Infantry Training Regiment at Camp Pendleton, California. As a corporal, you can actually fill out the request to get on the waiting list for housing as soon as you get orders to boot camp. Maybe it can all happen before the baby is due so it can be delivered free at the naval hospital at Camp Pendleton but it brings us back again to what you asked.

'Official' is whenever my boss, the officer selection officer, finds out you're not in school and that's kinda up to you." He opened his hands as if it was beyond his control, which I suppose it was.

"So I'm officially in school until whenever I let you know I'm not."

"Well, yes to the extent you actually do attend class up to the point you notify us. If you are not attending class and making reasonable progress toward graduation, you could be considered AWOL and orders would be automatically cut to send you to boot camp."

"How soon after you know can the orders be cut and I'd be on my way?"

"A new recruit company starts every week. If it's not full we can get you in whenever you're ready."

"Okay, Sergeant, thanks for the info. I'll letcha know as soon as I know but for now I'm gonna try to at least finish this semester," I said, pushing myself out of my seat across from his desk. As I left, I still had no idea what to do. How long would Bonnie be able to work? Would there be enough money for us to live on if she can't work and if I'm in boot camp on a private's pay? She'd have to go home and live with her folks or my folks until we can get base housing and corporal's pay.

A couple of weeks later, while I was still trying to figure out what to do next, attending class, going to reserve drill over one weekend and working six nights a week, she said in a sad quiet voice, "Bobby, I've had a miscarriage."

"Oh, honey, I'm so sorry." I hugged her and tried to console her as she cried, but somehow she detected the tension had slipped away from my body.

"You're relieved, aren't you? Sure you are," she accused. "I can tell."

"No, honey, I'm devastated," I lied. But she could tell I wasn't sincere.

"Did you sign the papers?" Her voice sounded matter-of-factly and distracted on the phone.

"Yes, they're on the dresser in the bedroom."

"I'll go by and pick them up later. I'm staying at Darrel and Dottie's until you find someplace else to live and then I'll stay in the apartment." Darrel was a friend from her work, and Dottie was his wife. Dottie was the one who had gone to court to testify we were "incompatible" due to irreconcilable differences. I didn't even know there was a court date. How stupid could I be?

The pain and misery sometimes eased off for short periods or were temporarily replaced with a driving will to succeed. More often though, they were drowned in the comfort of alcohol. Most of the time I got home from school and work, I was bone tired, dejected, demoralized and depressed.

On Sunday, a few days after the divorce, I found myself alone at home with a bottle of bourbon and a six-pack of Coke. Looking at the rapidly approaching holiday break and our four-year anniversary, I was even more depressed than usual. I tried to do some homework, but I was unable to concentrate. I couldn't think about anything except how screwed up my life had become. It is probable, if I continue at this rate, I will flunk out altogether. An obnoxious voice on the brain committee shouted, *Fuck it! Let's get drunk!* Another outraged member joined the fray. *You're an idiot, Pincer. It's obvious you can't stay drunk all the time. You may as well end it before you screw up even more.*

I concluded, with the help of some pretty poor input from the brain committee, that I had messed up my life to the point it was impossible to straighten out and, without alcohol, the constant pain of a knife slicing and twisting in my gut would be unbearable. I could not see any way back to sanity.

I calmly found the garden hose and shoved it into the exhaust of our Chevy and tied a wet T-shirt around the connection to seal it. I put the other end through the window, reached in to start the car, closed it up and left it running while I went back in to fix myself another good strong Jack Daniel's and cola. When I got back, I climbed in on the passenger side and closed the door quickly. The fumes were strong. The Chevy was running good. It was a very sharp, fire-engine red, '58, two-door, hardtop, V8 Impala, which I had "given" us as a present before we drove home for Christmas the year before. I traded the '53 Chevy her father had given us and made payments from my income at the bar as part of a deal with the seller.

The committee calmly wondered how long it would take to die. *Better finish this drink before we pass out. Don't want to waste good booze.*

I woke up flopping around in the flower bed on the side of the apartment. The neighbors heard the car running for so long, they became concerned. They pulled me out of the car and called an ambulance, but they couldn't keep me from flopping around when I started to wake up.

It seemed like I was having some sort of uncontrollable fit. I didn't know where I was or what was going on. It was dark, and I was scared. Just as the ambulance arrived, I stopped flopping, but the men in white dressed me in a straightjacket anyway and hauled me off to the university clinic.

The emergency nurse didn't say a word as she changed the oxygen connection from the ambulance emergency bottle to a large oxygen generator. After a while she untied the straightjacket and took it off.

"Sit there and breathe deeply," she said softly.

I did as she said, for a while. But when no one was watching, I just took off the mask and walked away. They were too busy with people who wanted to live to notice. I walked home even more dejected and depressed than I was before. I couldn't even do suicide right!

Temporary Insanity

I hitchhiked home to Oklahoma City for Christmas and found out later Bonnie was also home. I called her, and we had a long talk. She decided again. "It's better this way. We were too young. "We'll both be better off in the long run."

I bummed a ride back to Albuquerque with her, and we talked the entire 10-hour drive along U.S. Route 66. Probably more than we had talked since before we were married. She was right, I guess. We would probably both be better off going our separate ways, although I couldn't understand how I would live with the nagging pain in my gut.

Just a day later, I was tending bar and talking with Liana, a student and sorority girl who had been frequenting the bar a lot recently but would usually be at a table with a group. I knew her name, of course, and knew she was older than most of the other college girls, by a couple of years, because of the ID check. Sometimes she came with a date, but more often she would come in with one or two girlfriends and go home with one of the frat boys. We had spoken before but just amenities to say hello or to order a drink, but tonight she was alone and sat down at the end of the bar where I usually stood when I wasn't mixing drinks.

"Seven and Seven," she said casually as she climbed on the stool. "I hear you got divorced?" It wasn't really a question. More of a statement of fact with a teasing glance out of the corner of her eye. She was wearing a midthigh-length fitted black dress over dark hose leading down to matching high-heeled black pumps. The V neckline was cut far enough down the front to show all of her cleavage and most of the sides of her breasts. A gold chain with a green teardrop gem of some kind hung in the cleavage. Obviously, she was not wearing a bra. She was dressed up. *Way too dressy for this college toilet,* the committee chimed in.

"Yeah," I admitted, showing my depression. "It's been three weeks already. Seven and Seven coming up." I moved away to mix the drink.

"Looks like you've been out someplace pretty fancy tonight," I said as I returned with her drink.

She had large dark brown, nearly black, wide-open eyes, surrounded by long dark eyelashes, covered by lids lined with mascara and shaded with golden brown makeup under tailored, arched brows. Her long dark brown hair hung in wavy curls past her shoulders down to her shoulder blades and framed a beautifully balanced high-cheekbone face with a great smile, surrounded by full lips. Smooth naturally brown skin wrapped around a sensuous tall upright carriage that seemed to scream, "Come fuck me," whenever she moved.

"Not really too fancy but I went to the Officers Club at the air base for happy hour and dancing."

"How was it?"

"It was fun but mostly married couples, so not much action."

"How did ya know I got divorced?"

"I didn't know for sure." She smiled wryly, pointing at my hand. "I noticed you're no longer wearing your ring and I overheard some girls at the sorority house saying, 'Some good-looking jock just got divorced.' I just put two and two together and I thought it might be you."

"Yep," I said as I spread out my fingers and stared at the little untanned white line the ring had left. "So you're interested in a divorced guy?"

"Well, it's not a crime, you know. I'm divorced too."

I figured she was a musician, a local double-meaning term used to refer to women who were known to be players, or active participants in the ongoing campus dating games. She was also known to be available, because of her flirtatious manner and the company she kept. Tonight it was obvious by the cut of her dress, and the tune she was playing, she was ready to fiddle.

"I have to work 'til two but since there are no classes tomorrow, I don't have to get up early. You can stick around 'til closing if you want."

"Thanks," she said, as she flashed a broad smile. "I want."

When I closed and locked the door to the club, I made a drink and came to sit at the bar beside her, but she turned and slid off her stool. "I've been waiting all night for this," as she raised her arms around my neck and pulled herself close. The kiss was hot, wet and nearly continuous as she spoke simultaneously, "I've been sitting here all night with wet panties watching you move around the bar, mentally masturbating and dreaming of fucking you." *Girls always know when they are going to get laid.*

I was amazed at her frank admission, but I'd been turned on ever since she said she wanted to stay and realized I'd been doing similar mental calisthenics as I watched her sitting there waiting for me. I went instantly from semi hard to fully hard and pressed myself against her. "Do you want to go to my apartment? It's right around the corner behind the bar."

"Yes, eventually I do, but first I want to fuck you right now, right here." She stepped back, gathered the skirt part of her dress up to her waist and then pulled the dress off over her head and stood there in panties, garter belt, hose and high heels. She was gorgeous and confident as she looked into my eyes and shook her long wavy curls. She was stunning, and she knew it! She stood there smiling and turning her body slowly and basking in my gaze as if expecting my praise.

I had to say it, "Absolutely stunning, Liana!" She bent quickly to pull off her panties, and when she stood up, my hand went immediately down to stroke her huge neatly trimmed black bush.

Her smile turned to a devilish grin as she unbuttoned my jeans, reached into my underwear, stroked me a couple of times, pulled down my jeans enough to bend down to wet my cock for a few strokes, rose and turned around to lean over the barstool. The whole scenario hadn't taken more than maybe a minute from "I want to fuck you right now" to posing on the barstool, still smiling, looking at me over her shoulder across her butt like, "What are you waiting for?"

I let my jeans fall to the floor, rolled my underwear down and inched in close behind her while waving my aching erection up and down inside her cheeks.

When I moved near her butt, she said, "Not there now, Bobby, but I'd like it later if you want?" *If I want? What a question! We want it all!* The brain committee screamed.

I hadn't thought about it, since I'd never done it there before, but I'd heard it was different and good, and the idea intrigued me. "I will take you up on that, my sweet," I said, as I slid slowly down and into her wet vagina.

She groaned loudly, and it crossed my mind some people might still be within hearing range in the restaurant side of the business. "Oh, that's it, Bobby," she whispered loudly. "Start it nice and slow with long, easy strokes."

I'd never had anyone talk to me and tell me how to do it before, so I paid close attention and tried to do as she instructed.

"Deep, Bobby, and hold it. Then draw slowly almost all the way out and hold it. Good, now all the way in again and hold it."

A few of those strokes, and I was shaking—so ready to come I could barely hold it.

"Oh, that's good! Don't come yet, Bobby. Don't come!"

The more she said, "Don't," the more difficult it became to hold it.

"Wet your thumb and put it in my ass, Bobby!"

The new task distracted me just enough to take the immediate pressure off the need to let go. I continued to move in and out, long and slow, but not holding as long at either end of the stroke.

She began to shiver and lean back hard against the inward stroke and groan even louder. "Oh God, Bobby, put your thumb all the way in—that's it. Speed up now, Bobby. Harder, faster."

I obeyed and pulled hard against her hip with my other hand as I increased the speed.

"Now, shove it hard in my ass, Bobby! And come now, Bobby. In my ass."

Again, I obeyed. I pulled out quickly and reentered hard as directed and came almost instantly. The action was wild—frantic almost. My body convulsed, shook and shivered uncontrollably as she pressed her butt hard against me.

"Oh God," she yelled! "There it is! There it is! Ooooh, that's good! Oh God, it's soooo good, Bobby!" Her legs shook, and she leaned more heavily on the barstool to keep her balance. Breathing hard and resting for a couple of minutes, she eventually rose, pulled slowly away and turned around. Coming close and putting her arms around my neck, she smiled and tilted her head to one side. "It was worth the wait, Bobby."

"I didn't know it would be this soon when you said you would like it in your ass later—you got my cherry, Liana. I never did it like that before."

"Did you like it?"

"It was tight and smooth and I could feel the contractions when you came. So what's not to like?"

"Good, let's go to your house and do it again where I don't have to stand up." She smiled and wiggled and brushed her thick black bush against my leg.

She stayed that night and the next, giving more instructions on how she liked to do other stimulating positions. I enjoyed it all and learned to listen and respond to her desires.

A few days later, she said, in a matter-of-fact, almost distracted manner, "I've been sexually active since I was a teenager and I've always enjoyed more sex, more often than most people I know. I enjoy women sometimes too and it's even better if I can have a man and a woman at the same time."

Incredible. The brain committee was shocked.

"I married a kinky guy who enjoyed watching me with women at first and later with other men and we joined a swinging group of married couples. We were married for two years but it didn't work out for the long run because his travel schedules left me alone too much."

"Why? Didn't swinging work while he was gone?"

"Well, it wasn't just the lack of sex because I've always managed to get it whenever I want but it was a big part of it." She tilted her head, cut her eyes to the corners and gave me a sly, knowing, flirtatious smile, and I knew what she said was true.

"But when he was gone, I did get mostly shut out of the group. Everyone was married, as a prerequisite for belonging to the group and being invited to parties."

"What do you mean 'mostly'?"

"Most of the girls didn't like other wives hanging around solo when their husbands were gone but there were a few wives who liked to occasionally have a woman for themselves and one who wanted to have a threesome with her husband. After the divorce it was even worse. So, single again, I came back to school and hooked up with some old friends and found some new friends."

I was amazed and shocked at how open and frank she was as she lay there nude, propped up on the pillows, smoking a cigarette, alternately stroking her nipples and her bush near her clit and flashing me with her eyes and smile. Her legs were open, with one foot under the other knee, like a figure four. It was obvious she wanted more, and my body began to react again, sooner than I thought it would, although I was wondering how long this could continue.

We sipped our drinks and talked and joked for a while, and as I was dozing off I remembered, I'm so glad I don't have to get up early this morning and go to class.

"Happy New Year!" Her voice sang out the cheer!

Liana usually woke up with laughter and boisterous activity, but today was even more exuberant than these past few days we'd been together—though I couldn't figure out how she could drink so much and feel so good in the morning.

"What are you up to?" I smiled.

She feigned an arrogant and haughty attitude as she tilted her head back. "The question is, dahling, what are *you* up to?" She reacted to the skepticism in my eyes with laughter and a peculiar suggestion. "I need a husband so we need to get married!" And in reaction to my look of horror, "It wouldn't have to be a permanent thing—more a marriage of convenience."

"Why, a marriage of convenience?"

"So we can hook up with the swingers."

"You must be kidding!" I exclaimed, even more alarmed.!

"No, I'm not kidding. I still know at least one couple well enough so we could hook up with them and afterward maybe get an invitation to a key party or something and go from there."

Someone on the brain committee asked, *What's a key party?* I didn't want to show my total ignorance, and I could imagine, so I didn't ask.

A marriage of convenience, as such, or any marriage for that matter, would not have any sincere meaning for me. It would be a '60s open marriage arising out of my devastatingly painful divorce and subsequent total disillusionment of and disrespect for the institute of marriage. Her desire for a lifestyle that would satisfy her need for promiscuity would be interesting and exciting for me as well. So she stayed, and we planned a little wedding for the next weekend at a friend's house.

Time off for a honeymoon was out of the question, and the idea was really silly anyway. We didn't have any extra money, and I had to get into my classwork and get the last semester of college done in order to graduate. As it turned out, the wedding was just a short event in a revolving blur of classes, work, booze and sex followed by more of the same. Liana wanted something new and interesting to do every day. She was driven to be cooking up something all the time.

The bar made for a convenient rendezvous, and within a few weeks we met with several other couples, one at a time, and wound up swapping with all of them. It was obvious the girls were in charge of approval. Liana knew all of the couples from before and was highly desired by the men in the relationships. Her beauty far exceeded most of the other women, and her personality was more open and infectious. In addition, while all of the women had strong sexual desires, Liana's appetite and talents were renowned. In general, they were all shy compared to Liana, although as soon as the situation was determined to be amenable and the timing was right, they were more than willing.

"Bobby, this is Diane and Max. We call her Di and most of the guys say she is to 'die' for, and I agree." Liana was obviously in a good mood—smiling and presenting the couple like a model posing in a commercial with a fancy new washer and dryer.

"Hi, Max." I offered my hand.

"Hi, Bobby." He took my hand to shake. "I've watched you play ball for the Lobos and we've known Liana for a while now. We're both happy she's found you." Diane offered her hand to shake, and I swung my hand over to take hers. "Nice to meet you, Bobby." She was smiling and appeared to be at ease.

After one drink, Max and Liana left, and Diane stayed with me in the lounge. I was working but sat with her at the booth whenever I didn't have other duties. "I'm curious, Di, do you really like swapping or is it something you do because your husband wants it?"

"No, I like it. In fact, it was me who brought it up with him."

"How'd that happen?"

"Well . . . everyone knew there was a swinging group around but no one, except those in the group, knew exactly who else was in it. So to be in the group you had to be invited by someone and one day I was invited."

"You mean one of the husbands hit on you to join them?"

"No, actually, it's the girls who did the inviting. They pick out the couples they like and then find out if the wives are interested."

"Wow! That wasn't my view of what would happen at all. Obviously, it worked out for you two but how did he take it when you brought it up?"

"Actually, we had talked and sort of joked about it before it happened but we, like you, thought it would be the husbands doing the inviting. I'd said to him, 'I don't know how I'd feel, but if you get invited, we'll see, depending on who it is doing the inviting.'"

"So what happened?"

"Turns out, I had told him, I'd gotten wet panties at the New Year's Eve Ball dancing with the husband of the girl who was now inviting us. When I told him about the wife inviting me, he laughed and said, 'Great! I wouldn't mind tapping her!' We had a discussion about swapping in general and made some rules for us but it was a short leap from the invitation to closing the deal and accepting the date."

"What were your rules?"

"The main rule was that either of us could veto any swap. Also, there would be no getting together individually with others for outside sex. That meant, even though we had been with someone before in a swap, we would not get together again alone."

"What is it you like about swapping, Di?" She was a cute redhead with a lot of freckles surrounding bright blue eyes. Thin, with small hips with a bubble butt and small breasts, her initial impression was not sexy, but her attitude, clothes, hair and makeup surrounded her with a sensuous, flirtatious aura.

"Well, mostly, I like the adventure." She smiled and flirted with her eyes. "I get turned on by the idea . . . the thought or the daydreaming, sometimes even more than by the actual physical contact."

"Really. Why is that?"

"Occasionally, the actual sex can be disappointing."

"Disappointing how?"

"It's probably, well, at least partially my own fault, by anticipating or expecting more than some of the guys can give. Sometimes the guys are just into jumping in bed like we do sometimes at home like old married couples. It's a good physical relief, I do have orgasms and I do like it but I still like a little more petting, kissing, hugging and cuddling. You know, nice loving . . . caring, caressing."

"Yeah, I know what you mean and I like it that way too, but sometimes, especially the first time together, or after a long time between, it just gets too hot, too quick."

"True enough and I like the hot stuff very much too." She smiled shyly again. "And especially if the cuddling, sweet kisses and huggin' are between the hot stuff and the next round."

I smiled broadly at the suggestion and chuckled a little. "Okay, sweetheart, we'll see what can be done about your dreamin' later." I went back to work with half an erection for the last hour before closing, and every time I passed her, she smiled and nodded, and it got harder.

I ushered the last customers out, locked the doors, turned off the lights in the bar and lowered the dimmer to almost off in the lounge. It had been pretty dark already, but now the only area lit well enough to see much was by the jukebox and dance floor, which was next to her booth. Her red hair glowed in the soft light, and her eyes were shiny.

I slid into the booth next to her, turned sideways to put one hand in her hair and pulled it away from her neck. I nuzzled in close to kiss her neck and her ear while I began to stroke my other hand lightly under her dress over her hose on the inside of the top of her crossed leg. "I've gotten hornier and you've gotten even sexier every time I passed by," I whispered in her ear. "Whaddaya say we have a session here on the table and afterward we go to my apartment like an old married couple?"

"Ummm," she groaned and uncrossed her legs.

I turned around a little more and turned her face toward mine so I could kiss her lips. My hand moved softly and slowly up and down the inside of her thighs, teasing, above the top of her hose and eventually all the way up to her panties. As soon as my fingers touched her wet panties, she started to move. The movements got quicker and stronger almost immediately, and I responded with a little stronger pressure, pulled her panties aside and inserted two fingers.

I kissed her with all the tongue I could, and she sucked it hard. Occasionally, we softly bit each other's bottom lip and swapped tongues, and I sucked hers softly while she swirled it in my mouth. She twisted her body and bucked like a roped calf, and it became too rough to kiss her anymore. I held her hair at the back of her head and kept my other hand holding solidly against her and moved to put my thumb in her front and middle finger in the back. I watched her bounce and twist while she humped mightily.

"Oh God! There it is," she repeated in full voice with an expanded chest, arched back and exploding hips. "There it is! Don't quit, don't stop," she whispered loudly through clenched teeth. "Oh God!" She banged my arm hard against the underside of the table and continued to curl her hips back and lunge her pelvis powerfully against my hand.

Eventually, she began to slow and started to breathe more normally, although her hips continued to roll lazily against the palm of my hand.

"Well, my beauty, you sure burst out with a lot of power for a little girl and quick. You started to come as soon as I touched you. No wonder the boys have a hard time holding off and givin' you the lovin' you want. If I'd been inside you when all that started, I would have had a very difficult time holding off 'til you finished."

"I guess I forgot to mention that part." She smiled sheepishly. "So what about you now?"

"Oh, don't worry about me, sweetie. I love it this way. I love to see you come first, especially since I now know better what you want and I haven't even had you on the table yet. I get more pleasure out of making you come and it just makes me hornier. Are you ready for more?"

"Sure," she said a little breathlessly.

"Okay then." I slid out of the booth and held out my hand to her to help her up.

"Oh, where are we going?" She looked at me quizzically.

"Nowhere, sweetie. I just think it will be easier to undress you if you are standing up." I smiled, and she stood up quickly, almost jumping. I took off my shirt, and she started to unbutton the shirt top part of her dress. "Wait, turn around."

"Yes, sir!"

I stood behind her. "This looks like it buttons down the front to the waist and then lifts off over your head. Is that correct?"

"Yes again, sir."

I reached around and began unbuttoning the top of her dress and kissed her neck on the other side of the previous assault. She shivered.

Chuckling, I asked, "You cold?"

"No, you devil. You know, it's the kissing. It tingles all the way from my neck to my toes."

"Didn't skip the sensitive parts between, did it?"

"No, and you knew that too, smarty!"

I slipped the dress off over her head and laid it on the back of the booth. She turned around to face me and raised her arms to put them on my shoulders, but I took them by the wrist and held them up to look at her. *No bra.* "Nice." I smiled as I complimented her and brought her arms down and around to her back and held them there, and turned her slightly, as I kissed, licked and nibbled each of her breasts, one and then the other, several times back and forth. I pulled her hands back above her head and turned them softly so she would slowly spin around, as if dancing. "Very nice," I said again as she smoothly turned. Her breasts were small but firm with tiny areolas surrounding tiny nipples. Her waist was narrow from side to side and with a flat stomach. I stopped her turn with her back facing me the second time it came around and bent over to pull down her panties. She wiggled her legs, stepped out and turned around. A dark bush stood out against her white skin. I couldn't tell if it was dark red or black in the soft light of the lounge.

"Very pretty and cute overall and nice buns on your thin little body. Why don't you just bend over there and put your elbows on the table and stick those pretty buns out like you're a mare ready for a stallion?"

"Uuum," she mumbled softly. "I like it. How's this?" She wiggled her buns a little and looked over her shoulder, smiling as she bent over the end of the table.

I unbuttoned my jeans, let them fall to the floor, kicked them away and stepped out of my underwear.

Her nylons were dark sheer with a darker lace top up to about three-quarters of the way between her knees and the top of her thighs. She alternated between squeezing and loosening her cheeks nervously, and her legs quivered as she felt me moving up behind her. The garter belt around her waist, the straps on the sides and the hose below left her white buns looking like a beautiful target.

I spread her cheeks with one hand and dragged myself up and down until her wetness coated me. She trembled when I paused between her buns and shivered as I slowly went farther down and pressed in lightly—in a little—and pulled almost out and slowly went back in a little deeper. I repeated this action slowly several times as she rolled her hips down when I pulled out, and back up into me, when I started to push in. Finally, I pressed in as far as I could and held still. She continued to roll. I leaned down and reached around to massage her breasts and pinch her nipples. She leaned back hard against me, holding on to the sides of the table—almost sitting in my lap. After a while I rose to tease her butt and eventually put my moistened thumb in as far as it would go. I could feel her reaching for her clit as she shivered and bucked and bumped and came again even more violently than before.

As she was putting her dress back on, she asked, "You didn't come, did you?"

"No, sweetie, like I said before, I'm savin' it for when we get home."

"Why?"

"I have a lot more energy before I come the first time and I'm harder. I can usually come twice if it's a long session and the stimulation is right but it's better if I can get a ratio of at least two to one—if you know what I mean?"

"Well, I do, sorta, but don't you have to work really hard at holding off and wouldn't it be better to just let it go?"

"Yes and no. I do have to concentrate to keep from coming but in my first marriage we had little time for sex and were usually tired, so I got used to hopping on and off and going to sleep. She seemed to be okay with that—until, obviously, she wasn't. Liana taught me another way. She does not like quickies, unless you're gonna follow it right away with another."

"Well, I agree with Liana. She has taught you well." She chuckled and began to button the front of her dress.

I smiled and looked into her eyes and then down at her buttons. "Just a momentary peek at these little beauties," I requested, as I spread the opening to inspect her cute little breasts once more. I leaned her back and turned her a little so I could bend down to lick and nibble her obviously hard nipples again. It was a little awkward since she was so short and I was so tall.

"That's enough for now, my friend." She chuckled as she pushed me gently up and away. "We need to get to the old couple's horizontal position you were talking about earlier. What do you think will happen if I'm still here when Liana gets home?"

"Nothing strange like wild jealousy or anything, but I don't know exactly. It depends on what the situation is when she comes in I guess."

"Whaddaya mean?"

"I don't know because this is my first time doing this so I don't have any experience to draw from."

"Well, I've been on dates with her and her ex before but they were usually a lot earlier—like going home after dinner or a movie. Usually, the girls keep the cars so we can go home whenever we want and most of the time I would be home around midnight. Tonight, or this morning, as the case is, we didn't get started until after two when you closed the bar so I have no idea what's going to happen. I think you're right though. She won't be jealous. She knows what's happening."

I locked up the bar, and we walked around the corner about a half block on the side street to my little apartment. It was old, probably built in the 1930s, a tiny, one-story, one-bedroom, wood-frame, freestanding house that was owned by the same people who owned the bar. I took her hand and motioned at the corner. "This way." And at the door, "This is it." No conversation—just the necessary communication to get to the bedroom. The furnishings were also old and simple. The living room had a stuffed couch and chair and an old wooden coffee table. The kitchen had a small wood table and four chairs. The bedroom had a regular bed, a nightstand on one side and a valet chair in the corner by the other side—my side.

We each undressed ourselves on either side of the bed like we said, "like an old married couple," but that was the end of the anticipated routine sex. We met in the middle of the bed on our knees. When we hugged, her face was between my pectorals, and I turned to put my right nipple next to her lips. "Perfect height," I said as I rubbed it against her lips.

Surprised, she asked, "What? You like your nipples licked too?"

"Sure, my nipple nerves are connected to my prostate just like yours seem to be connected to your clit."

"Really, I've never known any guys who liked it."

"Well, maybe some wouldn't admit it if they did, I guess. And maybe it seems effeminate, I suppose, and some just wouldn't know it's good because they haven't tried it."

She latched onto my nipple like a sucker fish on the side of a tank. It was time for me to give instructions. "Easy, honey. It's sensitive and I don't like pain at all—just tongue, lips and maybe soft nibbles. Okay?"

"Uh-huh," she murmured between licks. She knew immediately what to do and did it very well as she switched back and forth between the little hard protrusions.

We rolled together onto the bed, and she pushed me over on my back and went down on me. "It's my turn now, Bobby!" She was excited and obviously well cultivated in the art of oral stimulation. Her bottom was still wet and nearby, so I began to shake hands with her privates, thumb in the back and as many fingers as would fit in front, just two in this case—she was small.

"Don't spend too much time down there, my lovely, or you will explode the cannon and spoil the party," I warned.

She continued with one more very deep immersion but not into her throat, bobbed a couple of times, and stayed as long as she could. "Enough for now then," she whispered as she turned back for a quick lick at my nipples.

"Oh yeah, it was great! The best—certainly the deepest I've ever had and it would be great for when I've already had an orgasm and when you want to evoke seconds but right now you almost wound up with a mouthful or a face full."

"Well, that's happened before." She laughed.

I rolled her over and went down on her after kissing her lips, nipples, belly button and licking the inside of her thighs. I pushed her legs up on my shoulders and reached around with both hands to massage her breasts and pinch her nipples lightly while I sucked and tongued her below. I had to let go with one hand to hold her down because she began bucking hard against my face. *She's coming again! She's so easily multiorgasmic! What fun!*

I rose and leaned forward on my arms and slowly lowered my pelvis down to hers. She curled her stomach and slammed her pelvic arch into me over and over again, and when she finished she eventually slowed down to lie still again.

"Roll over, Bobby, it's my turn on top." She was gentle but direct, and it was now clear she wanted to be in charge.

She rose straight and sat across my lap and lightly rubbed her wet hair against my swollen erection, teasing by rolling her hips back and forth. Her eyes were closed, and she was breathing hard with her mouth wide open, and she was stroking her own nipples with both hands. Finally, she reached down with one hand and pulled my erection upright and sat down on it. She sank all the way down and sat there for a moment, obviously enjoying the feeling of the deep penetration. She began slowly—teasing herself and me with long, slow strokes but in short order began banging again with her thinly covered pelvis and with an intensity belying her small body.

"Let it go, Bobby! I'm not going to come this time until you do."

I had been holding off—not working at it but just enjoying the moment—but when she spoke it was only a few seconds before I exploded, and so did she. It was so powerful it was almost violent. She pounded me so hard I thought we might crack our pelvic bones, but it didn't hurt at the time. She slowed to an easy roll and eventually stopped and stretched her legs out on top of mine. I stroked her back and rubbed her shoulders, and as her body relaxed, it seemed to melt into mine. She was still in that position when I fell asleep.

When I awoke in the morning I was already semihard and in her mouth. I was still on my back, and her thin body was curled up next to mine with her butt near my hand like it had been at one point the night before.

"Good morning," I said cheerfully.

She shoved her head down more forcefully and squeezed hard with her hand at the base before she rose and turned around. "Good morning to you also." She smiled as she continued to hold and stroke my wet erection.

My pelvis was very sore, and the pressure as she squeezed and pressed down to sit up was unpleasant. *But it's worth it!* the committee exclaimed.

Obviously, Liana had not yet come home, and it was daylight out. Hopefully, she was getting all she wanted because I was going to be worn-out.

"So, Little Miss to Die For, you're ready for some more, I take it?"

Her freckles stood out more in the daylight than they had in the dimly lit lounge, and her thin face shone brightly around her smiling blue eyes. Scanning the picture, I could now see that her thick bush was neatly trimmed and matched her dark red hair. Her areolas, like her freckles, were nearly orange—kind of a burnt sienna maybe. *How pretty! And unusual!* The committee was impressed. "I *am* ready! How could you tell?" She was enjoying the tease.

"I could tell by the way you hold your mouth, sweetie," I joked. "You're gonna have to roll over on your tummy though 'cause I'm gonna need your buns for padding."

"Oh, why—I like it like that but why do you say you need it?"

"Because I'm very sore in the pelvic area and I think it would hurt a lot to bang pelvic bones again this morning."

"Yeah, you're right! I'm sore there too but I hadn't thought about turning over—good idea!" She turned over and looked over her shoulder, trying to look at the disproportionate muscle on her gorgeous buns. "I do have plenty of padding, don't I?" She giggled.

"Just the right amount, sweetie, and you look great!" I rolled over, rose on my knees and spread her legs from behind.

This position was even better on the bed than it had been the night before at the table, and she was able to bounce against the bed and push her butt farther up and into me. I was right—her bulbous buns were firm and provided a great cushion for my bruised pelvic bone, and the soreness went almost unnoticed. I rested most of my weight on her buns but softened it with my knees and arms and worked her slow and easy into a rhythm that soon became involuntary convulsions for both of us. She was just as raucous as before, but I didn't try to hold off, and we shuddered, shivered and came together without conscious control.

"I've left you with a virgin butt, Di. We'll have to take care of that if there's a next time."

"Not quite virgin, Bobby. You've had your thumb and fingers in there several times already," she said, chuckling as she grabbed my hand to inspect it closely. "Odd shape, Bobby, where'd you get it? Is the other one the same?" She reached for my other hand, but I held both thumbs up.

"Yep, they're a matched pair, except the left one is scarred a little. Got 'em from my mother's side of the family."

"And whaddaya mean *if* there's a next time? There better be a next time or I'm gonna be *very* disappointed."

"Oh, I hope so but I'm graduating in June and heading for flight school in July so there's not a lot of time left."

"Okay, I understand but we'll make time, Bobby—at a party or another date. So you're gonna be a pilot, huh—air force?"

"No, Marine Corps—through the navy flight school in Pensacola, Florida."

"I didn't know the Marine Corps had airplanes."

"Yep, jet fighters and bombers, multiengine transports and helicopters."

"Wow! What will you fly?"

"Well, I didn't even know the Marine Corps had airplanes myself until a couple of years ago when a recruiter got hold of me. Hopefully I'll fly them all eventually. I'm partial to helicopters because of my time with the reserves but I won't know until I get most of the way through training."

"Why is that?"

"Well, I'm too tall for most fighter cockpits so it's not likely I will be going through the jet pipeline but maybe, in the future there will be aircraft with larger cockpits to accommodate my long legs. Anyway, you have to qualify with exceptional flying skills to fly jets and I've never flown anything, so I have no idea what will happen during training."

"Well, we still have a couple of months before you leave but I'll say good luck to you now—not that I don't think I'll have another opportunity but just in case I might forget later. Is that someone at the door? Is it Liana?" She jumped a little to start getting out of the bed. "I should get dressed."

"No, don't worry. She won't care and will probably like you just the way you are."

Liana burst delightfully into the house. "Good morning you two! I knew you were still here, Di, because you didn't come home last night. I was hoping you would show up there for a threesome, but since you didn't, I was hoping you'd still be here. Great!"

"Good morning, Liana," we chimed in together. And I continued, "Well, Liana, this little girl has completely worn me out and I'm pretty sore, so if you want, you two can do whatever you like and I'll just watch, if it's okay?" Visually stimulated and easily aroused by the sight of a shapely female body, the committee regretted the decision to not participate but heartily approved of watching.

"Ha!" Liana retorted. "I'm not surprised. She usually wears everyone out! We've been together several times before—with my ex on dates and at parties. Whaddaya think, Di, you up for a quickie?"

"I already had a session this morning, Li, and it was *not* a quickie but I can go again." She smiled and turned her bright blue eyes up to meet Liana's dark brown orbs.

"Great," Liana said as she started to peel off her clothes while not taking her eyes off Diane. "Bobby, why don't you put the coffee on, and yes, you can come back to watch if you want." *If we want?* the committee screamed again.

I waited until the coffee was ready and poured myself a cup before planting myself on my valet chair in the bedroom to enjoy the scene. My mind wandered as I watched the girls stroking, kissing and petting one another. The chair was a genuine antique and was the only piece of furniture in the apartment worth anything at all. The remainders of the sticks in the apartment were strictly functional necessities purchased at second hand stores or through personal newspaper ads and garage sales. I'd found myself in a situation after the divorce, which left me with little choice. Furnished apartments were more expensive than unfurnished, so I rented unfurnished and bought a mattress to throw on the floor to start. The valet chair was the second addition as a coincidental, but special, find in the corner of a garage sale. It looked kind of out of place, as if it wasn't considered worth being part of the sale. I queried while negotiating for an upholstered living room chair. "Why don't we throw in that old chair in the corner?" I nodded toward the dusty wooden chair with the shoulder-shaped hanger at the top of the back. The finish was faded, and it was scratched but otherwise looked okay. I was, at the time, taking a wood finishing and refinishing class at UNM. I figured refinishing it would be relatively easy.

"We could throw it in for another five bucks," she said, chuckling. She was asking $10 for the stuffed living room chair.

I chuckled also. "I figured I wouldn't charge you to haul it off—you know, I would do it as a favor."

She laughed. "Okay, if you give me ten bucks for the living room chair, I'll throw in the valet chair."

"Well, I was thinking five bucks for the living room chair. So that won't work. I'm not really impressed with the living room chair anyway but I'm kinda stuck with what's available."

"Okay, five bucks for the living room chair and two bucks for the valet chair." She smiled and threw her arms out in front like, "Here it is, take it."

"How about six bucks for both chairs?" *Good! Why not take a shot?*

She paused a few seconds, chuckled, shrugged her shoulders and finally said, "Okay, you got it. Six bucks for both." Her smile showed, as she stuck out her hand to shake on it. She enjoyed the negotiation and was satisfied.

I was proud of my negotiating skills and felt like I had accomplished a lot with very little of my $48 a week salary. In fact, a week of my occasional tips when serving as bartender probably covered the $6 expenditure.

The girls continued their escapade as if I wasn't even there. Although on several separate occasions, they each glanced to see if I was watching and smiled approvingly when we locked eyes. They came separately, and each of them locked eyes with me while they were coming. It was quite a show as evidenced by my ever increasingly hard erection. After they finished and noticed my condition, they invited me into the group and proceeded to work me over in the nicest way. It didn't take long when there were two talented ladies switching from the starter button and the finish button to the erection.

The spring of 1963 had been filled with the last semester of classes, monthly Marine Corps Reserve meetings and some exciting and erotic times with Liana's group while still working six nights a week at the bar. Most encounters were swap dates with various couples on Friday or Saturday nights or Sunday afternoon. One Sunday afternoon pool party at a private home resulted in multiple penetrations in groups, as well as some private situations. I watched Liana with another man for the first time that day because all of our previous experiences had been separate swaps. I had often wondered how I would feel on such an occasion. Would I be jealous? I knew what had been going on, of course, but how would the visual verification affect our relationship? It didn't of course. But somewhere along the line I felt this was not what I would want to have in my life for the long term. Certainly, our "marriage" only existed so that we could participate in these types of activities. So as it turned out, it was fun and erotically exciting to watch her and even more intense to be with another woman while watching her. Because she was the most attractive woman in the group, she was also the most active. There were five other men at the party, and I saw her with all of them at one time or another, including more than one at a time on at least one occasion.

Thursday night before graduation was scheduled to be held the following Tuesday, Liana brought a girl to the bar. "This is Joanie," she said, as she slid into a booth near the jukebox by the dance floor. Her husband's out of town, and we're not playing by the rules. "Can we have a couple of Seven and Sevens, Bobby?"

"Sure, on the way."

It was nearly closing time, and they sat talking quietly while I locked up, swept up and dusted the pool table. I finished putting the pool table cover on and put away the chalk and cues. Liana put some quarters in the jukebox and punched up some songs she liked.

The restaurant in the other half of the building was still open, so I went out to lower the sound, and when I came back, Liana was dancing slowly to the beat and unbuttoning her blouse. It was one of those white, almost see-through blouses she liked to wear over a lacy nearly see-through bra. She was beautiful and enjoyed showing off her assets. Her eyes were like large dark brown olives filled with excitement and daring, surrounded by long dark lashes. Her black hair was pulled back and up in a high ponytail that hung down below her shoulders. She was tall, about five feet nine inches and of medium build. She liked to go without a bra but occasionally wore a half-cup bra.

Joanie joined her on the dance floor, pulling off her shirt over her head, while looking at Liana, as if I wasn't there. She was bra-less and obviously very proud of her perky little B cups. They were white with little pink nipples and stood out from her tanned body like two small headlights pointing the way.

Liana seemed not to notice her as she glared at me with excited eyes—challenging me, teasing me, daring me. Although I had been married for four years, I was a sexual novice when I met Liana, and she knew it. She enjoyed teaching me new things that would give her pleasure, but even more, she enjoyed shocking me. I was also shy, and she loved to turn me on and embarrass me at the same time. I was about to take her challenge and started to unbutton my shirt when her skirt fell to the floor and she kicked it away. Liana almost always wore a skirt, half-slip and panties rather than jeans or slacks because she enjoyed sex in semipublic places like an out-of-the-way park bench, the back row of a balcony in a movie theater, the hood of the car in a somewhat remote place in the park. Actually, any new place where there were people around but far enough away so no one could see exactly what was going on. The danger of getting caught excited her, but she didn't want to actually get caught—but didn't mind if I got caught. She would arrange our action so she would be on top, with me in a sitting position, and she would sit in my lap, either facing me or facing away depending on the circumstances. If anyone got too close for her comfort, she would simply get up, drop the hem of her skirt, walk off with her panties neatly tucked in her purse as though absolutely nothing was unusual at all and leave me scrambling to button up my jeans over an erection.

The music stopped, and while the record changed, the two girls turned their backs to me and hovered over the jukebox. I could see Liana's garter belt through her slip, and I noticed the hose and black high heels. Pumps, I think they're called, and I loved them. She was six feet tall in those three-inch heels, and I loved her height also. You couldn't help but notice when Liana walked into a room. She towered over most of the other girls, and her beauty was breathtaking. She loomed over Joanie in a protective and unthreatening way.

Joanie was cute, not beautiful or gorgeous but sweet-pretty, about five feet four inches tall, with short bouncy blonde curls down to about the middle of her neck. She was quarter turned toward me with the pink and orange lights from the jukebox highlighting her little breasts. Her skin was a little darker than Liana's, but it was because of her tan, as evidenced by the strap lines across her back and the whiteness of her breasts. They were talking low, obviously enjoying themselves. Liana was smiling, and Joanie was giggling.

They continued to talk for a short while after the next record started, and Liana took off her slip and laid it across the back of the nearby booth while Joanie turned her back to me and seemed to be undoing the front of her jeans.

Liana's panties were obviously already in her purse, and I found myself wondering whether she had taken them off for this show or if she had found it necessary for an earlier occasion. Yes, I was a bit jealous, I suppose. I knew the "marriage" was "open," and with the swaps and the parties, I knew I could handle just about anything, but somehow it just didn't sit right with me that she could be off somewhere with someone else while I was working or in class. The brain committee discussed it and decided if we ever enter into this type of arrangement in the future, there would be a new rule. *She can do almost anything or anybody she wants but we have to approve and be actively participating.*

The music started again, and Liana could tell where my attention was focused, so she started to move her hips aggressively to the beat. The girls were sort of dancing together in a kind of little synchronized step while they were both staring at me. Joanie was now in pink lace panties and white socks. Next to Liana's long legs in a garter belt, hose and heels, she was almost childlike. I smiled at her, and she smiled back and seemed to relax a little. I don't know what kind of look I had on my face before, but I realized I hadn't been smiling, until then. I relaxed a bit myself, sipped my bourbon and Coke, kicked off my loafers and leaned back on the edge of the pool table to enjoy the show.

After the suicide attempt, I didn't drink much, but I was getting pretty high already. I didn't like the taste of booze, but I liked what it would do for me, so I usually mixed it with Coke in a tall glass. I had learned I could have two drinks during the last couple of hours before closing and not be drunk on the job. Then one drink after work would put me right on the step of a pleasant high.

The music stopped again and didn't start. Liana was out of change and came over to dig some quarters out of my jeans. "Make us a couple more drinks, will ya, Bobby?"

"Sure." I made us all fresh drinks and heard the music start as I headed back to the lounge, but they weren't dancing anymore. The girls had pulled out several seat cushions from the booths and made a crude bed on the dance floor in front of the jukebox.

Liana and Joanie were lying, half sitting, on the uneven cushions looking kind of awkward, and I chuckled at them as I handed them their drinks and asked, "What are you girls up to now?"

Liana laughed with a now familiar challenge in her eye and motioned for me to join them. "C'mon over here," she teased. I sat down on one of the cushions next to the base of the booth, leaned back against the side and crossed my outstretched legs. We talked and joked for a while, and I commented, "I'm so glad I don't have to get up in the morning and go to class." Was this déjà vu. I remembered thinking or saying the same thing on New Year's just about five months earlier. But no, I was finally finished with all of it. I had finished all of my finals and was going to graduate next Tuesday. There were no classes tomorrow, no reserve drill this weekend and no problems on the horizon. I was going to graduate in Marine Corps Dress Whites and be commissioned a second lieutenant immediately after the graduation ceremony. Mom and Dad were coming to the event. Flight school was next.

At one point early in the session, I was on my back, and the girls were facing each other, with Joanie hovering lightly over my face, enjoying my tongue, and Liana was in her favorite position in my lap, mounted on her favorite tool. I couldn't see what they were doing to each other—maybe kissing? Suddenly, Joanie's knee slipped between the cushions, and the full weight of her little body came pressing down on my face. She couldn't get up, and I couldn't breathe. I lifted her up by the bottom and tossed her gently off to the side, where she landed on another cushion, and it slid clear over on the other side of the room near the jukebox!

Liana tried to jump up, but her foot slipped on the cushion on the other side, and she fell off to the floor, not so gently, with her feet on me and her head on the cushion, which had slipped away on that side. I was laughing so hard I couldn't talk. Joanie had her hand over her mouth trying not to laugh, and Liana's expression was rapidly changing from fright to astonished disbelief before she also broke out in a fit of laughter.

We were finally able to stop laughing and kicked aside the rest of the cushions. "Well, that calls for another drink and a redo," Liana said jokingly after a short pause while we all caught our breaths.

"Sounds about right to me," I said, as I scrambled my scattered body together and got up off the floor.

After the drink and a cigarette, I found myself sitting on a cushion with my back against the wall and a girl on each side. Liana kissed me long and slow and played with my balls while Joanie licked my nipples for a while and worked her way down to engulf my hard erection. In this position the only part of each of the girls I could reach was their crotches, so that's where I started. I knew Liana liked the bowling ball grip because she's the one who taught it to me. So the girls played and licked and sucked, and I pressed my thumbs and fingers in their respective front and back openings until they both came.

Eventually, I folded my jeans to put under my head, folded Liana's skirt to put under my back and the girls proceeded to get back onto their previous positions.

The girls were in charge, as they always are, and eventually did everything two girls can do for a guy and I did everything one guy can do for two girls—at least as much as I knew. There was body rubbing, nude dancing to slow music, sexy, shimmy and shake dancing to fast music, cigarettes, drinks, jokes and stories. It lasted about two hours or so after we discarded the seat cushions. I think there was at least one more orgasm for each of them, although I held off and only came once—in Joanie's mouth while I watched Liana going down on her from behind.

I was certain I would never forget the night but knew it was sure to be one of the last, if not the last, with Liana. I think she knew it too because she was melancholy later when we got home and she had not shown that side before in these exciting but superficial six months.

I slept most of the next day and Liana was gone when I got up. I went to the restaurant to have a late lunch and shoot a couple of practice games of bumper pool in the lounge before I had to go to work.

Dutch came in early and we shot a couple of games against each other before the partner games started. When we played against each other we only played for a dollar. He won them both. When we played as partners, we usually played for five or ten dollars, per player, per game. Later in the evening a couple of guys we had played before came in and wanted to play us again. When we played at their bar, on their table, we broke even. Breaking even is not bad when playing on their turf where they know the table, the breaks, the speed of the cover and the bounce off the edges and the pegs. The table now being turned, so to speak, we accepted the challenge at ten dollars per player, per game.

A sophomore football player, I'd coached in spring ball a year ago, was curious and stepped up to ask about the game. Dutch began the game as we stood nearby watching.

I explained, "Bumper pool is played with five balls for each team, red or white solid colored balls. The first ball to be shot has a red or white dot. The playing area of the table is two and half feet wide and about four feet long, rail to rail with a hole in each end in the middle. There is one bumper peg on each side of each hole and eight pegs in the middle of the table which form a plus (+) sign squared toward the hole in the end and to the sides. This precludes shooting straight at the hole from the other end without banking the shot.

To begin the game, the balls are all lined up on the end of the table with two on each side of the pegs next to the hole and one in front of the hole. Each player shoots the center ball at the same time from the end toward the hole on the other end by banking past the right side of the pegs in the middle. The player with the opening ball closest to the hole, or in the hole, wins the shot and is allowed to continue until a shot is missed, after which, the second player on the opposing team would shoot. If both players sink the first ball, they both shoot a second ball of their choice at the same time and then a third if they both sink the second and so on, until one misses or both miss and one is closer to the hole than the other. Five balls sunk is the end of the game and if both players make all five balls in a row then the game is a tie, the bet is then carried over and another game proceeds with the same shooters." In less time than it took to explain the game, Dutch and his opponent had run the first set of balls. Then, within a little more than a half hour, they ran four sets of five, with added bets at the end of each game, making the fifth game worth fifty dollars per player and I hadn't even had to make a shot yet. This could be an interesting night! Dutch was hot and it was our table. We knew it like the back of our hands. The opponent finally missed the third ball in the fifth game and Dutch sank the last two just like he did the previous 23. The opponent was so incensed he said he couldn't play anymore. He and his partner paid up and left.

Sitting at the bar later, halfway into a beer Dutch said, "I wish those guys would have stuck around for a little while longer so we could rack up some real dough for a celebration in Juarez."

"Celebrate what?" I asked.

"Your goddamn graduation, you crazy bastard!"

"Dutch, I can't go to Juarez this weekend. I've got to work tonight and tomorrow night. Tomorrow is my last night here. Besides, you would not believe what Liana did to me last night. Why should I go to Juarez and pay for it?"

"Because it is your last weekend here and probably our last weekend together," he said. "And who says we have to go to get laid? We can just go down and get a room on the Mexican side, swim in the pool, throw back some tequila, catch some shows and shoot the bull about our times together."

"Why not?" I asked rhetorically.

Why not indeed! Now I know why not. Here I am in the Juarez jail with stitches in my head, blood on my shirt, grime on my body, the world is rapidly turning into Monday morning and I'm supposed to graduate from college in Albuquerque tomorrow.

It sounded like a good enough plan; I quit the job and the owner slipped me a fifty-dollar bonus. So I had the weeks' pay, the winnings and the bonus for about a hundred and fifty bucks. Dutch had about a hundred. We jumped in my new MGB, rounded up some clothes and shaving gear and went by Tony's for a free pizza to eat on the way.

Free pizza was one of the bennies for college athletes. Tony gave free pizzas to football, basketball and baseball players to help draw a crowd into his parlor after the games. If we didn't want a pizza on game night or if we shared pizzas, we would save the extra coupons for later. Also, Tony would forget to ask for the coupon so we always had extras for free pizzas.

The drive down was easy and fun. It was the first time I had taken the new MGB on a road trip. It was a graduation present to myself, but it was a surprise, even to me. After the divorce, I went to the dealership to see about getting some kind of used car to drive until graduation and until I got on the Marine Corps payroll. Being a well-known football player had its benefits. I had a job and good credit but I would not have the income to qualify for an expensive new car loan, until the Marine Corps paychecks start in July, if there weren't some privileges attached. The dealership owner was a fan of the Lobo's, a friend of the head coach and a former marine. I went to shop just for a cheap used car, mostly to get back and forth to classes but he offered a new car and a loaner while the new car was being shipped, no down payment and no payments until August 1st, when I would be on Marine Corps second lieutenant's pay.

The loaner was a '53 MG-TD while the new MGB was on its way, and I fell in love with it, except for the first gear—it was not a synchromesh. I liked to race in Gymkhana races sometimes on Sunday afternoon but could never get into a groove with the requirement to stop before downshifting to first gear or maybe lock up the rear wheels with the brakes and try to shift while the transmission is not turning. It failed more often than not and I was terrified of ripping out the transmission of the loaner car. Maybe, just maybe, the new one wouldn't have as many problems because it would have a new synchromesh first gear. The TR-3s were wiping me out. Not so much though—I never won a race, even with the new MGB but did get a third place one time because the actual third place winner, by time, was penalized.

We crossed the bridge into Mexico late Friday night—actually early, early Saturday morning but Juarez was still jumping. American tourists crowded the sidewalks wandering from bar to bar. The colorful people of Mexico still cluttered the streets and businesses were still trying to entice customers into their shops and restaurants. With the top down on the MGB we could hear the Mariachi bands wandering the streets and filling the narrow space between the buildings with the beautiful rhythm and resonance of their songs. The smells of chili peppers mixed with fried beef and fried chicken and onions blended with the sweat of the dancing and singing people and hung in the moist air like a sweet perfume.

The cabdrivers sat on the fenders of their cabs, crowded around each corner, whistling and waving. Each one would swear he knew the best bar and least expensive Blue Room in all of Mexico. "Hey mister, you want to go to my Blue Room? Only five dollars, American," they yelled. "Prettiest women, best bodies, youngest girls. Only the best for my gringo amigos."

Dutch was in a good mood, waving and joking with them at every opportunity. "How much for a quickie? What about all night?" They bantered back and forth and offered some prices but we were not interested. Our focus was to just relax and have a good time.

We wound our way on south through the neon lighted streets to a nice little motel where we stayed overnight about six months ago, between the divorce and Christmas. It was the only white building in the area which was a combination of apartments, tiny brown adobe houses and small daytime shops. A grocery store, filling station, drugstore and some others we didn't recognize, were all closed. The street was deserted and dark except for the English orange neon MOTEL sign and half a dozen small yellow lights bordering the sidewalk and driveway into the parking lot.

The desk clerk, who was probably also the owner, was somewhat amused at two crazy gringos looking for a motel room. Two rooms she could understand. One room, two beds and she just shook her head. Dutch spoke more Spanish than I did, but it was minimal, so he was having some difficulty. "Dos hombres, uno habitacion, dos camas, por favor," he said.

"Two men, one room, two beds, please," I understood.

"El mismo" she kept saying but he kept insisting on a lower price. He was able to clarify the situation but she still wanted to charge us the same as for two rooms. Everything in Mexico had an asking price which was totally negotiable and negotiating was part of the game. It wasn't that we were so cheap but we didn't have a lot of extra money to throw around. Finally, the two were able to compromise and we had a deal.

Dutch had a roll of paper pesos we had acquired at the border and peeled them off just like he knew what he was doing and paid cash for two nights. I was still trying to figure out the exchange rate and whether we were getting a good deal.

We decided to hit the pool, shower and shave before we headed back to town. The bars and shows would only be closed for one hour between six and seven in the morning so there was no hurry. The room was nice. Small but clean with two twin beds with the headboards against one wall and a little nightstand between with a lamp and a small AM radio. It reminded me of a similar little radio we had as kids. We used to fall asleep listening to it and never remember turning it off. Probably Dad did it. I wonder if we will actually do any sleeping in this room.

I was tired all the time and I'd lost weight because school, working, reserve drill and sexual escapades had left little time for nonessentials like eating and sleeping. I was having a supersize, sinking spell, so I turned the radio on, tuned it to a local Mexican music station and lay down.

Dutch was already in his swim suit and threatened, "I'm gonna throw you in the pool if you don't get a move on."

I knew he could do it too, if he really wanted. I didn't know if I had fallen asleep or not but I knew if I didn't keep going now I would sleep the whole weekend away. "Okay, Dutch, I'm already half way there. Don't get too rambunctious."

The pool was cool and refreshing. "Well, I'm awake now Dutch. I don't know if it was worth the effort instead of just taking a shower but it has served the purpose." We headed for town and parked the car on the main street headed back toward the bridge we had come across.

Dutch started speaking in his broken Spanish to some kids on the street who were admiring my car, but they laughed and answered in English, so he gave up. "Okay, I'll give you five pesos to watch the car while we're gone and another five when we get back." Of course, he knew they wouldn't actually watch over and protect the car but the payment and promise would probably keep them from messing it up and then offering to wash it when we got back.

We headed to a bar with a continuous strip show where we'd been the last time we were here and recognized it when we passed it on the way to the motel. The stage was a large half circle with a polished wooden floor and recessed footlights all around the outer edge. It was the same height as the square wooden tables pushed up against it and scattered around the large room. Straight back wooden chairs around the tables provided seating and we found a deuce right next to the stage. We ordered our first tequila shooters, with beer chasers, as we watched the dancing girls peeling down to bare tops and tiny G-string bottoms.

Certainly nothing exceptional but pretty girls who moved in a tantalizing and inviting way. They all had great smiles and seemed to enjoy themselves. All just part of the act. *Not bad, the committee chimed in, showing no particular interest.*

"You want company senor," the dancer asked Dutch? She had just finished her show and was headed out to dance at another bar but would have enough time to hustle a few drinks, to make some extra money, if she could. She wouldn't actually drink of course. The bartender would serve her water with a lime or soda or anything cheap and split whatever they charged the customer.

"No thanks, we're just here to celebrate his graduation," he answered, as he nodded at me. "No women this time." He smiled.

She smiled and moved on.

We talked for hours, about our teammates, coaches, wives, girlfriends and a myriad other subjects, stories and history. The MC announced the show would start again when they reopened in an hour. "Wow, quick! It seems like we just got here! Give us a shooter and a beer to go," I yelled. The waitress delivered and we threw down the shooters in the bar and took the beer with us in a paper cup. The parting was jovial and cordial. They invited us back, explaining it was the law and they needed to clean up.

Outside the sun was shining and the day was starting to warm up fast. We walked a while and then stepped into a clean looking little café to get some breakfast. The Mexican seasoning smelled good and I remembered Liana's Mexican cooking and the party she had arranged with Joanie. I smiled, and Dutch, thinking I was impressed with the waitress, said, "She's too young, Bob."

"I am impressed but it wasn't why I was smiling, Dutch. I was thinking about Liana and Joanie. Remember? I told you about it on the drive down here."

The waitress brought strong coffee and took our empty beer cups. I could see a lot of her cleavage clearly as she bent over the table. She was full breasted, narrow around the waist and the peasant dress accentuated her hips. The top was cut in an arc from the top outside edge of her shoulders across the front about three-quarters of the way down her cleavage but the edge was covered with an embroidered white lace just above her areolas, through which the outline could be seen through the flower patterned lace material. She wasn't tall but she wasn't as short as most of the Mexican girls. Her hair was pulled back and down into a clip at the back of her neck which made her face look open and vulnerable.

She was young, as Dutch had said, maybe 17 or 18 or so, I thought. The brain committee wondered, *How she would look if she raised the clip up into a ponytail.* I had not been turned on by the nearly naked dancers but now the pretty young waitress was having a definite effect on me. I just told Dutch I was all out of energy and wasn't it just last night I was with Liana and Joanie? No. That was Thursday night and this was Saturday morning. Jeez, I'm having trouble keeping track of what day it is and the weekend has just started.

"Are you working all day?" I asked.

"No," she smiled.

Encouraged, I asked, "would you like to come over to our place for a swim this afternoon?"

"I'd like to but my father won't let me out yet. I'm 17 but he says I have to wait until I'm 18."

"Well good for him and for you. I'll come back in a couple of years and check you out."

"I'll probably still be working here, since it's my father's business, but not as much. I will be going to college across the river in El Paso" she volunteered proudly.

She reminded me of myself. Driven to graduate from college no matter what the difficulty and odds.

Dutch reminded me, "No girls this weekend." He laughed and joked with her, "Wanna get married for the weekend, chiquita bonita?" She knew he was joking and laughed with us. A very cute and sweet girl. How precious and innocent.

We ate our breakfast of ranchos huevos and headed back to the bar. It was quiet when we got back and we decided to slow down a bit ourselves.

Dutch ordered, "Dos frio Dos Equis por favor. Grande!" He also counted our green and our pesos to see where we stood. "We have about forty-five dollars each," he estimated, "and the hotel bill is already paid."

"I have another twenty hidden in my shoe for emergencies and gasoline home and I also tied my car keys in my shoe lace for safe keeping." I had gotten drunk and lost them once before and I didn't want to lose them again, especially down here.

We relaxed—everything was going well. The shooters were less than a dollar each and the big beers were about seventy-five cents. It was obvious we could drink ourselves into oblivion and not run out of money. The "continuous" show hadn't actually started yet when we got back to the bar and wasn't due to start for another half hour.

The waitress brought more beer and we were hitting the nachos again. The show started and the girls were dancing just for us because the place was still almost empty this early in the morning except for the waitress and the doorman. The girls were rotating between our stage and other stages in other bars and the same ones kept coming again and again in the repeat of the shows during the day. Different costume, different music, same girls.

We would tip them if they were really good or were really friendly during their dance. We put a dollar bill folded length-wise in the top of a beer bottle and set it on the edge of the stage. They would come over at the end of the dance and squat down over it and pick it up by squeezing their butt cheeks together. One girl picked up the whole bottle and we roared. They were hustling tricks between shows and after we had been there a while they would stop by and see if we were "ready for some action yet?" We kept telling them no thanks but they kept coming back anyway.

Sometime in the afternoon we started doing the shooters again. The tequila had no taste and we had long since given up the lime and salt. The routine order had become a shooter with beer back and the beer was just to kill time between shooters so we wouldn't spend our money too fast.

We never made it back to the pool and the afternoon slipped into evening and the Saturday night crowd filled up the room. The girls didn't pay any attention to us anymore and played to the rest of the crowd. We talked about ball games, bumper pool, toga parties, girls, cars, wives, school, problems past, potential future alternatives and full circle again and again.

Dutch thought he might join the army. I tried to talk him into going back to school so he could graduate and go in as an officer.

"What if there is a continuation of the war in Korea or an expansion in Vietnam. Do you want to go as a mudslinging doggie?"

"Why not," he said. "Who the hell cares? If I have to listen to one more narrow minded professor pontificate on the accomplishments of his specialty narrowed world, I'll literally puke all over the classroom."

"I'll drink to that." I laughed, and we dropped it.

Somehow, the evening slipped into late night and early morning without my noticing it. The crowd went away and the girls came back to us. "You still here?" one of them asked. "Aren't you boys ready for a little company yet?" another questioned. Then later the sarcasm. "What's the matter, boys? Did you drink all your dinero? Or did the tequila fix it so you can't get it up?" They must have known we were getting low on money because we had quit tipping. At first we just laughed it off politely and just said no, but as it continued, our patience began to wear. Dutch was curt with the last few, "Not only no, but hell no and beat it!"

I wasn't paying much attention when one of them stopped and was having a longer than usual conversation with Dutch. All I heard was "Fuck off bitch! Can't you understand? We are not interested!"

Suddenly, she hit him with her purse and Dutch, in a flash reflex, backhanded her in the shoulder. She was knocked off balance reeling into the empty tables behind her screaming as she stumbled.

I was thinking the place was almost empty but the locals seemed to come from everywhere. It was like someone had poured turpentine in an ant hole and everybody was scrambling to get out. The whole place was an instant madhouse. One of them picked up a chair to swing at Dutch.

I saw it coming and jumped up to block it with my forearms in front of my face and over my head. It shattered around me like it was one of those mock up stage props. I didn't feel it at all. It ended up as two pieces of wood about two inches square by three feet long which used to be the back and legs of the chair. I grabbed them both and tossed one to Dutch.

The bouncer, in a policeman's uniform, pulled his gun out, but before he could point it at either of us, Dutch swung his stick sharply down and across the forearm of the gun hand. The gun fell to the floor and Dutch grabbed it. He didn't point it at anyone but everyone suddenly stopped and stared. He threw the gun on the stage and jumped up himself.

I joined him, facing the angry crowd.

The noise started again as they tried to get to the gun so Dutch picked it up and everyone stopped again. He unloaded it and threw the bullets at the crowd and threw the gun across the room behind the bar breaking some bottles and cracking a mirror.

The crowd was quieter now. They seemed to be deciding whether to continue or not. The bouncer was not in sight and I figured he'd gone for help. We didn't have much time left if we were going to get out of there. We jumped down from the stage and started chasing the crowd back toward the bar. Then we threw the sticks at them and raced out the door.

I was surprised. It was daylight as we headed down the stairs for the street. The sun wasn't up yet but it was definitely morning. The sidewalk hawkers were on the corners and we headed down the sidewalk away from them which just happened to be in the direction of the car. We did pretty well for about a block but at the first intersection a bunch of cabdrivers started trying to grab and tackle us. I could hear the cops blowing their whistles behind us. It was like running the gauntlet. Everybody took a try at stopping us as we went by. I noticed after a couple of blocks, Dutch was not with me. I figured he'd been caught. He is big and strong so he could run over them but he wasn't too fast or light on his feet so he could be tripped. *We better get away so we can get him out later.*

I finally made it to the car and was bending over to untie the key out of my shoelaces when I heard a hard thump against the left side of my head just above the ear. It didn't hurt but it knocked me off balance. When I straightened up there was this little fat Mexican policeman standing there with a very surprised look on his face. The pistol in his hand had blood and hair on the butt. I noticed the blood dripping down my neck into the collar of my shirt.

I shook my finger at him like a schoolmarm and yelled, "You better not hit me again you little son-of-a-bitch or I'll break you into little pieces and throw you in the street!"

He stepped back about a yard and watched me take the key out of my laces. I kept one eye on him but the look on his face convinced me he had taken his best shot and wasn't about to try it again.

The top was down on the MGB so I jumped in and stuck the key in the ignition but the street people were all over me. They were pulling on my arm and shoulder, turning off the ignition as soon as I turned it on, jumping back as I swung my arms to chase them away. All of a sudden there was a dark flash in front of my eyes. I thought someone had swung something at me but I knew instantly what it was when the horse collar began to choke me. I was out in a second.

I woke up in the back seat of a police car across the lap of two policemen. They were all laughing about something. I was handcuffed behind my back and laying on my stomach. I couldn't see what was going on and was trying to raise my head to get a look. I could hear Dutch. He was up front laughing with them.

The guys in the back tugged on my shoulders and pushed on my feet until I was sitting up between them. They were waving the collar in front of me and speaking excited, rapid Spanish. The one with the collar demonstrated to me by putting the collar over his head, laughing and pointing at me. They were obviously very proud of themselves for having figured out how to capture me. I smiled and nodded. It was obviously time to try to get on their better side. They drove slowly back through the crowded streets toward the police station, waving the horse collar out the window and laughing. The number in the crowd grew larger as we approached the entrance to the station.

They didn't finger print us like they do in the states. They just took our money, wallets, cigarettes, lighters and belts. Dutch was complaining to them about the wound on my head which was beginning to hurt. They just smiled and nodded and led us off to the tank.

A few hours later they came and took me to an office where there was a doctor who washed, shaved and stitched my head. It stung a little when he cleaned it with alcohol but I didn't even feel the stitches. I passed out and slept the rest of the day until about dusk.

Dinner came just after dark when they brought in a big barrel of bean soup and handed out some metal cups. It was terrible but I ate it anyway. Now, I knew what they did with left over refried beans. I had always thought they just refried them again and again. I barfed up the beans about half an hour after I ate them, as did many of the others. I was tired, depressed, miserable, sore and feeling very sorry for myself. The pain in my gut, the guilt, the heartbreak, and sorrow were all with me as strong as ever. It seemed they were to be constant companions of reality whenever I was not drunk. My mind wandered and I drifted off to sleep. *Passed out, again.*

"Dutch, wake up!" I whispered excitedly as I shook him. "Dutch, listen! They're calling for U.S. military personnel to come out to the courtyard and they're opening the door! I heard an American voice." I was so excited I was shaking. We might walk out of here after all.

"Forget it Bobby. We're not in the service."

"C'mon, Dutch, get with it! Do you want to spend the rest of your life in a filthy, smelly, Mexican prison?"

"Hell no!"

"Then fake it! You were in ROTC. You know how to get into formation. Make up a service number with six digits and follow me. Start the number with zero and tell them you're a second lieutenant in the Marine Corps. Line up next to me on my left side."

We hustled out to the far right of the line, where marines and officers, in this kind of formation, would be located.

The American Army Military Police sergeant came sauntering across the courtyard toward me. I knew I would be first. Military people are very predictable. Inspections always started on the far left side, as the inspecting officer faced the formation. "Name?" He sounded bored and tired.

"Pincer, Robert K. Sergeant," I replied.

"Rank?"

"Second lieutenant, United States Marine Corps, Sergeant."

He stopped writing on the clipboard and looked up, surprised, not believing what he heard. "You got an ID, Lieutenant?"

I didn't have an active duty ID yet. I possessed what was known as a pink card, which was a reserve ID, and it showed my rank as a corporal. "It's in my wallet, Sergeant. They took it when I was arrested—and my orders are there!" I just remembered the orders as the words came out of my mouth. One copy was neatly folded and put there for safekeeping as I'd been told to do when I was previously reporting for Reserve Training and Officer Candidate School. "The ID card shows I'm a corporal but the orders show I've been commissioned and to report for flight school."

He nodded to the corporal with him who understood and took off to go verify the claim. "What's your service number, Lieutenant?"

"It's 081810, Sergeant," I replied. It had been an easy one to memorize.

"What are ya in for?" I didn't answer. I had been standing at attention with head and eyes looking straight ahead, because he would not have known I was an officer, but at this point, I turned and looked defiantly directly in the eyes. He stiffened slightly and said, "Sir, on what charge is the lieutenant being held?"

I focused my eyes back on the top of his white helmet liner. "They were speaking Spanish, Sergeant, so I'm not sure, but probably along the lines of drunk and disorderly. Lieutenant Dutch, on my left, might know better because he understands more Spanish than I do."

I could feel Dutch's head turn toward the sergeant.

The sergeant faced sharply to his right, took one long step, stopped, faced sharply to his left and stood directly in front of Dutch. "Name?"

"Dutch, second lieutenant, United States Marine Corps, sir."

I cringed inside.

"Don't call me sir, Lieutenant, I work for a living." I could see him surveying the line out of the corner of my eye. "Have I got a whole mess of you people here, or just you two?"

"Just the two of us. We were in a bar fight, Sergeant," Dutch replied.

The corporal came back carrying my wallet in one hand and the copy of my orders in the other.

The sergeant compared the information he had written on the clipboard with the orders. "OK, Lieutenants. Fallout and get on the van. I'll see if we can get you out of here."

The relief was so great my knees almost buckled. I tried to move sharply out of the formation but I felt very clumsy.

Dutch didn't wait for the sergeant to move on and bumped into him as he tried to move out behind me. We're gonna make it! He didn't even ask for a serial number or check Dutch for ID.

The green van had been modified into a paddy wagon. The big yellow letters on the side said, "MILITARY POLICE." The driver and shot gun front bucket seats were separated from the back by heavy wire, like chain link fencing. The bench seats in the back were parallel to the sides and I was sitting with my back to the right side of the van right behind the wire separating me from the sergeant. The corporal was driving and Dutch was sitting across from me behind the driver's seat. There were six other prisoners with four on the seats and two on the floor.

"Sergeant," I said tentatively as we parked on the U.S. side of the border, "before we go inside I have to tell you Dutch is not in the service. I talked him into getting into the formation so I could get him out of jail."

He stiffened up and swung his head around so fast I was sure he would have a permanent crick in his neck.

"I'll take full responsibility," I said quickly. "I'd a whole lot rather spend time in an American brig than in a Mexican jail. I won't let this cause you any problem."

He got out and stomped into the building under a green sign with big yellow letters reading PROVOST MARSHAL.

We had been in the van for about thirty minutes. It was nothing like being in jail but it seemed like a long time. The sergeant came back for the rest of the prisoners shortly after he first went in, so Dutch and I were alone for the first time since the incident began. He looked terrible and I suppose his mouth, tongue and lips were coated and as dry as mine.

"Dutch, are my eyes as red as yours? If I look as bad as you do, I must be a sight."

His shirt was torn and a couple of buttons were missing, but otherwise there were no signs he'd been in a fight. "How the hell would I know? I haven't seen my eyes in more than two days."

I felt optimistic and relaxed for the first time since before it all started. I unbuttoned my jeans and stretched to tuck in my shirt. The corporal, the driver, who stayed nearby just outside the vehicle, was leaning against the front and felt it move. He slowly turned to see what was causing the motion and saw me tucking in my shirt. He took a long slow drag on his cigarette, threw down his butt, and started pacing. I wondered if he would give us a cigarette if we asked. Probably not, judging from the look of contempt in his eyes.

"We gotta get out of here Dutch. We need to start trying to find out what it will take to get my car out of Mexico. Then start gettin' our act together. We'll call my Dad in Arlington. I'm probably going to need an attorney, and he can help, but we'll probably need more money to get out of this than he will have on him."

"Also, we need get hold of the local marine recruiter. See if there is an officer selection officer in the area. If there is, maybe we can ask if they know what the situation is and ask if anything can be done to get us out. And listen, don't you dare take off and let me sweat it out here or I'll break your neck when I get out!"

Dutch laughed for the first time since he was laughing with police holding the horse collar out the window of the car. "You do bounce back don't you?"

"What do you mean?"

"Hell, we're still locked up in this shiny green paddy wagon and you're already figuring what to do, *if* we get out."

"Yeah, well, the army can't hold you, Dutch. We put one over on them and they might be pissed but the worst they can do is hand you over to the El Paso police and how long can they hold you? You haven't broken any laws in Texas have you?"

He pondered the question for a moment. "No, I've only been through Texas to get to Mexico and to play football." He smiled ruefully.

"On the other hand the Marine Corps can try me for a bunch of things under military law but it'll take time. Eventually, I'll probably be released to report to flight school and wait for this mess to catch up with me. I'd still like to make it to graduation tomorrow. Jesus, I hope Dad and Mom haven't already left for Albuquerque."

"OK," Dutch said as the sergeant unlocked the back of the van, "I'll give it my best shot if I get out before you do."

There were markings on the floor showing where to stand in front of the desk sergeant, the camera, and the fingerprinting desk. The gunnery sergeant behind the high booking desk was one of the grizzliest I had ever seen. I thought only the Marine Corps grew them this hard and tough looking. I paused in front of the desk, "Good morning, Gunny."

"Good morning, sir." He seemed surprised at the greeting. I tried to sound confident and matter-of-fact, but it was obvious from the slightly annoyed "sir" in his reply he already knew what was going on which was definitely not good for us. Our MP sergeant motioned us to follow him and passed through a door on the other side of the room over which there was a sign that read OIC (officer in charge). No fingerprints and no booking yet—could be a break.

I entered as smartly as I was capable of at the time and noticed the officer in charge was a warrant officer. I was not familiar with how to distinguish the rank from warrant officer one, two, or three and chief warrant officer and the army bar he was wearing seemed to be different than those I had seen worn by marine warrants. Also, I was unsure how to address him. Navy warrants were called *mister*; marine warrants were called *gunner*. I didn't have the foggiest idea what to call this one. I fumbled, "Second Lieutenant Pincer reporting, sir." *Shit! Why did I say* sir?

He was squared away—short, flat topped, salt-and-pepper hair, wiry body, lots of ribbons, probably from the Korean War, and appeared to be tall though he was seated behind a polished mahogany desk. Probably a chief warrant officer with the experience of holding all the enlisted ranks from private to at least gunnery sergeant plus three junior warrants before receiving his chief warrant.

"Lieutenant, I've talked to my counter-part on the Mexican side. I know what happened. He was short and to the point, not sarcastic or vindictive, more tired and disbelieving, as though he had been through this many more times than he desired. Did you know you made the front page of the Juarez newspaper this morning?"

"No, sir, I didn't."

"How long have you been in the Marine Corps, Lieutenant?"

"Sir, I've been in the Marine Corps Reserve since November '59, on active duty for training several times since then, but I was just commissioned and ordered to active duty for flight school last week."

"Lieutenant, we have these fucking incidents with soldiers all the time. It's almost routine and we handle it, but we do not expect it from officers and I strongly suggest, if you've had any training in how to conduct yourself as an officer, you should start remembering it." His stern manner demonstrated a leader who is thoroughly disappointed at the conduct he has been forced to observe and the situation with which he must deal.

"I'm not going to handle this one, he continued. I've told the Juarez Police I'm handing you over to the Marine Corps I and I staff at Fort Bliss. The unit there has been notified and they're waiting for you. My driver will take you over there when we're finished here."

He briefly studied the papers on his desk. "The bar owner wants sixty dollars U.S. for the damages and the Mexican Police will release your car. You can pick up your personal belongings at the cage across from the booking room." He nodded and gestured toward the door.

I took one step back, did as sharp an about face as I could, in bare feet, and beat it through the open door. I could not believe it! They are going to let us off for sixty bucks. No mention of the guard's broken arm. This is unreal! Well, there is still the Marine Corps to think about. What will they do?

We followed the yellow line on the floor across to a chain link wire cage painted green and stood on the red X in front of a half door. The soldier inside had one of those funny-looking army patches on the sleeve of his shirt, which meant he was a specialist in something or another. I chuckled inside, Specialist in Charge of Prisoner's Personal Affects.

We signed for the bag in which the Military Police had put our gear and sat down on a nearby bench to put on our shoes and socks. I don't think I've ever put socks on my feet when they were as filthy as they were now, and the disgust started another spiral of depression. But when I stuck my right foot in the shoe, I was amazed. There, way down at the end of the toe, was the twenty-dollar bill I had tucked away. I was up and at 'em again! I remembered saying the usual deal making prayer in the stinking jail. "God, get me out of this and I'll never, ever do anything as foolish and dumb as this never, ever again so long as I live, so help me God, and I mean it. I know and you know I've said things like this before and I really meant it then and this time I really, really mean it." And as I looked at the twenty-dollar bill, I reaffirmed it. "God, I will make it up someday. I promise I will."

Right now though there were battles to fight. The twenty meant seed money for food, phone calls and gasoline. Operating capital and time were all we needed to get this show on the road and with a little luck we could still make it to graduation. The corporal, who had been driving the van, was outside, this time with a jeep and drove us to a part of the army base where the signs turned from green and yellow to red and yellow. It read, Marine Reserve Training Unit, Headquarters I & I (Inspector and Instructor) Staff Reserved Parking.

The time was 1000, and there wouldn't be any reserves around on a Monday morning. Just the active duty staff. The sergeant carried the record of the morning's events and delivered it to the marine sergeant who was obviously expecting us. He was a young E-5 with only a National Defense Ribbon, which everyone on active duty is awarded whenever there is any action anywhere, and a Good Conduct Medal which is only awarded after 3 years of continuous active duty. "Good morning, sir," he said politely.

I could tell he was trying to stifle a smile. "Good Morning, Sergeant." It was a little easier now to act self-assured. I couldn't tell if the smothered grin was sarcastic or if he were genuinely amused. His greeting was official and respectful but his face eventually broke out into a big smile.

The staff sergeant behind him now had a big grin on his face as well.

"What the hell is the amusement all about?"

"Well, Lieutenant," the staff sergeant offered, "it seems these young marines don't get along too well with the Mexican Police in Juarez and several of them have been busted for getting into fights over there. They think maybe, after what the paper said this morning, you're a hero."

"Staff Sergeant, if you've read the Juarez paper would you please tell me what it said we did?"

"It was the El Paso paper, sir, but we didn't put it all together until we got the call from the army this morning. The paper said you beat up a bar full of Mexicans and ran the cops all over town before they could arrest you, er, uh, the lieutenant, sir." He stumbled over the second "you" in the sentence as he realized he hadn't been addressing me in the third person, as junior marines are supposed to do when addressing seniors. Up to this point, I figured my half Irish luck had been all bad, but things seemed to be turning my way again.

"Sir, the colonel is on his way in and wants to see the lieutenant when he gets here. This past weekend was drill for the unit and the colonel usually takes Monday off afterward, but he said he would be in ASAP and the lieutenant should wait for him."

Good news. Bad news. The colonel directed I wait for him, which probably meant, if he hadn't asked, I would have been free to go. Also, it means I probably would not be held. Good news. But the colonel wants to see me. Probably to inform me of my rights under the Uniform Code of Military Justice. Bad news.

"Would the lieutenant like to clean up before the colonel gets here?" A suggestion which I'm sure included the intent of good advice.

"Yes, Sergeant. Thank you."

"The head and showers are two bulkheads down the passageway, sir. I'll send someone down with towels and a razor." He nodded at Dutch indicating he was also invited.

"Okay, Sergeant, but first I would like to use the phone."

I had called Dad for help before and he had always been there for me to do whatever he could to help. Basically he had been there in my corner every time since I first got in trouble as a kid. I hated the pain it would cause him much more than I regretted the pain it caused me. I always swore I would make it up to him but it seemed every time I got on track to something good I would somehow find a way to derail myself.

"Hello," it was Dad who answered. I was relieved because I really did not want to talk to Mom. Communication with Mom had basically stopped at age fourteen when I wouldn't pray out-loud for forgiveness for stealing cars from neighbors. I had a paper route in the evenings and Sunday morning, and when it was cold on Sunday morning, I would look for a car with the keys in it. At first, I just started the car to warm up with the heater but soon I decided to just drive the car on the paper route and take it back afterward. I figured I wouldn't get caught, and eventually, if I did get caught, nobody would care much, since I hadn't really stolen the cars. I just borrowed them for a while. When I did get caught, Mom took me around to the families whose cars I had taken and made me apologize. They were very nice about the whole thing and said they strongly suspected it was me burning up their gas. One of them had shot at me one time when I almost got caught red handed and said he was glad he didn't hit me. I was uncomfortable making the apologies and I was truly sorry for causing problems for everyone but I was not filled with overwhelming spiritual guilt and or remorse. *To the contrary my brain committee reckoned the car owners were stupid for leaving their keys in their cars and deserved to have them "borrowed."* But I had learned a lesson. The pain and embarrassment I had caused my parents, especially my father, was enough to let me know I would never steal again but I did not believe God was going to burn me in hell for it—until Mom jumped on the bandwagon.

When we got back from visiting the neighbors Mom took me in her bedroom and turned off the lights, had me kneel beside her bed in the dark and told me to pray out loud for forgiveness because, if I didn't, I was surely going to hell. But I prayed silently, "God please forgive me and let this pass. Let the pain go away from me and my parents.

And I tried to make a deal. "God," I said, "I don't think I deserve to go to hell but if you're thinking about it please don't make your decision just yet. I promise I will be good from now on. I will not cause anybody anymore problems and I will make it up to you and everyone else someday! I promise I will. We stayed there a long time. Mom alternately cried, shook me and hissed at me through clenched teeth, "Pray," exhorting me to pray and eventually, "Pray, damn you!" I tried but I could not force myself to speak.

Finally, she sighed in disgust, stood up and said, in a slow, deliberate, contemptuous tone, "Goddamn your soul to hell, Robert Keith Pincer Jr.!" She paused for a second and then stomped out of the room, slammed the door and left me there in the dark.

Now, her damnation scared the Devil out of me for sure. She was gone and I was shaking and I was very ready to pray out loud now, "God don't listen to her! I'm not even real sure exactly what my soul is but I know I don't want it damned to hell already. She doesn't know what she's saying and she'll probably get over being mad in a few days and take it all back anyway."

No one else seemed to wield as much power as she did. Even more than God, it seemed, most of the time. I certainly did not want God and Mom to get together on this deal.

"Hello, Dad," I said. "It's Bob."
"Well hi, number one! You caught us just as we were headed out the door for your graduation. What's up?"

He sounded cheerful and I hated to ruin his day. "Dad," I started. The pain was back in my chest and in my gut. I took a deep breath to try and relieve it.

"You OK?"

"Yeah Dad, I'm OK but I fouled up. I'm in El Paso and my car is in Juarez and I need sixty bucks to get it out."

There was a long pause and I could feel him coming down from his happy mood and I could hear the pain in his voice. "Well, I guess I can handle it. What happened?"

"Dad, it's not a big deal at this point. We got into a hassle in a bar and there were some damages and they're holding my car as ransom. I'll explain in detail tonight in Albuquerque, okay?"

He' didn't hesitate long. "Okay, but are you sure this will take care of it? Shouldn't I wait here until you've gotten your car and you're on your way, so you can call, if you need me?"

"No, Dad, the money will do it. I have help here, gas to get back and food money. I'll see you tonight. Okay?"

"Yes, okay" he sounded suddenly tired. "I'll send it to El Paso by Western Union on the way out of town. You drive careful, ya hear?"

"You too," I said, "Bye, Dad. Thanks."

As he said goodbye and hung up I wondered how much and how he would tell Mom and what they would think of their number one son now? I had done some things they were proud of but I felt like the trouble outweighed them by far. Well, things would get better. Wouldn't they? After all I was going to be a marine pilot. Dad was a marine in WWII. He would be proud of me for also being a marine. It would all balance out sooner or later. It would all even up someday. Wouldn't it?

The colonel was polished and sharp. Not a hair, thread, button or ribbon was a fraction of a millimeter out of line. The triple creases in the back of his shirt, the double creases in the front and his trouser creases were all very sharply defined and not a wrinkle anywhere. How do they do it I wondered? Did he just put them on before he walked through the door? *The brain committee wondered if I would look as good when the Marine Corps got through with me.* When he moved, he had a crisp and deliberate manner which presented the essence of complete self-confidence, control and power. As he looked me up and down I could see the contempt in his eyes. When he spoke, his voice and manner commanded respect. He said in mock disbelief, "You . . . are a lieutenant in MY United States Marine Corps?"

"Yes, sir," I said quietly. I was embarrassed again, and the pain in my gut was back in full force. I had been able to shave and clean up a little, thanks to the sergeant, but I was still a mess. "These are my orders, sir," I said, as I handed him the folded paper.

"Sergeant! Make a copy of these orders for our files."

"Lieutenant, I will write a report on you to my own files. This report and a copy of the article in the Mexican newspaper will stay in my files unless you show up here again on my watch, and if you do, the shit will hit the fan like you've never seen it before and I guarantee you will not have a career in *my* Marine Corps. My advice to you is to get your act together, forget about booze, parties and women and make an intense effort to learn about and live up to the standards of an officer of marines.

"On the other hand, one of our traditions, making the Marine Corps what it is, is marines take care of marines. What do you think it will take to get you squared away and outside my perimeter?"

"Sir, my father is wiring the money I need to get my car out of the Mexican Police impound. I just need a ride to Western Union and to the Mexican border and I'll be good to go."

I had skated again. The Marine Corps wouldn't officially know about the incident unless I screwed up inside this colonel's perimeter again and I would avoid El Paso and Juarez like the plague.

The trip back was uneventful, and unlike the trip down, Dutch was quiet.

"You too hungover to talk, Dutch?"

He just nodded.

Quiet was okay. I didn't feel like talking either. I was thinking mostly about Dad. He had been a good father and didn't deserve continued bad news from his first born son.

Dad had been in Albuquerque often on his sales travels before I wound up going to college there and he was there for all of my home football games. These days, he always stayed at the Western Skies Hotel because it was where the team stayed on Friday nights before the home games on Saturday and he wanted to be close by. I knew he would be there waiting for me to show up from our Juarez escapade. I was very tired and badly in need of sleep after the drive but had sense enough to go by the apartment to get cleaned up before going to see him.

Liana was at the apartment but in no mood to have a civil discussion about where I had been for the past three days and why I hadn't come home on Sunday like I said I would in the note I left. She didn't offer to say where she had been Friday night when we left. I didn't care and I didn't ask.

I hadn't been to the Western Skies Hotel since the last home game of the '61 season and I didn't recognize the desk clerk. "Hi, Thomas." I read the name tag on his jacket. "Do you have a Bob Pincer registered?"

The clerk was friendly. "Yep, he checked in about an hour ago. I'll let him know you're here."

"Either that or I can just go there."

"Well, hotel policy, I can't give out his room number without his permission."

"Okay, I'll wait here then."

A few minutes later Dad appeared in the lobby. "You don't look too much the worse for wear after such a hard weekend. You want a cup of coffee?"

"Sure. Where's Mom?"

"She's gone to bed already. She can't sleep while we're driving and she's worn-out."

We proceeded to the hotel coffee shop and spent the next hour or so going over the details of the Juarez story.

"Okay, that's that," he said finally. "It sounds like there isn't any more to do at this point. What are your plans for tomorrow and the near future before going to flight school?"

"Dad, if it's okay with you and Mom, I'd like to go home to Arlington with you until I have to report to Pensacola. I'm splitting with Liana. It was never intended to be a permanent relationship and I'd just as soon get things settled with her before I get launched into my career."

"Sure, son. Your baby brother is gone to the navy so we have plenty of room. What about tomorrow and the graduation ceremony?"

"Nothing special there. I have my dress white uniform all set up at the apartment. Liana is supposed to be there and wants to pin on my lieutenant's bars after the graduation. The rent is paid at the apartment through the end of the week. Liana is planning to stay at her father's house after that. I've told her she can't join me at flight school until after ground school and until after I can get base housing. Both of these are not quite true and . . . sometime, after I get to Pensacola I'll tell her she won't be joining me there. I'll file for divorce in Arlington shortly after we get home."

"Do you think it's wise to keep her in the dark about your plans?" Dad always seemed to be able to get to the crux of a problem—pointing the way with his question.

"Dad, she is a wild woman, especially when she's been drinking. I was at work when I brought up the question of how we should actually end the relationship, which was never intended to be permanent in the first place. She picked up a cue ball off the table and threw it across the lounge at me and I wasn't looking. It was very lucky she missed my head by just a few inches. It crashed harmlessly into the wall and she stomped out. Later when I got home she had my shotgun out and loaded lying across her lap. It seemed like a long time but it was probably only a few minutes to talk her down from a very tense situation.

"Wow, what a story! What's next?"

"Well, I've been very cautious around her ever since. I just need to get out of here after graduation and get to Texas to file for divorce as soon as possible."

"Will that be all there is to it?"

"No, I have to come back in July to take the Graduate Records Exam and she knows when, so I have to dodge her at that point."

"Well, we'll have to handle the exam when we get to it. One thing at a time, I suppose," and he did then, as he always had, assumed the burden of my problems.

It was a typically beautiful bright sunny June morning saturated with fresh, crisp mile high air that greeted the 1963 graduates of the University of New Mexico. We lined up outside and waited for the procession to begin as it has time and time again—through the lobby, down the center aisle and into our seats one by one. It was a scenario I had projected over and over again and eventually it happened just the way it was supposed happen.

I didn't see Mom and Dad before the graduation ceremony but they were in the lobby as I walked out with the rest of the uniformed military graduates. There were some navy, some air force and some army, but I was the only marine.

Liana was also there but she was not with my parents. Of course, they had not met each other so they could not have gotten together. After the introductions, Liana pinned on one of my gold bars and Mom pinned on the other. Dad watched and took the pictures. Afterward, he saluted, shook my hand and said, "Congratulations, Lieutenant!"

Surprised, I returned his salute and said, "Thank you, sir, but now I've broken a tradition for my first act as an officer."

"Yes, what's that, Lieutenant?" He smiled knowingly, as he asked the question.

"I don't have a silver dollar or even another coin to present to the first marine to salute me."

"You can catch me later, son. It's an honor and a privilege to be the first."

"Thanks, Dad."

Relief overwhelmed my mind and body suddenly. I was a little dizzy and kind of weak. The lobby of the auditorium seemed strange. I had never been in the building before but it was not that kind of unfamiliarity. It was as if the ceremony, the moment, the event, the scope of what I had finally accomplished, was not real. In fact, the rolled-up piece of white paper that was given as I walked across the stage and shook the hand of the president of the university and the dean of the College of Education was indeed blank. The actual diploma would be sent in the mail after I would take the Graduate Record Exam in July. Not that one has to pass the GRE to graduate but the administration holds the actual diploma like a club over the head of anyone who has not actually taken the exam. *What if I die before I take the exam? Will the diploma be forever withheld?*

Pensacola Found

The diner was set back about 40 feet off the highway and about ten feet down a sloping gravel driveway leading to a flat spot of grass and gravel in a clearing which formed a sort of make-shift parking lot. It was dark along this stretch of the road and I would have missed it entirely, except for the small orange neon "DINER" sign hanging on a post near the highway shoulder.

I pulled in toward one of the many huge pine trees on the edge of the clearing, next to one of the two cars in the lot, and pulled my six foot, two-inch body out of the new black MGB to stretch.

The building looked like it was made out of a couple of busses stuck together on the sides. The floor level was raised above ground on concrete blocks and faded wooden steps lead up to a small wooden, covered porch. The only light came from the glow of the bar lights through the row of bus windows and a clear glass pane in the upper half of a wooden entry door. *The brain committee suggested it doesn't look like a place where ladies would be found. A woman in here might be a drunk, desperate, a hooker or all of the above.*

The steps creaked and the porch groaned as I pressed my lean 205 pounds onto my size 13 shoes and ascended to the door.

A weathered little man, hunched over his beer mug at the end of the bar, spouted off when he heard me ask the bartender for directions to the Naval Air Station. "Well, there goes another candy ass, navy squid off to see the world and looking for his magic wings of gold."

My head swiveled quickly to the left as my body automatically stiffened at the insults. He was the only customer in the diner. I was in no mood to fight after the long drive but I was not about to take any crap either. Fight a little man and win, you get ridiculed for picking on him. Fight a little man and lose, you become the laughing stock of the universe. As a college bar bouncer I'd learned, a strong reprisal would usually shut down the weaker, so a fight would not have to ensue. "Listen up you scrawny, wrinkled-up, pitiful-looking excuse for a human being, unless you want to get your head screwed off and a load of crap dumped down your neck, you better shut your beer funnel and mind your own business!"

"Hello, Marine," he jumped up and shouted! His face filled with a huge toothy grin of yellowing teeth as the wrinkles seemed to deepen in his face. He stood by his barstool, his wiry body weaving a bit, swung his arms open wide, and waved me toward him. His bald head beamed like a headlight as he rose nearer the hanging bar lights and his sparkling, steely blue eyes seemed to indicate he had solved some mystery others could not. "Welcome to Pensacola lad, where the Naval Aviation Flight School produces the world's finest Marine Corps pilots and the women are flinging themselves in your path. Let me buy you a beer lad." It was not a question—more like a command.

"Are you a candidate or a second lieutenant?"

"Second lieutenant, sir," I replied. I added the "sir" because if he were an officer, he would obviously be senior to the lowest of the low-down, brown-bar lieutenants. Navy and Marine Corps officers are commissioned in order of seniority based on Naval Academy graduates by standing in their class, followed by West Point and Air Force Academy graduates who choose navy or marine commissions, followed by other military schools such as the Virginia Military Academy and then by graduates of other public or private schools through ROTC or other various commissioning programs. As a graduate of the University of New Mexico, commissioned upon graduation through a program called "Platoon Leaders Course" I was at, or near the bottom of this long list. The only rate in flight school lower than mine would be aviation candidates who were recruited out of junior college and signed up as enlisted men who would be commissioned as second lieutenants only when they completed officer's candidate school and flight school.

"Major Locke," he said proudly as he offered his hand to shake. "Carl Locke but everyone calls me Lucky. I'm XO of the Instrument

Training Squadron at Whiting Field, flying the TC 45J or SNB, nicknamed and more commonly known as the Super Navy Bomber. You'll learn to fly instruments in my squadron, if you get that far along."

I was rapidly reaching information overload. I'd never heard of Whiting Field or the SNB and didn't have the faintest clue about how far along in the 18-month syllabus I would be if I reached instrument training. I had never even flown any kind of airplane. "Bob Pincer, sir," I replied, as I took his hand. His grip was stronger than I expected.

"Bring the lad a beer Andy," he said to the bartender. "Where did you come in from, lad?"

Why is he referring to me as "lad"? Is he Irish or Scottish? "I spent a few days with my folks in Arlington, Texas, sir, and started out from there yesterday. I stayed in a little motel just this side of Houston last night. Slept in a while this morning and drove the rest of the way here today."

"When do you have to report to ground school?"

"My classes don't start 'til the 15th, a week from Monday, but I thought I'd get checked in early, get settled in my quarters this weekend and get some uniforms ordered early next week."

"Nah! We'll take the weekend to show you around. You'll have plenty of time to get squared away. Are you a reserve with a uniform allowance?"

"Yes, sir, I'll get three hundred.

"Stay away from the PX. It's cheaper there but they will fix you up with stuff you don't need and the tailoring is mediocre. I know an excellent tailor shop in downtown Pensacola which can have you dressed out smartly in three or four days with all the uniforms you'll need and with money left over."

Scottish for sure, the brain committee chimed in.

"Let's head to town for some action, Bobby. I want to show you the most famous aviation libation location and kitty lair in the world. There are other parts of the world where the action is better and somewhere the booze costs less but in Pensacola, the combination of plentiful, liberated, tight American pussy and smooth American bourbon are beyond comparison."

"Yeah, but how's the competition with all the single male flight students here, and tons of single navy and marine support personnel?"

"Well, the single men are a well-known attraction in the southeastern states but the girls are drawn like nails to a magnet and there are plenty of 'em. A new crop shows up every year looking for husbands, and these days, they are not shy about sex and sexual relationships."

"I'll be avoiding the marriage ambush. I did that already."

"Really? You're just out of college and you've already done the marriage and divorce thing?" He looked at me with surprise, and if I'm not mistaken, not without a little empathy.

"Yep, twice. I got married during my second year of college and divorced four years later and then married again just before I graduated. I'm not free of the second one yet but I've filed for divorce," I answered only a slight bit wistfully.

"Wow! I'm only a one-time loser and it took a few more years." I was married here in Pensacola when I got my wings, and divorced after eight years, when we were transferred back here a year ago."

"What happened?"

"You mean what caused the divorce?"

"Yes, sir, if you don't mind talking about it?" I was genuinely curious.

"Hell no. I don't mind. It was the typical thing that happens to military couples, especially marines," he shrugged. "She got tired of me being sent off to faraway places while leaving her stuck at home with the kids. It was okay at first when I did a six-month cruise on a ship, but after only a year at home, I had to do a 13-month tour in Okinawa. Recently though, just before we were transferred back to Pensacola, I was sent to Okinawa for my second unaccompanied tour. She was really upset and wanted me to get out of the Marine Corps, but by the time the tour was complete, it was over with us and I had half a career done. We argued terribly for several weeks before I left on the tour and she said she was going to file for divorce while I was gone."

"But she didn't?"

"Well, she filed but when we found out I would be sent back to Pensacola for a three-year tour as an instructor in Flight School, she said she would stay because it looked like we would be stabilized for at least three years."

"Well, that plan sounds reasonable. What happened?" I leaned forward, realizing I wanted to know something about how to make a relationship last.

"I think maybe she just wanted to get back here to the southeast, where she's from. She started the divorce procedure again within a couple of months after we got back and the whole thing was done within a year. I don't know if she knew in advance or not but an old flame of hers was stationed here and they wound up getting together."

"A convenient liaison."

"Yeah, it was actually. He wound up with all of the responsibilities, my wife, my kids, the car and the dog. I don't even have to pay alimony or child support," he shook his head in disbelief and folded his arms across his chest.

"Looks like she just wanted out?" I surmised.

"Well, yes out of the service lifestyle in particular, and she found a perfect alternative. He's seven years older, divorced with no kids and was within a year of finishing a 20-year career as a navy pilot and ready to go with the airlines. Already hired, in fact—just waiting for his final release from active duty."

"Are they gone?"

"Yeah, they were married at the chapel at the air station about three months ago and left shortly afterward. A honeymoon, of sorts, and on to Atlanta, where he will be based with the airline."

"Sad times, I suppose. Sad you had to go through it I mean."

"Not so bad. Lots of marines go through the same thing. It's a tough life for the women and a lot of 'em can't handle it. Never knowing what's coming next. How long she will be left alone next time and how soon? It's better if marines stay single, if we can, and just work at being married to the Corps. You know, the old saying, 'If the Marine Corps wanted you to have a wife, you would be issued one.' What happened with you twice?" He raised an eyebrow and scrunched his wrinkly face even more.

"The first one's a long story of being too young, too much in love and too stupid to wait until the right time. The second was a result of the first broken heart and broken spirit. I stopped thinking of marriage as any kind of real commitment after the first one fell apart and wound up getting temporarily married, just as matter of convenience . . . so to speak."

"As a matter of convenience?" Obviously, my characterization puzzled him.

"Yes, sir. It was her idea. She needed to be married to carry out a plan of rejoining a group of married couples she had known during her previous marriage. At least that was the way she presented it although it may have been just an excuse to push me into a marriage. She was beautiful, very sexy and I figured what the hell. Marriage doesn't mean anything anyway, really. At least not to me. I didn't give a shit about vows at the time or meaningful relationships. It was just a legal piece of paper. So we did it and stayed together for the last semester of my college days and then we split the blanket."

"That was it? Six months?"

"Yes, sir, at least that was it for me for sure but she wasn't really happy about it. She wanted to stay together and come to Pensacola with me."

"So you're divorced?" He pulled a cigarette from his pack on the bar and offered me one.

"No, sir, not officially—just separated," I muttered as I accepted the cigarette. I filed for divorce in Texas while I was home after graduation and it will probably be finalized by the time I go home for Christmas."

"Well, it sounds like you have some stories to tell but they can wait. It's time to start a new chapter and this town is full of opportunity. Come on, Marine—let's go chase some pussy. Follow me downtown and I'll introduce you to the greatest meat market in the country.

It was late in the evening when we arrived at the busy nightclub and it looked like most of the patrons had settled into groups ranging from three to five or six at a table. The Major stopped just inside the entrance and scanned the room. He ignored the people while he began pointing out items of special interest. "That's the T-34 trainer, which will be the first aircraft you will learn to fly. That's the T-28, a great flying WWII vintage trainer you will master and learn to fly precision aerobatics, formations, and make arrested landings on an aircraft carrier. And there's the SNB over there with the twin engines and twin tails in which you will learn to fly on instruments only."

Trader Jon's, a downtown bar with an aviation decor including every kind of aircraft and flight-related memorabilia imaginable, was an amazing scene to behold. Models of every flight trainer in the U.S.

Naval Training Command and every operational aircraft in the navy, Marine Corps and coast guard hung from the ceiling. Plaques and patches and decals adorned the faded grey wood walls identifying every navy and Marine Corps squadron in existence from World War I to Korea. Flight helmets, leather flight jackets, goggles, gloves, sun glasses, boots, flight suits, and even parts of flight suits and squadron identifying patches were stuck to the walls and doors and hung from every conceivable hook, nook and cranny.

The atmosphere was electric with the energy of the crowded ocean of charged bodies. A small wave of young men in their late teens and early twenties pushed for access to the bar between the ones seated on the stools. Others sat at tall tables near the bar, at booths along the walls, or at tables for two or four near the dance floor, and a few elbowed for room to pull their cue at pool tables on the other side of the room. Half a dozen waitresses with black high heeled shoes on the tips of their long legs and low-cut red, white and blue striped hot pants, hustled draft beer by the glass or pitcher between the sweaty battlefield of bodies. They swung their arms up and out from fluffy sleeved, white cotton tops, to lift the drink trays above the crowd. They slid, swayed and twisted their flat, bare bellies through the sea of patrons, brushing braless breasts on back and front of appreciative sailors and marines, bumping hips like choreographed dancers.

The polished hardwood dance floor was slick with oiled saw dust but beyond the border, the main wood floor was rough and gray with age and permanently infused with the stale smell of spilled beer.

Beautiful girls, and some not so beautiful but cute—all types—nicely attired in hot pants or brightly colored miniskirts with matching panties and ponytails, were plentiful. They had pilot-hunting on their minds and were not shy, according to the Major. Tall, short, medium, voluptuous, skinny, buxom, average, chubby, athletic—take your pick. The music was loud and the dance floor was full of writhing torsos appearing to enjoy the crush—or at least not minding it. Some were obviously couples, but others were dancing without a particular partner, although there was no girl-girl dancing like you might see at a wedding. No, even when girls touched while dancing with or next to each other, it was a hot, sexy, teasing experience. The constant briny fray of openly exposed hard bodies and grinding moves provided more than a suggestion of desire.

Some girls from all over the country were there on vacation "just for fun." Others had moved to the Pensacola area and gotten local jobs while looking for a long-term relationship and, eventually, marriage. Of course, the fun part would happen sooner rather than later and marriage would be anticipated, even expected, before the boys finished flight school and were shipped off to other parts of the world. Some more forward explorers, by way of exhibiting their most immediate desires and the latest in sexual liberation movement would mention, in casual conversation, "I'm on the pill."

No single item or historical event seemed to have changed the social dynamic of young people so much since World War II as the birth control pill did in the 60's. WWII liberated women to enter the work force in huge numbers, although many returned to the kitchen when the warriors came home. Such was not the case in the 60's climate.

The 60's girls were suddenly and forever free to enter the workforce at will, according to their talents, and were freed from the stigma and shame of accidental pregnancy, which also offered, for those who wanted, the opportunity for open and direct expression of their sexual desires. Long before the Masters and Johnson book on Human Sexuality hit the shelves in 1966, describing sex as a healthy and natural activity, the cat was out of the bag. This new generation, liberated from the fear of pregnancy, relished the idea sex could be openly and safely enjoyed as a source of pleasure and intimacy. Coy and vague skirmishes in introductory situations gave way sometimes quickly, sometimes slowly, but almost inevitably, to frank and sometimes blunt discussions, which often led straightaway to passionate encounters, especially with those on short vacations or weekend visits. A few glasses of wine or a couple of cold draft beers enhanced the probability of a successful connection.

My previous work experience in a college-town bar, to help pay expenses not covered by a football scholarship, had presented many opportunities to hear every cajoling pick-up line imaginable and most of the flirtatious and coy responses, as well as, some more dismissive and blunt rejections. When the tables turned at flight school, with many girls on offense, it was sometimes necessary to call upon memories of gentle rejections, in an attempt to avoid hurting someone's feelings.

The Major motioned for me to follow him over to a table near the dance floor where two girls and one guy were seated. "Hi, Angie!" He was jovial and friendly with her and appeared relaxed and open toward the other two. "What are you doin' over on this side of the bay?"

Angie replied casually, "Relaxing and having a good time. I have the night off and don't have to be at work 'til 1800 tomorrow. What are you up to, Lucky?"

"I'm showin' this greenhorn second lieutenant around town—Bobby, this is Angie—a friend from the beach?"

"Hi, Angie, nice to meet you." I smiled.

She smiled and nodded. "These folks are Louis and Barbara. Louis is an aircraft mechanic at Whiting Field and Barbara is a full-time mother of their two kids."

The major leaned across to offer his hand. "Pleasure to meet you, Louis." And nodding toward Barbara, he added, "And you too, ma'am. You working on the T-28 or the SNB out there, Louis?"

Louis stood and offered his hand, as the major was speaking. "The SNB, sir, I'm an engine mech—Petty Officer Second Class Daniel Barns, sir. I recognized you—uh, when the major came in."

"Sorry, Louis, I didn't recognize you out of uniform."

I followed suit and offered my hand. "Nice to meet you, Louis . . . and Barbara," as I also nodded in her direction.

"My pleasure, sir. Do you all want to join us, Major?"

"I don't know Louis. We don't want to interrupt your evening."

"C'mon, Lucky," Angie chided, "there's two chairs available and anyway you ought to be good for at least one round of drinks for your squadron mate." She was cute as she chuckled and bounced her solid body up and down in the chair. Her loose halter-top revealed ample unbridled bouncing breasts. I noticed the wedding rings on her left hand against the background of blue shorts—not hot-pants like some of the girls were wearing, but regular shorts about half way down her thin but strong and shapely thighs. Her crossed leg held a black flat shoe, hanging loosely from the toes of her right foot, which was flipping up and down quickly in my direction.

"Okay, a round of drinks it is for my squadron mate and friends. Only, no more ranks and 'sirs' for tonight. Okay?"

"Yes, sir," Louis said automatically.

"Yes, sir, Major," I followed, joking with a small half-ass salute.

He crossed his body with his arms right to left and left to right and stuck out his forefingers like pistols, pointing to both of us at the same time—thumbs up like firing the hammer. "Enough," he admonished jokingly, and we all laughed. "How is it you three wound up here together?" He sat down next to Louis and motioned for a waitress.

I sat in the empty chair between Lucky Locke and Angie. *Nice, the brain committee approved.*

Louis answered as the major sat down next to him. "Well, Angie doesn't get Friday nights off very often, and when she does, she likes to get out and have some fun but she doesn't like to go alone. We're next-door neighbors in Milton, near Whiting Field. We became friends and we BBQ or have dinner at each other's homes and sometimes go out to dinner and dancing. When we go out, we share a baby sitter with the kids at their house or ours, and the arrangement is still working for us while Bill, her husband, is gone. It saves a little money and everyone gets to have a good time."

Lucky seemed to have no comment so I interjected, "Where is it you usually work on Friday nights, Angie."

"At the Schooner. It's a smaller bar over on the beach. I'm a waitress there."

"Which beach?"

"Well"—she chuckled a little—"pretty much when anyone around here says 'the beach' they're talkin' 'bout Pensacola Beach but you have to go across the bay bridge to Gulf Breeze and to Santa Rosa Island to get there." She lit up a cigarette as she spoke, blowing a whiff of smoke away from my face.

"How far is it from here to the beach?"

"A little more than three miles. In fact, the bridge is locally known as the three-mile bridge because it replaced two old narrow bridges that were about a mile and a half each—then you have to go across the sound on another short bridge to get to Santa Rosa Island," she said, inhaling a long drag.

"How far is it to commute from Milton to work?"

"About 45 minutes but it's worth it for a good job."

I continued grilling her, "What about your kids?"

"Well, when Bill's home, he can usually make arrangements so he doesn't have to work nights so he takes care of them. When he's gone or if he should unexpectedly have to pull night duty at the squadron, we have a nanny who comes to stay at the house. She's at our house taking care of our two, and their two, tonight." She smiled, reaching for the ashtray.

"Sounds like a great arrangement but complicated."

"Not really. You wanna dance?" she asked, stubbing the butt of her cigarette out.

"Sure!" Though I'd been focused on her, I was surprised by her invitation.

On the dance floor she was tall enough to lean in and talk close to my ear without me having to bend over much. Her breasts were the first to make contact as she raised her arms to wrap around my neck and the rest of her body settled in close as she moved smoothly to the music. *Very comfortable, the committee observed.* "I wanted to talk to you but not in front of Lucky. He's a friend but I don't want him knowing about my personal business and I'm sure Louis doesn't want him to know about his business because of their squadron relationship."

"I don't blame you on the personal score but what's Louis's involvement and why is it so important now?"

"Well, our setup is so we can go out and enjoy ourselves without nosy busy bodies knowing what's going on and without my husband finding out. We take their car, and if I decide to stay out, they go pick up their kids at my house and tell the nanny I won't be back until later or in the morning. Otherwise, if I decide to go home, we call it a night and just go home together."

"Nice! And you're telling me this because?" I smiled knowingly as she leaned back and pulled her upper body away slightly. I enjoyed the increased pressure of her pelvis and returned it with a rub of the swelling in my jeans.

"Because, smart aleck, I've been turned on ever since you said hello and I'm not the kind of girl who wants to go home alone with wet panties, unless I have to."

"Wow, I like your spirit!"

"So ya think ya can handle it?" She smiled wickedly.

"Sure, just think of the story—scoring with a beautiful girl on my first night in town and I'm not even checked into flight school, yet! Wow!"

"Well, since you're in, I'll tell you, I'm just as happy about scoring as you are but we'll talk about it later."

"So how does this work for now?"

"When we get back to the table I'll invite Barbara to the ladies' room and tell her I'm going out with you. She'll give the high sign to Louis, and in a few minutes, they will finish the round of drinks Lucky ordered and excuse themselves."

The music changed to a faster beat and we headed for the table but I stopped her at the edge of the dance floor. "And what are our plans, exactly? Just so I know," I smiled.

"Oops, I forgot to ask. Did you come with Lucky or did you drive your own car?"

"I drove my own and he drove his."

"Oh, good. Another detail then. I'm assuming, since you're an officer, you have enough money for a motel?"

"Yes, actually, I probably do have enough but not because of my military pay. I haven't drawn my first active duty pay check yet but I'll get reimbursed for travel and draw my uniform allowance next week."

"Okay. I know a cabin motel on the way to Milton. After they leave we can also excuse ourselves. You can tell Lucky whatever you want."

"I'll play it by ear but I'll probably just say goodnight and thanks for the tour or something to that effect."

The plans to escape worked out almost exactly as she calculated. Louis and Barbara excused themselves after finishing their drinks. A few minutes later, seeing Angie and I engaged in conversation, Lucky excused himself and went to try to score at the bar where a couple of girls still appeared to be unaccompanied. A few minutes later we made our way to the bar to say good night.

"Thanks for a great evening, Major."

"Wait, let me give you my card and my phone number—you can call to let me know the phone number at your quarters and so I can give you the info on the uniforms."

He pulled a card from his wallet and wrote his number on the back. "Good luck, Marine."

"Thanks Major, but I've already had so much luck since I arrived in this town I can hardly believe it."

"I was referring to flight school, Lieutenant," he admonished jokingly while nodding at Angie. "You're gonna need all you can get."

"In that case, thanks again, sir."

He flashed his big yellow-toothed grin and gave an enthusiastic thumbs-up as his face broke into a million rugged wrinkles again. "Take care, Marine!"

I smiled and returned his thumbs up as I took Angie's arm and headed toward the door.

"This is it."

"Ooooh, I love it!" The new MGB always impresses the girls.

I opened the door on her side and helped her in. "Thanks, sweetie. It's been a lot of fun to drive so far."

"Just turn right at the corner and head out to the highway. Then go north and follow the signs toward Pace. It's about 20 minutes from here"

"Okay—you seem to know your way around pretty well?"

"I grew up near here, Bobby. I'm not the typical Pensacola girl who moved here to find a husband. I was born and raised here and I've been dating sailors since I turned 16."

"No marines?"

"Not 'til I was older. The younger men I started dating when I was 16, those still in their teens, were almost 100 percent enlisted sailors. I met a few younger marines stationed here as marine cadet instructors at ground school but I never dated any. Most of the marines here are aviation cadets or officers in flight school or flight instructors, like Lucky."

"How old were you when you got married?"

"I had just turned 20. He was 22. We met at the enlisted club at Whiting Field. That was five years and two kids ago."

As we turned north onto the highway the wind made it difficult to talk and she leaned her head back. Her black curls shook in the wind and her face relaxed with a contented smile.

"Pace is one mile ahead the sign says, I said." *Did she doze off?*

"It's on the left side just after you pass the city limit sign—a little off the road in the trees so go slow or you'll miss it," she warned me.

"Aaaah, there it is. Rustic, isn't it?" I parked the MGB near the building with the orange neon "Vacancy" sign.

"Yeah, but the bungalows are nice. I'll wait here while you check in."

"Okay, be back shortly."

The door to the office was locked and I couldn't see anyone through the glass in the upper half of the door but when I rang the bell a lady in a nightgown and robe appeared shortly.

"I'm sorry to disturb you this late ma'am."

"Oh, that's okay. We get lots of late check-ins on Friday. You just staying the night?"

"Well . . . I really don't know where I'm staying for the weekend. I might stay Saturday and Sunday nights, if there's a room available but I don't want to guarantee it." *How's this going to work out with Angie? I thought.* "I really don't have to check out 'til Monday but I don't know if I need to stay 'til then."

"I understand. I'll put you in a cabin I can reserve for the weekend and you just let me know before 1300 tomorrow if you're gonna check out." She handed me the registration card to fill out along with a pen.

"1300? Do all the civilians use 24-hour time around here?"

"Yes, a lot do but my husband is in the navy so I come by it more naturally than most." She smiled, and I could see the beauty of her shiny, cleansed face and soft natural lips. Her long wavy auburn hair framed the glimmer in her kind brown eyes. She was maybe 35 to 40. Nice shape as far as could be told under the robe. I found myself wondering if her auburn hair was natural.

I handed her back the filled out registration card and picked up the business card from the holder on the desk. "Is this your name on the card?"

"Yes, I'm the night manager. Here's your key Mr. Pincer. Do you need another?" She glanced out the window at the girl in the MGB.

"No, Laura. Thanks." I'll pick up another tomorrow if I need it.

"Okay, Mr. Pincer. Your cabin is all the way at the back off the highway. It will be more quiet in the morning when the other guests are leaving."

"That's good, thanks, Laura."

"Have a good night."
"You too. Good night."
"Did you doze off? I didn't take too long did I?"
"Oh no! Just closing my eyes—thinking about what's to come and I'm still just as excited as I was."
"Okay." I chuckled at the way she seemed a little flustered by my accusation as I started the engine and headed for the cabin. "I showered this morning but I drove all day in the heat and then out tonight—so I'm a little overdue for a shower. Do you mind?"
"Oh no, you go right ahead but don't use the motel soap. I can't stand the strong smell."
"I have some body wash and some Old Spice cologne in my kit. Is that okay?"
"The body wash is okay but you don't need the cologne. I actually prefer a natural clean smell."

I parked and reached behind the seat to pull out my Dopp kit before I went around to her side. She smiled and took my hand as I helped her step out.

"Are you gonna put the top up?"
"I don't know—it doesn't look like rain, does it?"
"No, but you've got a lot of stuff behind the seats and it's pretty exposed."
"Shit, everything I own is in the car."
"I'll help. Let's put it up," she advised.
"Leave it to you girls to be completely down-to-earth and conscious of the right thing to do, even at momentous times." I chuckled.

With the top up we headed into the cabin again. It was a clean, recently remodeled room and bathroom with a large bed and the refrigerated window air conditioner was already on—probably set at about 72, versus the moist July night air at probably 85 degrees.

"I have to go to the bathroom before you get into the shower, Bobby."
"Okay, no problem."

She was quickly out, went directly to the bed, sat down, and crossed her legs as I checked out the bathroom. I'll wait for you here." She smiled and interlocked her fingers across her knee.

"Okay—be out shortly."

She did wait for me there but not exactly as she had been. In my experience, married women, especially mothers, can be counted on to be very practical. There would be no torn button holes, lost buttons, or ripped zippers in the passion of new found excitement. No, her clothes were neatly folded on the chair in the corner and she was propped up on the pillows in the middle of the bed, smiling like she had invented sexiness. Maybe she had. The spread was folded at the foot and the sheet was pulled up to just below her naval.

I stopped abruptly when I saw her and returned her smile—feeling dazed and probably acting like a silly fool as I walked to the side of the bed and dropped my towel. The bedside lamp on the other side was on and the shadows created by her breasts made the scene even more alluring.

"You like, Marine?" She tilted her head and smiled as she looked me directly in the eyes.

"I do like. Very much, madam. May I remove this?" I reached for the sheet.

"Or you can just get in under."

"Removal is better. I'm glad you left the light on. I want to see you as I kiss every bit of you—one inch at a time."

"Ooookay . . . I'm definitely looking forward to that." She smiled broadly and rolled her eyes.

I slowly pulled the sheet all the way down to reveal the rest of her luscious naked body. I hadn't seen her panties on the chair so she either hadn't been wearing any or she hid them under her shorts. From nose to toes she was simply stunning. "You have no idea how good it is to be able to just look and admire your beauty."

I mounted the bed on my knees, scooted over next to her, sat down on my haunches and started tracing my fingers over her body as I viewed the detail of each fraction and talked to her. "Your wavy black hair perfectly frames your blue eyes and gorgeous face." She pressed her lips into a cute tight smile, turned her face away and looked at me out of the corner of her eyes.

My fingers followed my words, "Your neck is long and narrow and flares out to smooth, graceful shoulders. Your breasts are gorgeously firm with perfect little rings of burnt sienna around your hard nipples. Your tummy and naval are sunken down from your ribs and narrowed to your hips where the lines of your body curve out and rise up to a little mound where you have a perfectly trimmed thick, black, powder puff with kinky curls." *There's a little line like a long scar across from side to side below her belly button.*

She shivered as my fingers crossed the powder puff and continued down to the inside of her thighs. "Your legs are long and strong. I can't wait to have them wrapped around my body." *Who could possibly ask for more?*

I went back to her head and gently turned her face to plant little kisses on her eyes, nose, cheeks, ears, and neck before I found her lips with my tongue. I traced her mouth around and around softly, nibbled her lips and finally buried my tongue deep in her mouth.

"Ummm," she moaned. Her stomach curled and her pelvis rose to press against my palm as I moved my hand below the powder puff.

I continued to slowly caress her body with my hands and with little kisses, along the path my fingers had just traced, but lingering a little while, with nibbles and licks on one hard nipple, while I squeezed, massaged and pinched the other. *A man should have two tongues, two cocks and four hands to adequately pleasure one woman.* I continued down her body with my tongue and lips but stopped short of the powder puff as I turned and raised my leg over her head.

"Don't do anything—I just want to be next to your face. I don't want to come this way, but let me feel your lips. Lick if you want—stroke and squeeze if you want but don't put it in your mouth." I licked her thighs, spread them apart and buried my face below the power puff. She was wet before my tongue ever touched her and she shivered mightily when I licked her. *Will she have an orgasm like this, if I continue?*

"Oh God, don't quit!"

Wow, is she reading my mind? I redoubled my efforts as her stomach curled and her hips bucked involuntarily into my face. "Let it go precious. Come for me now!"

She continued to spontaneously shiver and buck her hips in a violent orgasm as she dug her fingers into my back and pressed her face against me. Eventually, she slowed and relaxed.

"Oh God, Bobby, that was wonderful," she said softly. "I really needed that," as her hot breath blew against me.

I rose and rolled off to her side and lay there on my back for a while with my feet on the pillow near her face. Her legs were spread slightly and my arm was lying naturally inside her thighs with my fingers on the powder puff. I gently stroked her curly short hair with my fingers and lightly pressed against her warm moist pelvic arch with my palm. I rose to see her face but instead I saw her cupping her breasts and stroking her nipples with her thumbs. She stopped when she felt me move.

"Would you like to roll over and put those in my mouth?"

"I would," she smiled. She sat up and gave her breasts a few strong massages ending with pinching nipple tweaks as she stared into my eyes and smiled again warmly. "The first one was so good I want another but I want you inside when it happens."

"Sounds great to me! I shall not refuse your desires, gorgeous!"

She brought the pillow from behind her head and put it behind mine and put the other one under my butt. *We know what that means!*

She turned, licked me, and dragged her tongue from my thighs, across my erection and up my stomach toward the middle of my chest. "Here, sweetie, don't skip these on the way," as I put my hands on the side of her head and guided her tongue to one nipple and then the other. "I like it too, and when you're ready, your tongue on the right one is my come button."

My erection had relaxed some after she came but was swelling again and aching to be inside her as she moved up to lick my nipples. She matched her breasts to my nipples and held herself up to wave them back and forth across my chest and rolled her lower belly and powder puff on my erection. She stretched farther up to kiss me, and her tongue wallowed softly in and around my mouth playing with my tongue. I pushed up a little on her hips, to get room to pull my erection up between her legs and she squeezed her thighs together to keep it there like a prisoner. Eventually, she whispered, "I want you inside me now, Bobby, but I want you on top." She began to roll off to the side. "Are you ready?"

"I'm more than ready, sweetie, but I'm gonna wait for you to come again before I let go."

She rolled off and over onto her back, but she was off the pillow, so I rose on my knees and moved between her legs. I picked her up by the hips and rested her bottom on my thighs and slid the pillow under. I took a moment to appreciate her beauty again as I moved just close enough to rub my erection on her raised mound, tapping softly and then rubbing just inside again. She was wet as I slid between her lips. I began to slowly penetrate as I stared at her face and then at the entry and back to her face again. "Amazing," I whispered.

She smiled and bit her lower lip.

"You are one hell-of-a beauty, Angie. I love watching you and I love watching me enter you." Each time I pulled almost all the way out, I eased back in a little deeper. "Angie, you're wet but you're really tight. Are you okay?"

"I'm good, Bobby. I'm just small and you're doin' great! Just keep on comin' in slow."

Two babies and she's still so tight? The brain committee was surprised and impressed.

I let the weight of my hips slide slowly down and pressed into her gently. She showed no sign of pain—just pleasure as I sank fully in, to the bottom. I held there for a few seconds before I pulled nearly all the way out again and held just inside, as I scanned her body from where my brown hair met the curly powder puff, to the matching wavy hair on her head. Her face was shiny with tiny beads of perspiration. She licked her lips when she saw me looking. She shivered, bit her bottom lip again and smiled as I stared into her eyes. What an absolute doll. *How do we get so lucky?*

I pushed all the way back in again and held there. My erection was throbbing and I knew I wouldn't be able to hold off for long after I started stroking so I reached down and started rubbing her softly with my thumb and pressing my fingers into her abdomen. She groaned a little and started to rotate her hips up toward my hand.

"Don't move or I'll come right now," I commanded softly. She completed her rotation but stopped when my erection hit bottom.

"I don't want to come until you do," I explained. I took her hands in mine and placed them on her nipples like she had done before while holding myself above her with the other.

"Tease and hold still as long as you can—then let it go, when you can't stand it anymore." She turned her head to the side and closed her eyes as she began to comply. Is she embarrassed or concentrating?

I was concentrating, but with my eyes open, watching her—holding my body in a state of limbo to prolong the pleasure and to create a powerful crescendo. I started massaging her again as she began teasing her nipples. After a few minutes, I pulled her left leg up and under my shoulder to give me even more penetration. I didn't move to pull out or start a rhythm but the new position gave me a little more inward pressure.

"Oh my God!" she whispered hotly, as she moved just a little. "Oh God! Fuck me, Bobby. Please do it, Bobby! Fuck me! Fuck me! Fuck me—*now*!"

I let go of her leg and caught myself on my arms and then on my elbows as she rolled and bucked like a newly saddled filly and went into an involuntary rhythm as strong as any I'd ever experienced. Thank God she has some padding on her pelvic bone. I could feel her tight squeezing and hot pulsing as she quickly curled and uncurled her stomach and hips and bounced her body against me so hard I thought she might hurt herself.

I had no choice, except to match her rhythm as I arched my back and flung my hips into her and met her thrust with all the energy I could muster. I came for a long time and continued to thrust as long as she did. It felt like she was milking me with her pulsing and squeezing. We slowed eventually and I relaxed on top of her but kept most of my weight on my elbows. We relaxed and lay a long time together until she coughed and the strength of the contraction in her belly pushed me out like a pitiful worn-out worm.

"Oh my God, Bobby. I've never had it like that before! I never knew it could be this good. What the hell have you done to me? How the devil am I ever going to be satisfied with less?"

"Geez, Angie, what have you done to me? You are the tightest I've ever felt, not to mention the strength of your muscles. How am I going to be satisfied with less? How did it happen with two kids, you're still so tight?"

"It's because I'm so small in that area, the babies had to be born by C-section."

"Aaaah, I see. I felt the little scar on your tummy but I didn't know what it was. You've had two?"

"Well, they're twins. I can't have any more because the doctor said it's not good to have more than one C-section."

"Oh, how great is that? Since you can't have more, I mean, you had two at once." Are they identical?"

"No, they're a boy and a girl."

How does that work? One egg, two sperm, or two eggs, two sperm? Why can't I remember? Why don't I know that?

"And even better you got one of each—perfect family."

"Yes, I'm blessed really. You noticed my scar?"

"No, not really. I felt it, but I didn't see it. It's tiny and probably below your bikini line but I felt it as I went across your tummy with my fingers."

"Oh, and what a trip that began." She smiled, reminiscing... "We must do it again, sometime ... soon."

"How about in the morning, my lovely? What time do you need to be up to go home?"

"Of course, my sweet marine. I should be home by ten 'cause the nanny has a day job on Saturday and she needs to get there by noon. Let's get these pillows back in place and turn you around so you can spoon me to sleep and be ready to take me from behind when you wake up."

"And by 'from behind' you mean ... ?"

"Any way you want it, honey—I'm not a virgin there either and I like it either way, so if you want it, take it."

"Now, Angie. How do you expect me to sleep with your ass on my mind?" Just the mention of it caused my flaccid worn-out snake to awaken and begin to resemble a shaft again. We fluffed the pillows and put them at the head of the bed, turned around and pulled up the sheets. Watching her fluid naked body move, kissing her goodnight, and fondling her breast made me semihard again.

When she rolled over, curled into a fetal position and rolled her butt into me I was fully hard again. I snuggled up to her back and used my hand to guide myself between her cheeks as I squeezed my belly up tight against her butt. "I want to sleep inside you, Angie."

"I doubt if I can sleep with you inside me, Bobby, but it's okay if you want to try."

I felt her hand reach and push me in and I pressed farther by curling my hips below as she curled her back more to bring her closer to me. Inside, she was just as hot as she had been before, but not quite as tight, so I was able to slip in. I pushed into her and sunk all the way up to the base of my erection by leaning back and away and then came up again to wrap my free arm around her. She sucked in her breath through her teeth as I cupped her breast and kissed her back.

She shivered again just a little. "I'll never be able to go to sleep if you don't quit moving, Bobby."

Is it possible to lie still when it feels so good? I forced my body not to move, but I pulsated my partial erection inside her. I knew she could feel it although her body was not moving but after a while I could feel her fingers massaging her clit. Eventually, she couldn't hold still any longer and began sliding herself slowly along my shaft until she started softly shivering and shaking quietly. I knew she was coming and I couldn't stand any more so I pumped her quickly only about a half dozen times and we came together again.

When it was over, I just lay still holding her breast softly and kissing her back. Dozing, I whispered, "Goodnight, my lovely lady."

"Goodnight, my handsome marine."

Sometime during the night we separated. I was asleep and I suppose she was also. I woke up with my back to her and rolled out quietly to go to the bathroom. Her curly black hair motionless on the pillow and the shape of the sheets confirmed she probably had not moved all night.

I washed up—pits and tits and brushed my teeth. The thought of jumping back in bed with her began building in my mind as I performed the morning tasks. I pulled a little jar of Vaseline out of my Dopp Kit and took it with me.

She was still asleep, so I stood by the bed looking at her as I put a light coat of Vaseline on what I now termed the "one-eyed monster" who would ravage her. Gently, of course but still, most women I'd known considered giving up their ass as another case of submission and loss of virginity almost as important as surrendering their hymen. Hers was not virgin, of course, like she said, but it still seems special to give it up on a first time, one night-stand.

I left a little of the lube on my left ring and middle fingers as I pulled the sheet off and climbed back in next to her. We had fallen asleep with the light on but the morning sun sneaking around the edges of the window shades lit her tanned fair skin exposing faint bikini lines I had not noticed last night. I sat down on my knees and haunches next to her but far enough away to give my hand an angle and slipped my oiled fingers between her cheeks.

"Oh my God! What's that?" She was startled.

"It's me, my lovely and I'm taking what you promised." I began to stroke back and forth and around the target.

"When I went to sleep you were still inside me, Bobby and you came twice. Where do you get all the energy?"

"You give it to me, lovely. Everything about you is so sexy I can hardly stand it." I began to press in one finger.

"I don't feel sexy right now and I can't even see you."

"Did you forget what I look like already?" I pressed the one finger in and out a few times and then replaced it with my thumb.

"Oh my God! What are you doing to me?"

"Ah, well, you should know. You said you're not a virgin." I spread her cheeks with my other hand and pressed my thick thumb slowly in as far as I could and rotated my hand down.

"I'm not a virgin, but it was only once before and it was a while ago."

I rotated my hand again and slid my ring and middle finger between her legs. I continued to slide my fingers back and forth while my thumb rotated. "I assume you liked it or you wouldn't have offered it again."

"I did. But it was different."

I could feel she was very wet so I rotated my wrist and thumb and inserted both fingers into her front and held her like a bowling ball. "Oh God! Oh God! It can't be this good!"

With my free hand I grabbed her lower hip and rolled her over onto her stomach and began to twist, push and rock my thumb and both fingers in and out. She pushed up against my hand. Fingers in—thumb out. Thumb in—fingers out. She bucked and humped again and again and moaned loudly.

"Go, lovely," I urged her. "Let it go." Her arrival was violent and long. The convulsions seemed as though she was attacking the bed and bouncing back to my hand. Afterward, she lay breathing heavily, for a while and then was quiet.

I let her relax for a moment and then moved behind to spread her legs apart and inched up close. She was like a limp doll. I spread her cheeks, exposing her completely and spanked her with my shaft. She raised her buttocks just a little as if asking for more. As I leaned forward, I pushed in and adjusted my weight forward onto my arms and lowered myself into her slowly. She was well prepared and I was well lubricated so the penetration went smoothly. Her solid buttocks felt good against my lower abdomen and sore pelvis. I let my full weight press into her for the deepest penetration and held it there.

"Aaaah, Bobby," She moaned. "It feels so different, so good—fuck me slow, Bobby."

I began to pump her slowly and she started to talk and make little sounds of pleasure and maybe pain? I stopped mid stroke. "Are you okay?" I was concerned it was hurting her.

"Oh, Bobby. Yes, I'm more than okay. Fuck me, Bobby. Don't stop."

I started again and pushed her for quite a while but I wasn't getting to a crescendo and neither was she. I could tell it was good and she was enjoying it, but something was missing.

I pulled the loose pillow over next to her hip and pulled out. I rose on my knees, reached for her hips and pulled her up, lifted my knees over her leg and rolled her on her back with her hips on the pillow.

She smiled. "Had enough of my backside, sweetie?" She's teasing a little, I think.

"No, Angie." I smiled. "I've just begun with your 'backside' but I want to finish looking into your gorgeous eyes and eyeballing the front of your gorgeous body."

I pulled her legs up and inside my arms to rest on my chest and rolled my weight forward. My weight on her legs pulled her right up to a perfect position to enter her backside as I relaxed her right leg to reach down between to start the penetration. I was still hard and getting harder as I sunk down and down. I reached and pulled her hips up even more and rolled her up farther like a pretzel.

She sucked in a deep breath again and let out a little surprise squeak. "Oh God, don't stop! That's even deeper than it was! Oh God, fuck me now, Bobby! Don't stop!"

I gazed into her eyes. Her face reflected the morning light in little beads of sweat across her forehead and the bridge of her nose, highlighted with pink flushed cheeks. Her blues were even brighter in the light of day. I watched intently, scanning between her wide open vulva and her wide open eyes, as she masterfully manipulated herself. One of her hands squeezed her breasts and teased her nipples while the other rubbed her clitoris and rimmed her vulva and occasionally stroked into her vagina. She had little room to move her trapped body with her legs under my arms and her feet next to my neck and my weight on my pelvic bone against her but she managed to pulsate even more than she had squeezed last night. Now we were getting somewhere! The stroke length was long and deep but not fast. The slower rhythm seemed to tantalize her more and she began to shiver and convulse just as violently as she had before. "Oh God, that's good," she whispered loudly in her passion, closing her eyes and turning her head to the side.

"Look at me, Angie! I want to see your eyes and I want you to see mine. When you see me looking into your eyes tomorrow or the next day or the next, I want you to know my eyes will be fucking you then, just as they are now."

"Oh yes, that's perfect," I whispered, and stared intently into her wide eyes as she relaxed with a huge toothy smile. "I love it when you smile while I'm fucking you. I love knowing you're enjoying it.

"Oh, give it to me, Bobby," she whispered loudly again and as she started to whimper and shake I pumped hard and came with her. I nearly lost my balance as the violence of my ejaculation exploded. I relaxed, leaned back and put her legs down around my hips with her butt on my thighs. Her curly black powder puff was the highest point on the convex shape her body produced, so I pressed the palm of my hand there and gently rotated my wrist to stroke her with my fingers.

"Oh yes, that was perfect," she whispered as she continued to look into my eyes and smiled her loving smile again.

I put one leg over and rolled her lower half onto her side and then lay down next to her. "Good morning, lovely lady." I turned the upper half of her body toward me, kissed her wet, soft lips, breathed the hot air from the depths of her lungs and fondled both her breasts while alternately brushing her powder puff.

"Don't start with me again or I'll be late getting home."

"You mean you would want more?"

"Well, no—it's not that I'm not satisfied, because I am. We've done just about everything that can be done and it's been great. The problem is, I just don't want it to end. And if you start teasing me again, I won't be able to resist."

"All good to know for next time," I answered with a tender smile.

"I know, and I really wanted to taste you but I didn't get the chance the way things happened."

"You never know what opportunities may arise," I said and sat up on my knees again and flapped my mostly flaccid penis on her hips. "Although this one-eyed monster looks mostly dead right now, I'm sure he'd come alive fairly quickly at the thought of some new experience with you." I rolled over, got up and headed toward the bathroom but stopped. "Do you want to go before I get dressed?"

"Yes, thanks. You don't need to go?" She popped out of bed and marched to the bathroom without an apparent thought about her nudity. *Kudos to a lovely lady who is not shy and either likes it when she's admired or just doesn't mind if we look.*

"Nope, I went already, before you woke up. I just need to get my clothes out of there."

"Okay, hand me mine off the chair and I'll hand you yours."

"Works for me." As I handed over her clothes, I grabbed her forearm and pulled her toward me. "Let me feel your naked body against me one more time, gorgeous." I wrapped my arms around her and kissed her wet and long before I let her go. "Just a taste to remember until next time"

I left the top up on the MGB because it was a little windy and also so we could talk more easily. "There may not be a next time, Bobby. My husband will be home in a couple of weeks and I only have Sunday nights off work. You'll be starting ground school soon and may not be able to take time away from your studies. I've heard those classes are not easy."

"Well, I know they're not easy but I've already had all but Navigation as college courses. I have an Associate Degree in Civil Engineering, two years in upper level engineering courses and a bachelor of science degree in industrial science. Anyway, compared to six years of daytime college with five years of football and a full-time night job, going only to aviation and engineering classes for eight hours a day, five days a week, sounds more like a part-time job."

"What did you mean 'until next time'?" She seemed a little confused.

"Does that mean you think there will be 'a next time'?" I chuckled.

"I think it does, if you want to make the effort. So what happens?"

She was persistent in a pleasant way but I ducked the question anyway. "There could be a lot of things left on the list but I've already done most so I don't see setting out to accomplish an agenda, rather letting whatever happens, happen spontaneously over time if it does."

"So have you done it on a beach?"

"No, sweetie. I just got here, remember? I grew up in Oklahoma and went to school in New Mexico. I haven't even seen a beach, much less had sex on one. The closest I've come is making out on a blanket in the grass by the lake but that was a completely private area. Not like a beach where someone might come walking by."

She was quiet for a moment . . . maybe like she was contemplating the idea.

"So . . . Angie, my sweet, tell me about the 'other circumstances' when you lost your anal virginity."

She smiled and looked across the car out of the corner of her eye like she was a little surprised I asked. "That requires a pretty frank story and I'm not sure I'm ready for that yet."

I laughed. "C'mon, Angie. I did you twice last night and once this morning. Isn't that like maybe we're on our third date already? And we've been about as 'frank' as you can get, haven't we?"

"It just seems more personal and I don't know how you would feel about it."

"You mean like if I would disapprove of something you did?

"Yes."

"And what right would I have to judge you? I'll answer—*none*. The way I feel, you have a right to do and be and act in any way and with anyone you want, as long as you're not hurting someone else." *And besides, the committee surmised, if we were to judge your actions as inferior, would we not then have to take a much closer look at our own behavior—and we're not nearly ready to do that are we?*

She was quiet again but said, "Well, if you want.

"I do," I said softly as I turned and smiled at her.

"We, Bill and I, have a very close relationship with Louis and Barbara. We've swapped with them—only a few times." She quickly added and paused to look at me for a sign and then continued, "One night the boys decided they'd like to double up on us—a double penetration—one in the front and one in the back door, so to speak. There was a long discussion about who should be in front and who should be in back and which wife should go first. Barbara and I were both virgins there but I am, by far, the most adventurous. By the time it was decided that we would try it they also decided I should go first. Bill would be in front and Louis would be in back, I would be on top of Bill with my butt in the air for Louis. Louis was so excited he was clumsy and rough. He didn't prepare me enough so I wasn't stretched as much as I could have been and neither of us were lubricated enough so it hurt a lot at first, but finally, he got it together and it was okay."

"And how was Barbara's experience?"

"Both guys came when I did and it took nearly an hour of rest and foreplay for them to get it up together again. When they were ready, I made sure Bill was lubricated and that he took his time to stretch her slowly with his fingers. She came when Bill first entered, and again when the two boys came, so I think hers was better than mine."

"And you were concerned I was going to condemn you for swapping or having a DP?"

"Something like that, yes."

"I would never do that, even if I'd not done it myself, but I have with my second wife."

"Second wife? How many times have you been married? How old are you?"

"Well, just twice, so far anyway and I'm 24."

"So, I'm a year older than you are and you've been married and divorced twice?"

"Not exactly. I've been married twice but only divorced once. I'm in the process of getting divorced from the second one right now. It should be final when I go to court at home over Christmas leave. I filed there this summer when I was staying with my folks."

"You've been a busy man, Bobby," she said as she smiled coyly and started twirling a lock of her black waves. "What happened?"

"Suffice to say, the marriages didn't work out. Well, the first one didn't work out but the second was an open marriage of convenience and it was supposed to end just like it did. We can talk about the details later if you like?"

"Of course, you liked the open marriage though?"

"Mixed feelings I guess you would say. Long term, I don't see it as way of life for me. Sure, as far as sex is concerned it's the best of all worlds. You're married but not monogamous. You have sex with all kinds of sexy and kinky women with no effort to chase them and no consequences. I'm sure you know how much more exciting first time sex can be as compared to routine sex with your husband. You've obviously enjoyed the encounters with Louis and Barbara. Right?"

"Yes, of course, or we wouldn't have continued. But they are the first and the only ones we've ever shared."

"But maybe not the last."

"We are still young so I guess we'll just have to wait and find out. Turn left up here at the next corner and then right in two blocks."

"Okay, but before we get there, what are we going to do about us?"

"I don't know exactly. I have to work tonight from 1800 'til 0200 when the bar closes."

"I don't know the situation with the kids and the nanny and your schedule but you could stop by the motel on the way to work or on the way home, or both, if you like and you don't have to work on Sunday, do you?"

"Oh my God, Bobby! I'm not sore but I can still feel you inside me. I was sure I'd be satisfied for at least a week and now you're stirring me up again. Stop here. That's Louis and Barbara's house and this is mine."

"Like you said, Angie, we may not get another chance and I don't want to miss this opportunity."

"Oh Jesus, what do I do now?" She paused looking down at her hands in her lap.

"Do you know the lady at the motel?"

"Yes, why?"

"Is she someone you can trust with your secrets?" Most motel managers are discreet when asked. It's good for business.

"Yes, she's a friend but what made you think so?"

"Well, because I figured you'd been there before?"

"How did you figure?"

"A couple of things. You said it was nice and remodeled which just may have been hearsay but mostly because you told me not to use the smelly soap."

"Really, the soap was it?" She looked dumbfounded.

I laughed. "Yes, I figured you must have used the soap or have been there with someone who used it in order to know how it smelled. Anyway, what I was getting at is, you don't have to tell me right now what you want to do. You can see how you're feeling and make your plans accordingly and let me know by calling the motel. If I'm not there, just leave a message and I'll check with her to see if you're coming or not."

"So just make my own plans and let you know?"

"You have several options. Come early before work this afternoon—come after work and go on home later, or sleep over, or don't come this evening or tonight at all and come anytime Sunday and stay 'til Monday if you want. Your choice."

"Boy, this is a complicated menu. I think . . . just because I'm tired, I know already I won't come before work tonight, but if my nanny can handle it, I'll come after work tonight, and since you offered, and I don't have to work Sunday, I'll stay tonight after work and Sunday night, and go home Monday morning, if it's okay with you?"

"Of course, sweetie. Whatever you want is okay with me. Do you mind if I show up at the Schooner tonight?"

"That would be great and I can confirm the plan then—rather than calling the motel."

"Okay, I'll see you tonight then."

"Don't get out, Bobby." She leaned across the car to kiss me. "I don't want the neighbors to see me being brought home by such a good looking man. They would be full of questions." She smiled, winked and slipped out of the car. I watched her until she was inside and closed the door.

The Schooner, a small bar, is located on Santa Rosa Island on the inland side as opposed to the side on the Gulf of Mexico. It's smaller than Trader Jon's and adorned with beach regalia rather than aviation memorabilia. The decor includes the typical fishing nets, seashells, paintings of beaches, sailboats and sunsets over the water. The atmosphere is more homey, and the bartenders and waitresses are more friendly than the more commercial Trader Jon's. Not to mention, the beer is colder and cheaper. As such, it was destined to become the bar of choice for regular patrons who wanted to spend more time at the beach and for tourists who were primarily coming to the area to visit the beach.

I arrived around nine o'clock in the evening so Angie had been working three hours already. The Saturday night crowd was already lit up pretty well, and noisy. As I walked in, a young man, probably a flight student or at least a serviceman, judging by his looks, was playing a guitar and singing "Michael Row the Boat Ashore," which had become a number one hit song a couple of years earlier. I cut a path through the smell of stale beer mixed with heavy cigarette smoke as it drifted through the room like a dim lit cloud. I headed across the old wooden floor to an empty table for two by the wall near the music, and sat down facing the singer with my back to the entry door. The bar was on the other side of the room about 25 feet away, extending in an "L" shape from the front wall with a waitress station at the short end on the "L."

Angie was at the waitress station, waiting for an order and apparently didn't see me come in. She was cute in the uniform, which consisted of a light blue strip of cloth across her breasts and all the way around her body with elastic on the top and bottom gathering the material. There were no straps to hold it up—just the breasts and the elastic. Bare shoulders, no sleeves and bare midriff down to her dark blue shorts. Interesting, I thought, remembering her perfect breasts as they were last night—sitting there with proud, hard nipples, pointing at me when I came out of the bathroom.

The song ended and I focused in on the entertainer and clapped. He started another not so familiar song and I turned back to watch Angie but she was gone from the station—probably in the back or serving tables around the corner on the other side of the bar. I listened to the music and was lost in some kind of trance remembering the events since graduation from college when she came up beside me and put her hand on my shoulder, "Hello, Marine!"

I half turned in surprise and stood up. "Hi, Angie! I was watching you but you disappeared."

"I saw you come in but I was busy with an order I had to deliver. How are you?"

"I'm good, thanks. I went back to the cabin and let the lady know I would be staying for the weekend and then took a nap. How are you?"

"I'm tired. I had to do some grocery shopping and give the kids a bath and get ready to go to work. The time just flew by and here I am."

"I got up, took a shower and called Lucky. He wanted me to meet him at the diner for a quick dinner and then we went to Trader Jon's for a while. He said he might come over here later."

"Yeah, if he comes over here to the island, he usually shows up around midnight because he struck out over there. He'll come in and hit on any of the females who might still be unattached and if he doesn't have any luck there, he'll hit on the waitresses."

"So he hits on you?"

"Yeah, but he knows it won't do him any good. He's too little and too old for me. I don't think he's ever been out with any of the waitresses here but that doesn't stop him from trying. He does get lucky every once in a while with the older tourists though. Hey, I gotta get back to work. You want a beer?"

"Sure, Angie but I can get it at the bar. You don't have to wait on me."

"No, I'll be going back and forth anyway. I'll get it—what do you want?"

"Coors draft?"

"Nope, all you westerners ask for Coors but we don't have it here in the east. Next choice?"

"Bud draft?"

"Sure."

"Thanks, Angie!" I smiled and sat back down at my table.

She returned shortly with my beer and bent over facing me.

"Very nice view, Angie!" Her top was about half way down her breasts as she leaned over more than necessary to put the beer on the table.

"The view is free for you, Marine, but that's how this sailor's wife makes her tips." She smiled pleasantly, adjusted her top down just a tiny bit more and shook her shoulders to wave her breasts in my face. The closer look at her breasts revealed a roll of bills neatly tucked in the cleavage between. "I'll be seeing you after closing, if it's still okay?"

"Absolutely, it's still okay!" The brain committee screamed in amazement, *Why wouldn't it be okay?*

"But, Bobby, I'll probably be so tired I won't be able to do much after last night, this morning and working all night."

"I understand, sweetie. I used to work eight hour shifts until 0200, six nights a week just like you do. I'll rub your feet, your back and your shoulders, let you fall asleep spooning and let you sleep in tomorrow morning."

"Ooooh, I remember how you spoon." She smiled and shook her head playfully, as if she would disagree with the proposition.

"Well, that episode included falling asleep connected which I wouldn't do if you're too tired."

"I'd never be too tired for falling asleep that way."

"It's settled then. Connected spooning as soon as you can get there."

"Nope. After today's schedule I'll have to shower first."

"Okay, but I also want you to remember what I said about my eyes watching you and thinking about you as you work tonight."

"Yeah, but you didn't say watching. You said fucking and I've already been doing it."

"And so I did. I stand corrected and the intensity of the action just went up another notch."

I nursed three or four beers until about midnight. The music was good but the time seemed to just creep along. Lucky never showed up so he must have scored at Trader Jon's. I watched Angie move around the room—swinging her narrow hips gracefully in the tight aisles between the tables and chairs as she waited on and seduced her mostly male clientele—allowing them to fold and tuck their tips in her cleavage alongside the continually growing roll.

"Do you want another beer, Bobby?"

"No, Angie, I think I'm gonna go on back to the cabin and take a shower. At this point, you'll only be an hour or so behind me."

"Sure, that's okay." She smiled her approval.

I stood up and gave her a kind of public kiss on the cheek and headed out. "Okay, see ya later then."

After my shower I decided to wait for her the way she had waited for me the night before—I unlocked the door to the cabin, turned off the light on my side of the bed, leaving her side light on, propped up the pillows, climbed in under the sheets and fell asleep waiting for her knock.

"Come on in," I said. "It's open."

"Hi there, Handsome," she said cheerfully as she bent over to kiss me.

I teased her nipples and pulled her top down to see them. She had removed the roll of bills from her cleavage.

"Aaaah, don't start with me yet—I still have to shower," she protested.

"If I'm asleep, just wake me up."

"Right." She pulled herself away and headed to the bathroom without pulling the top up.

Daylight illuminated the room in shades of gray when I was conscious again. It was 0900 on Sunday morning. Apparently, I fell asleep as soon as she closed the door to the bathroom and she didn't wake me up. *Speaking of the bathroom, the one eyed monster needs draining.* I also washed my face and brushed my teeth and when I returned to the room she was awake. "Good morning, Lovely!

She peeked out from under the sheet. "Good morning!"

"Obviously, you didn't wake me last night after your shower—or did you try unsuccessfully?"

No, Bobby, I was just simply too tired and you looked so peaceful lying there without a care in the world. I think I remember one of the options was to crash after work and sleep-in on Sunday morning. Right?"

"Of course, that's right and it's fine."

"Let me go to the bathroom and wash up and I'll be right back." Unabashed, she threw the sheet away from her nude body, bounced up and marched off.

"I'll wait for you here," I said jokingly as I climbed in bed and pulled the sheet up to my waist. This protocol seemed to have become the standard rhetoric and setting for the scene. The sight of her naked body flouncing across the room had an instant swelling effect on me but it soon waned because she was gone a long time. When she returned at a much slower and more teasing pace, I became almost instantly erect. Her approach to the bed was smooth and deliberate as she pulled back the sheet and ravished my body with her mouth. *Having a hot dog at the Y, the committee joked. Yea!* Angie licked and tickled and stroked and stayed a long time, just generally teasing, and playing around, eventually working her way up to my left nipple—a.k.a. the starter button.

"I'm comin' up on top, Bobby. I want you inside me and I want to ride."

"You've got it, lovely! You do whatever you want. I'm at your disposal."

She put one leg over on the other side and hovered with her powder puff just touching me and rolled her hips forward to drag herself along my erection. She balanced herself with her hands on my chest but was able to use her thumbs to stroke both my nipples.

"Jesus, Angie! You've got both my starter button and my come button goin' nuts and you're gonna make me come before we even get started." She rose a little on her knees and used one hand to guide me inside. She was very wet, so I slipped easily into her tight vagina, as she sat back down and pressed smoothly, all the way to the bottom. I stared into her eyes as she persisted for another couple of minutes with her fingers on my nipples and then put her arms down to the side and curled her body so she could reach my come button with her lips and tongue and urged, "It's okay, honey. Let it go. Come for me now!"

She didn't have to say it twice. It was going to be a quickie but I was on the verge of exploding and could not have held off much longer anyway. The explosion of muscle and bone grinding was as strong as possible. I felt the shakes all the way down to my toes and shivers were running rampant in my legs, back and shoulders. She sat up during the quake and rested herself almost entirely on her pelvic bone, which was at the base of my erection and then proceeded to bounce into me as I thrust toward her. I tightened my buttocks and held my pelvis up to her for deeper penetration and let her bounce to her hearts content. I let go as soon she began to convulse and shake.

She shook and shivered for a long time until she was finally able to settle down.

"I've been thinking about that all day yesterday and all night last night at work, Bobby. I had wet pants several times just thinking about you looking at me and fucking me."

"And I was sitting there in the lounge with an erection, watching you, waiting on the customers, shaking your boobs and collecting your tips. I was mentally fucking you, just like you thought I was."

She pushed her legs back alongside mine and rocked forward to lower her body onto mine. She cuddled there with her head just below my chin as I wrapped my arms around her, squeezed lightly and rubbed her back. I stroked her hair and kissed her thick black waves and she rose to pull herself higher and kiss me. She was kissing softly with wet lips and moving around my face to my cheeks, eyes and forehead and then came back to my mouth for a long time. She sucked gently on my tongue and my lower lip and then left her tongue in my mouth moving softly, as though she didn't ever want to take it out. Eventually, she stopped and climbed off to the side and lay on her stomach.

When I was able to talk I rolled toward her, patted her bubble butt and asked, "Are you hungry?"

"Yes, Bobby, I am hungry but first I want your fingers and thumb in me like they were yesterday." She raised her hips and pushed her buttocks up to show me the target.

I chuckled. "Aaaah, a different kind of hungry. You want to be the bowling ball again. Yes?"

If that's what you call it, yes?

"Great! Let me see if you're still wet enough without lube." I pushed myself up and pulled my legs underneath so I could sit on my haunches by the side of her butt. I slid my hand between her buttocks and down between her legs. Her cheeks were dry but there was still plenty of slick liquid remaining inside.

"Uuum," she groaned softly when I touched her. I worked my thumb into her until it was wet and then replaced it with my ring and middle fingers while dragging my thumb up. I worked my fingers deeper and began rimming her with my wet thumb. Occasionally, I dragged more liquid up and worked my thumb in more deeply. She began to move and wiggle as the stretching continued and as the sensations built, she became more vocal. Eventually, I worked my thumb all the way in the back and my fingers all the way into the front.

"Oh God, Bobby! I've been wanting this again! Give it to me, Bobby!"

"Aaaah, yes, my sweet. I love watching your butt bounce and feeling your tightness on my thumb and fingers and the power in the palm of my hand."

"Ooooh my God! How could it be any better?" I knew she was asking a rhetorical question but I couldn't resist. "Roll over on your back and we'll try."

"I don't want to move. It feels too good the way it is!"

"Okay, next time then." I redoubled the strength, depth and speed of the rhythmic penetrations and she became lost in the passion of her orgasm. As is the case with most men, I had reached a level of satisfaction and a number of recent orgasms, which left me excited and mentally ready to participate but with about half an erection. Such a condition might sometimes work into another orgasm if she were able to get her tongue on my starter and come buttons but the circumstances right now were not conducive.

She bounced into the bed and back into my hand harder and harder and I met her with aggressive pressure in a regular pounding rhythm as she shook and shivered through a very wild climax.

I left my hand in the bowling ball position and moved my thumb and fingers slowly around and in and out and massaged her ass and vulva lightly. She lay still and I thought maybe she was dozing but as I began to scratch and rub her back with my other hand, she said, "Is it next time yet?"

"You're insatiable, my sweet!" I laughed. My fingers were still inside her and I tweaked her a little by squeezing my thumb and fingers toward each other. "You really want more?"

"Well, I was just thinking about what you said—about showing me how it could be better?"

"I don't know if it would actually be better than what you just had but it could be, because it would be a better position for me and I can tease your clit."

"Let's see." She rolled away onto her back and my hand slipped out and rolled around her hip and onto her black curly bush.

I stroked her easy a couple of times, and she raised her hips into my hand. "Let's put a pillow under here, sweetie." She raised her knees and bridged her body upward and I put my pillow under her hips and repositioned her pillow under her head. I stopped to take a moment and admire her composite beauty stretched out before me. There were no flaws from head to toe except the tiny cesarean scar line on her lower tummy. Light creamy skin wrapped tautly around slightly defined muscles on a solid frame provided an almost sturdy manikin-like appearance. Her wavy black hair spread out on the pillow framed an almost porcelain doll facial quality with bright blue eyes, dark eyebrows, high cheekbones and rosy lips. *How do we get so lucky?*

I leaned over and kissed her and sucked her lower lip softly and then buried my tongue as deeply as I could in her mouth. I leaned back to look her in the eyes again and dreamed of fucking her beautiful face. I leaned down again and kissed her ear, sucked her lobe and kissed her neck down across her shoulder to her breast. I licked and sucked her nipple and stroked her breast with my right hand while I reached down to press lightly below with my other thumb.

"Ooooh, that's good," she whispered and I watched her face as I began to press my thumb into her. She closed her eyes and pressed her lips tightly together.

"I want to see your eyes, Angie." She opened them wide and smiled as she rolled her pelvic arch up to meet my hand as I pressed my thumb fully in and began to work my fingers into her backside.

"Ooooh my God," she whispered. "It *is* better!"

I sank my thumb and fingers fully into her openings and leaned over to lick her nipple again and then sat back up beside her to play her like a piano. I rolled my left wrist up and down providing motion in and out with thumb and fingers while I squeezed her breasts and pinched her nipples with my other hand and then turned to play her clit instead.

"Oh God," she groaned. "Don't quit! Don't stop! She whispered loudly and often, with wide-open eyes, looking directly into mine. She continued to moan and encourage me while she writhed and bucked under my hands. Watching and listening to her, I was now fully hard again, aching to be inside her as I stared back into her eyes when suddenly she came. It was just as violent as before and lasted just as long and afterward she lay completely still with her eyes closed. I gently removed my hand and sat still, waiting. Breathing less hard with each heave of her chest she eventually seemed to become aware of her surroundings again.

Finally, she said, "That *was* even better than before, Bobby. What the hell have you done to me? I don't think I'll ever be able to have sex again without thinking about this time."

I chuckled. "And I hope you'll never be able to look me in the eyes again without thinking of this time. I absolutely adore the way you look when you're about to come. The wide-open brightness of your eyes and the beauty of the passion in your face is overwhelming.

She was quiet and the serenity on her face and in her eyes was as calm as a windless lake.

I was all of a sudden very hungry. "How about brunch on the beach? Are there any places with good food?"

"Yes, there are a couple of places that specialize in brunches on Sunday. They have all the usual stuff—bacon, ham, eggs, omelets, waffles, pancakes and all kinds of seafood."

"Do we need to call for reservations?"

"No, they don't take reservations at restaurants on the beach. Everyone has to stand in line but the lines usually aren't too long. Let's hustle so we can beat the families getting out of church."

"Okay, should I just take my suit or wear it under my jeans?"

"Wear it under your jeans so you don't have to look for a place to change—and grab a couple of towels."

The drive to Pensacola Beach took almost an hour with the traffic so it was almost noon by the time we got there. The line wasn't too long though because the church crowd wouldn't get across the bridge and park until a little after noon. Our table was next to a huge floor-to-ceiling glass window so I was able to see the beach and the Gulf of Mexico for the first time. The sweep of white sand was wondrous and the occasional dunes between the restaurant and the water line were spotted with tufts of green and brown grass sticking up and waving in the breeze. The shoreline was replete with people of all shapes and sizes adorned with skimpy swim suits spread out on bright colored blankets.

The smell of bacon frying drew me to the buffet line where the extent of the spread was overwhelming. How could I possible enjoy all of this? Should I just pick out the stuff I know I like or should I try out some of the things I've never eaten before? Reading the tags, I was tempted to try them all. Fresh oysters, clams, mussels. Fried calamari, *lox*, prosciutto—what the fuck are these things? Does "Fresh" mean raw or as in recently caught and cooked?

"Angie, is this an all you can eat buffet or do you just go through the line once and that's it?

"It's all you can eat, Bobby. Are you really hungry?"

"Well, ya know, I really am pretty hungry and the fabulous smell and sight of all this food makes me even hungrier but there's no way I can even sample so many things."

"Well, just pick a few new ones to go with the old standbys. It's not all that expensive so you can afford to come back often and try the rest at another time."

I started out with coffee and a Bloody Mary followed by an omelet and a Belgian waffle and a dozen ice cold fresh oysters. Everything was delicious and I went back for more oysters, as well as, some steamed mussels, fried calamari and French toast. A third trip was mostly the same as the second.

"I'm so stuffed I'm a bit nauseous. It must be time for my first walk on a beach and close look at the ocean."

"Technically it's not an ocean, Bobby. It's the Gulf of Mexico." She was sweet—like a kind tutor, who wouldn't want to hurt my feelings but wanted me to know the correct terminology.

I chuckled. "Now, Angie, how would you expect an Okie who's never even seen the ocean or the Gulf to know the difference. What is the difference anyway?"

"Well, mostly I guess the gulf is surrounded by about 80 percent land consisting of the east coast of Mexico and the Yucatan Peninsula, the southern coast of the United States and the west coast of Florida. The mouth of the Gulf on the east side is partially blocked by Cuba, and the Haiti-Dominican Republic Island, along with Puerto Rico, and the Antilles Islands which are located in or on the edge of the Caribbean Sea and the Gulf. The southern perimeter is bordered by South America and the Caribbean Sea."

"Okay, that's about as clear as mud. I'll look at a map later and figure it out."

"The differences I see are the Gulf has warmer water with smaller waves than the Atlantic and the Caribbean has warm water like the Gulf but it is also clearer than the Gulf or the Atlantic. The sand and sun are beautiful no matter where you are. I don't know much about the Pacific west coast of California or Mexico but I've heard the waves are bigger and the water is very cold by comparison."

"Okay, my lovely professor. Let's go walk on the soft white sand, swim in the warm salty water, feel the cool fresh breezes and revel in the great beauty of the Gulf shore!"

"Sounds like a good idea to me!" She laughed and almost skipped happily as we headed out to the MGB to ditch our clothes. The trunk was still full of my stuff but we managed to stuff her little shorts and top and my jeans, shirt and socks into a corner where the towels had been. Have I only been here two days? It seems like time has stopped. I marveled again at the shape of her body as she peeled off the outer layer down to her red bikini. The material was thin and taut which clearly showed her prominent nipples. The strings tied behind her neck and across her back. Her breasts were a little fuller than most of the women I'd known but very shapely and firm. The front of the bottom was a straight band with the top just above the little cesarean scar. The sharp ends of her short curly pubes plainly demonstrated the presence of her powder puff through the thin red material. The rear was form fitted and stretched tightly over her bowling ball butt. I'm gonna have an erection all day, I thought!

"I should have brought a t-shirt—I think I'm gonna get too much sun on my back and shoulders," she pondered.

"Here, I'm sure I have a clean one in my sea bag. Mom washed everything before I left home and I haven't even had the bag out of the car yet." I pulled the big green bag out of the trunk, went fishing and pulled out two. They smelled fresh and clean. "I'd better wear one too."

"Thanks," she said as she smiled and slipped the shirt over her head.

I put on my t-shirt, locked the trunk, put the key in the pocket of my trunks and slipped my tennis shoes back on. "I have to say I like the bikini look much better than the t-shirt but this view is probably easier to handle."

"What do you mean?"

"I started to get an erection while inspecting your bikini and it could be uncomfortable walking around on the beach all day with a hard on."

She laughed out loud. "So I'm still turning you on, eh? I thought maybe you were tired and worn-out by now."

"My pelvic bone is so bruised I'm not sure I could do much physically, but mentally, when I look at your gorgeous face and your nearly naked body, I'm as horny as I've ever been." I leaned down to kiss her, stroked her powder puff and tweaked her through the bikini. Her first reaction was to draw away but it was immediately followed by an involuntary bump into my hand. I held the kiss, grabbed her tightly with the heel of my hand on her pelvic arch and my fingers pressing below.

She whispered, "Stop, Bobby," as she turned away from the kiss but didn't pull her body away. "Bobby, please," she persisted. "You'll give me a wet bikini right here in the middle of a public parking lot." I relaxed my hand and reluctantly let her go as she pulled her hips away slowly.

She wrapped the towel around her waist and put her purse on her shoulder. "Now, let's go, Marine. I guarantee you're gonna get all the action you want later."

"Guarantee?" I teased, pulled her close and patted her butt.

"Absolutely, I want it just as much and maybe more than you do!"

We held hands and walked toward the beach from the parking lot, past the restaurant, straight across the sand to the water's edge. This area of the beach was crowded but I spotted an open space at the edge of the dry sand where I took off my tennis shoes and put them on my towel with my t-shirt. The waves were very small—not much bigger than the lake waves I'd grown up with in Oklahoma. The expanse of the water though, was much more than I'd expected. The weather and the visibility were so perfect I could see the curvature of the planet on the far southern horizon. The breeze coming off the water seemed fresh and cool but it also imparted an aroma a little like fish or something. No, it didn't stink like dead fish or stagnant water, but I could smell something. Angie didn't take her shoes off and just stood there, watching me.

"Don't you wanna go in?" I asked.

"No, not now. You go on in and check it out but don't stay in too long. I want to go on down the beach and look for a good spot to sunbathe."

"We can't sunbathe here?"

"It's a little crowded here."

"Okay, I'll be back shortly then."

The water was warm. Warmer even than some of the lake water where I'd grown up and certainly a lot warmer than the 60-degree creek water at Platt National Park where we used to camp when I was young. I swam slowly away from the beach for a while—maybe ten minutes. I'd heard it was easier to swim in salt water than in freshwater because of the greater buoyancy the density of the salt water provided. It seemed to be true. I usually had to work pretty hard to swim and Dad always said, "Son, you swim like a rock," and he would laugh mightily at his own joke and punch my shoulder or playfully pick me up and throw me into the deep water or dunk me.

I learned to swim much better later and learned all the basic strokes in swim class during a physical education course in college.

Suddenly, I wandered how far out I had swum. I stopped, turned around and looked back for the shore and discovered I was a lot farther out than I thought I would go. But as I changed direction, my feet hit sand on the bottom. When I stood up, the water was just above my stomach—maybe only four feet deep. So as I stood there amazed, I wondered if the water was that shallow all the way to the beach. Probably not, I concluded. This must be some kind of underwater island or something. I walked a few steps farther out, and it got deeper. I walked a few steps back toward the beach, and it got deeper. I must have stopped right on a ridge.

Just as I turned back to look out again there were two huge fish, maybe five or six feet long, jumping out of the water, heading from my right to my left, no more than 20 feet from me. I had no idea what kind of fish they were. Maybe they're sharks? I wasn't about to stick around to find out. I didn't want to make a big splash so I quickly but smoothly arched over backward and rolled into an underwater breaststroke. Shortly afterward, when I was out of breath, I emerged quietly and started a smooth crawl without kicking and then shortly into a full crawl, pulling and kicking as fast as I could. I think it only took two or three minutes to propel myself back to shore.

Angie was right where I left her. "I watched you go out to the sand bar but why did you come back so fast?"

So it was a sandbar. "Did you see those huge fish jumping out there?" She could tell I was excited.

"Yes, but they're not fish they're dolphins. They go by out there on the other side of the sandbar all the time. It seems like they go west in the morning and east in the afternoon or evening. They're harmless."

"Well, I didn't know what they were and I didn't know they were harmless, so I came back quickly because I didn't want to stay out there and find out." *Why don't I ask questions about things I've never done before? I'd never swum in an ocean or gulf before. I didn't know what to expect but I didn't even think about asking. Why didn't I think?*

"Well, let's go walk down the beach."

"Which way?" I was still a little unsettled and walking would probably be a good idea.

"This way." She waved her hand and pointed east. "The other way is commercial and crowded. This way is residential and there are areas where there are no houses and bigger sand dunes between the highway so the beach gets very quiet and private."

We walked about a mile east along the mostly straight waterline into an area almost identical to the one she had described. She suddenly turned away from the water and into a flat area where three sand dunes formed a U shape with the open end toward the water.

"Nicely arranged!" I chuckled. "You've been here before, I take it?"

"Yes, I have—a couple of times. And I've been thinking about it ever since we left this morning."

"Thinking about it how—what happened before?"

"No, I wasn't thinking about what happened here before but about being here with you now."

"But what happened here before?" It was like squeezing a raw potato to get her to talk about it.

"We used to come here a lot when I was young and dating, I lost my virginity here."

"Was it a good experience?"

"It was okay. I was ready for it to happen. He was a very handsome sailor I had dated several times before. It had gotten dark and we'd done about everything else already. He gave me a petting orgasm and as I started to go down on him, I said, 'Bring a condom next time if you want to go further.' He grinned and magically produced one on the spot and that's the story of the end of my virginity."

"Was it painful?"

"Yes, a little. I didn't come again and the rubber broke and he came inside me and I wound up worrying my head off until my period started a week later."

We spread our towels on the sand and she pulled a bottle of brown colored baby oil out of her purse. "What's that?"

"It's baby oil and iodine. It helps to give you a quicker tan and makes you look tanner almost immediately. Would you put some on my back?"

"Back and front and legs and the bottom of your feet if you want."

"Later, big boy!" She lifted her sun glasses, winked and gave me a big smile. She slipped off the t-shirt, sat down, untied the strings on the bikini top and put it on her purse. She didn't try to hide her breasts as she turned to lie on her stomach.

"Thanks."

"For what?"

"For the nice view, although it was too brief."

"You're welcome," she chuckled. "But haven't you seen enough already?"

"I'll never get enough of those beauties. In fact, you have to promise, whenever you get a chance, to flash me."

"Sure. Like when?"

"Like now," I said. Or whenever you get a chance or whenever you feel like it."

"Okay, I'll try to keep it in mind." She turned her face to the side and folded her hands under her cheek. "Oil me up, Marine."

I spread the homemade suntan oil all over the exposed skin on her back side from neck to feet and then did the same to my front side. I lay down on my back on my towel next to her, took off my sunglasses and closed my eyes. "So, my beautiful friend, what were you thinking about today?"

"Well, it's too early to do what I'd like, because there are too many people around that may come walking by, and if we wait all afternoon until it gets late enough for the crowds to thin out, we will be cooked."

"Okay, I understand. So the timing is off but we can take the sun, take a swim or two and call it a day before we get burned and head back to the bungalow."

"I suppose that will be the plan then," she concluded smiling.

I dozed off until she woke me. "Do you want me to do your back before I roll over?"

"Sure, thanks," I replied sleepily but I was enjoying the view so much I didn't turn over.

She was sitting cross-legged, Indian style, facing me, oiling her breasts with her back toward the water and the people walking by. I couldn't see her eyes through her sun-glasses but she was smiling and teasing me with her tongue curled up to her upper lip as she massaged and squeezed her breasts and occasionally pinched and tickled her hard nipples.

"Do you want to hit the water before we turn over," I queried.

"No, the breeze is keeping me cool enough. You go ahead if you want."

And leave this amazing view. What am I, nuts? "No, I'm okay for now." I put on my sun glasses and offered to help. "Do you want me to do that for you?"

"No, I'm done"—she smiled knowingly—"but I should do your back or you'll wind up burning red instead of browning."

"Okay, my practical girl." I rolled over on my stomach and she oiled my back and the back of my legs.

"There you go, Marine—all done." She turned and straightened her legs out as she rolled onto her back.

"Thanks, Angie. Not just for the view and the oil but for everything." I could see her closed eyes under the edge of her sunglasses as I lay there, on my side, propped up on my elbow, staring at her. What a pretty woman. Not just her body and facial features but pretty all around and inside. A nice package of personality, common sense, feelings, and sensitivity. Lucky man, her husband. *Yeah, I know, she's out fooling around but why does that make a difference if she's loving and caring and a good wife and mother? Who is hurt by her promiscuity? Who am I to judge?*

"It's been my great pleasure, Bobby."

I daydreamed about the unusual and fascinating weekend until I fell asleep and it turned into a dream about hot, sweaty bodies and the evening yet to come. My prediction turned out to be right—I'd been mostly hard all afternoon.

"Hey, Marine, are you getting hungry?" I heard her voice as if it were part of the dream in which she was the star.

I stirred sleepily out of the fantasy world into reality to see her facing me, cross-legged again, but with her top on as she was tying the strings around the back of her neck. "Still a nice scene to wake up to but not as good as when you were oiling up a while ago."

"Well, here's the first of the flashes you asked for then." She quickly pulled the strings she was tying and flipped them forward and down, pulling the top out and holding it down momentarily while she pulled her shoulders back and shook her breast proudly. She smiled, almost shyly, as she pulled the top back up and began tying the strings again. "Look what you've done to me, Bobby. What a shameless hussy I've become—I'm not usually so brazen."

"You have no idea how much I admire and appreciate the way you are. Not just for this flash, which I certainly appreciate, of course, but for all of what makes up the exciting and terrific person you are. I don't think this weekend could have been better if I had dreamed it up and I hope we can do it again whenever it's possible for you."

"Ooooh, ya think we can? Of course, we can't do weekends when he's home but there are occasions when he has to stand duty overnight and we could meet after I get off work."

"Sure, we can. How could I resist?" *Why would I want to resist? I resolved to keep in touch.*

The drive back to the bungalow was quiet. I was lost in thoughts about the first ex-wife and the soon to be second ex-wife which had comprised my entire sexual education up to this point.

The brain committee pondered, *Bonnie and I didn't have a good sexual relationship and we never talked about it. Liana was all about sex and we talked about it all the time. She taught me everything I should already have known but the continuous escapades were also more than I wanted on a long term basis. Liana was the only woman who drank more than I did and wanted sex more than I did and, as a result of her beauty, was way more promiscuous than I ever thought could be possible until she showed me. Having a comfortable ongoing affair with a beautiful, sensible woman when she's available seemed to present a reasonable alternative to constantly chasing women. Looks like Pensacola is going to be a very interesting home for the next couple of years.*

Sudden Shift

The first weekend in Pensacola had been too good to believe. It didn't become a part of my story telling until other almost equally unbelievable stories began to pile up. Friends would say, "The way things happen to you, Pincer, you're gonna have to write a book." In the first weekend, I'd met a good friend, who happened to be a Marine Corps major, who introduced me to the city, to a great tailor and to another great friend who happened to be a sensuous and very sexually open woman who, in turn, introduced me to the beach and a neat little hide-away bungalow motel.

Monday, I checked into Flight School and got my Ground School schedule and quarters assignment for the next eight weeks. I decided to find the room and unload the stuff in my car before heading out to do the rest of the check in procedures. The room was small but had its own wash bowl so I wouldn't have to go to the head or shower room to shave and brush my teeth. It was obviously a single room since it was furnished with only one twin size bed.

The check-in list included the Dispersing Office where I found out I was entitled to more money than I'd thought. My record showed I was married because I'd been married when I'd signed up in 1959 and it had not been officially changed since, even though I'd been divorced and remarried.

"I've filed for divorce in Texas at my home of record and it is expected to be final in December when I go home for Christmas leave," I told the Disbursing Clerk. "Won't it be more trouble than it's worth, to set it up for less than six months?"

"No, sir, and if you wind up paying alimony or child support you'll still be entitled."

"Well, there won't be any child support because there aren't any children and I don't expect to be paying any alimony."

"In that case you just let us know when the divorce is final, and if you don't have to make any payments, we can stop it at that point."

Nice surprise. Maybe I'll be flying and drawing flight pay by then and it will even out.

The rest of the check-in took the bulk of Monday and I called the tailor to set up an appointment to be measured for my uniforms before I went in search of the Officers Club. An inspection of the facilities and few beers later I was buzzed and tired and done for the day.

Tuesday, I hunted down the tailor for the 0900 appointment, and I was done by 1100. I didn't have anything else to do until classes would start on the following Monday, except to go for a final uniform fitting sometime Thursday afternoon and pick up the new uniforms on Friday, which wouldn't be ready until late afternoon. The summer heat and humidity suggested a visit to the beach and the light sunburn from Sunday was all but gone. I drove leisurely to the parking lot at the restaurant where I had enjoyed breakfast with Angie on Sunday morning.

Tuesday at Pensacola Beach in the middle of summer was only slightly less crowded than Sunday. Numerous families, couples and singles were on the beach and in the restaurants and bars mingling, eating, drinking and swimming by the time I arrived a little after noon. Sunbathers lounged on chairs and towels soaking up the sun and a few hid from the fiery rays beneath large umbrellas.

Bare backs shined with little droplets of moisture and a momentary calm in the breeze allowed mixed aromas of oils, sweat, beer, and all sorts of snacks and chips to waft up gently as I walked by. White-chested men were turning pink and red, and some almost purple as the burns went deeper. The straps or strings that would mar the ladies' bodies with lines were neatly tucked into the cups or rolled up and pushed down into the cleavage and the ladies appeared to be struggling to keep the patch of cloth covering their nipples in place. To the delight of the male passers-by, some didn't struggle so much, allowing a peek at colorful areola or a nipple here and there. *Nice!*

I decided to walk east on the beach toward the sand dunes where we'd been on Sunday to see if the view was better. Sure enough, there were two topless girls lying together on a blanket but one was shy and rolled onto her stomach as I walked by. The other was half sitting up on her elbows and didn't move so I waved and gave her an enthusiastic two thumbs up. She smiled and waved back—not moving her body or arms she discreetly raised her palm at the wrist toward me without lifting her forearm from the sand. And then, just as discreetly, she rolled her arm at the elbow and wriggled her fingers calling me to her.

I stopped and turned slightly. Pretty brazen of her to issue an invite. She nodded her head toward the wiggling fingers and then stared at me like she was affirming the signal. As I took a few slow steps toward her—still 20 feet or so away—she rolled toward her friend and said something which caused her to reach back looking for the ties to her top, which she promptly tied. As I approached, she rolled over and sat up.

"Hello." I smiled and nodded at the uninhibited topless form stretched out in full view seeming to be without a care in the world. "You must be on vacation?" It was more of a statement than a question.

"Yes, we are but how did you know?"

I felt she was just being cordial but I decided to answer anyway in order to start a conversation. "Well, it's Tuesday so you're not weekenders and again it's Tuesday so you're not locals with a job or school to go to. "So it seems pretty safe to guess vacation." I smiled, shrugged my shoulders and raised my palms up as if to say, "What else could it be?"

She chuckled, and her little breasts bounced a little. They were small with very small pink areolas and slightly darker nipples. I noticed the nipples were hard. *Is it the breeze or is she a little excited?"*

Yes, a good guess," she said. "We're on vacation. We have to be back at work next Monday."

"Back to work where?"

"In Birmingham, Alabama."

"Doing what?"

"I work at a bank and Sandy is a hair dresser." She nodded toward her companion.

I nodded toward her as well and said, "Hi Sandy, the modest one—I'm Bobby."

"Oh, I'm not so modest. I just didn't want to turn over half naked not knowing who was coming up."

I turned back to the one who waved me over, "And you are?"

"Pattie, its Patricia but I prefer Pattie or just Pat."

"Well, since you started with Pattie, we'll just hold on to that for now. What are your plans for the vacation?"

She smiled and looked at Sandy before she answered, "Well, we'll get some sun, have a few drinks, dance, and meet some people. You know, have some fun. The same stuff most people do when they're on vacation."

"How's it going so far?"

"I had to work yesterday so we drove down after work. We were tired so we just checked into the motel, got a pizza and a beer and took it to our room and crashed. We slept in this morning and just finished breakfast about two hours ago, so we really haven't been here long enough to tell yet but so far, so good." She looked me directly in the eyes and stared.

Holy crap! Is this going to be the regular fare? I just came to look—kinda like window shopping! "How far away is Birmingham?"

"It's about four hours, more or less depending on how aggressive you want to be on the road. Some of the roads are not too great."

She was cute. Blonde hair but streaked with darker natural strands. It was cut shorter in the back and sloping down toward her chin line. Nice brown eyes and a pretty smile. Her lips were not thin like the rest of her lanky body.

"Close enough to come down on the weekends sometimes then, isn't it?"

"Yes, we we're here on a weekend once but it was very tiring and really, really hard to go back to work on Monday afterward. We had to leave after work on Friday so we didn't get here until ten o'clock and it was eleven thirty before we got to the bar. We had to leave Sunday evening early so we could get home and get some rest. Saturday was really the only day we had to get anything accomplished and it was a bust."

"Yeah, a weekender can be really tiring. Three day weekends are a little better but still, a week, like you have now, is a lot better. We used to do occasional weekends in Juarez, Mexico when I was in college in Albuquerque. It was about the same distance as between here and Birmingham but the roads were great. It was an easy drive."

"What college is in Albuquerque?"

"The University of New Mexico."

"Did you graduate? Are you a flight student here now?"

"Yes and yes." I chuckled. She was like an excited little girl at Christmas. Cute and bubbly.

"Well, I have to go—I have an appointment later this afternoon," I lied. "Maybe we can meet later? That is, if you're still unattached."

"I could be intentionally unattached—if you like?" She seemed slightly embarrassed at her own brazen invitation.

"Sounds like fun to me!" I laughed and stood up. "D'ya know the Schooner?"

"Yeah, sure. We're at the Beach Inn just a little way down the street. We were planning to go there anyway."

"Oh good! Don't plan on being intentionally unattached though because I don't know if I can make it."

Actually, as soon as the word "schooner" left my mouth, I started to feel odd about setting up a meeting where Angie would be working. I didn't want to hurt her feelings by just leaving or by just not showing up so I immediately concocted the meeting and the possibility I wouldn't be there tonight.

The shy one took her top off again, smiled and turned to lie back down on her stomach but not before she flashed a nice long look at her more bulbous set. She's right—she's not shy and better built than the blonde. *Hmmm—nope too tired for now. Maybe later in the week, if she's still available—but not likely.*

The summer sped on with ground school classes, drinking, parties and women. Some weekends were super memorable and some were ordinary successes and others were lonely busts. *But why would we waste our time talking about the latter?*

A few weeks later, sitting alone at Trader Jon's, I was contemplating my good fortune since arriving in Pensacola. I was sitting at a table for two adjacent to the in and out aisle alongside the dance floor facing the entrance. I was across the room from the door but I could easily see everyone who entered to determine if they were with someone.

The large and lively dance floor was swirling with a great mix of couples and singles. There was always someone on the dance floor but it was not too crowded. Most of the girls wore a mix of short shorts or mini-skirts with a shirt-blouse or crop top and tennis shoes with short white sox or no sox but some wore midthigh or slightly longer pleated skirts and high heels with hose. *We prefer the latter.*

I saw her as soon as she stepped inside. The most striking beauty of the evening and maybe for several weeks. *Careful, she looks like Liana. Oh shit! It is Liana.* I decided to take the initiative as she came closer. She was smiling broadly and I knew she had seen me already. I stood up as she approached. "Hi, would you like to dance?"

"Sure," she said as she went around me and turned through the opening to the dance floor.

"How've ya been?" I was being casual and pleasant, although I had a good idea what was coming.

"I've been okay, I guess. I had to ride the bus all the way down here, which was a royal pain in the ass. I've been here two days with no place to stay really—looking for you!"

"Well, don't look at me for a place to stay, Liana. I told you there are no quarters for you here."

"But you're a second lieutenant now and you should be able to afford an apartment."

"No, I'm on the lowest rung on the ladder. At the bottom of the officers' pay grades as a second lieutenant." I'm makin' about the same as when I was working at the bar in Albuquerque and it's gonna stay that way until I start gettin' flight pay."

"Well then, what about when you do start drawin' flight pay?"

"It's just not gonna happen for us, Liana," I avoided answering. "It was never intended to be permanent and you know it. That was your idea. Remember? I filed for divorce when I was in Arlington and it will be final in December when I go home for Christmas leave."

She stepped back at arm's length and her face did the most amazing transformation from unmatched beauty into a ferocious looking beast. Her eyebrows arched, her lips curled as she bared her teeth and her eyes flashed with hatred. "Well, that's it then," she snarled. She stomped off the dance floor and out the door with two guys who were waiting there. I hadn't seen them when she came in. I was genuinely scared. I knew she could probably do something to try to wreck my life. I stayed a while at the bar because I didn't want to run into her outside. One more drink led to another so I stayed longer than I should have. I was drunk when I went into the parking lot and saw my car. The hood was up and the engine was completely trashed with wires torn out and hanging loose and the distributor was missing. Nothing to do until morning when I could call a garage and get some help.

I slowly sank down by the front wheel and leaned back as the old agonizing pain enveloped me like a roll of barbed wire. It was a pleasant fall night and there were lots of stars to see but I was depressed to the point of not wanting to put up with all the crap anymore. This was different than the last time I was so depressed. I felt like the situation with Bonnie had been beyond my control but here, in this case, with Liana, it was all my own fault. I mulled it over for more than an hour.

As the last couple of cars pulled out of the gravel parking lot, one of the drivers asked if I needed any help. I told him, "I do but I'll manage on my own in the morning—thanks." His headlights shined on a piece of broken glass as he turned away toward the street. I picked it up and examined it closely. It's really sharp on this pointy end on this side. *Why not?*

Without a second thought I stuck the pointed edge into my left wrist and dragged the sharp edge across. A neat clean cut, about a quarter inch deep, began to bleed. I closed my eyes and waited for the inevitable and eventually passed out.

When I woke up I was still alone in the parking lot but the sun was shining brightly and it was obvious I had not succeeded, again. The cut had congealed and dried. I found out later, if you want to kill yourself that way you have to cut along the artery, not across. Apparently, I didn't even cut deep enough to cut the artery at all. *I guess we'll have to find a way to put up with life until someone or something else kills us.* The committee was matter-of-fact about the whole scene.

When the cleanup crew arrived at the dance hall on Saturday morning they let me in to use the phone and recommended a nearby mechanic's shop. I described the situation and the mechanic said, "it probably won't take too long if we can find a distributor cap. Do ya have car insurance?"

"Yes."

"Good, you kin probably file a claim for vandalism."

When he and his mechanic showed up they were smiling and waving a distributor cap out the pickup window. "Looka heah whut we spotted alongside the road. Somebudy musta thown it out and I'll bet it's youns!"

I never appreciated the strong southern dialect more. He was done in less than half an hour. And it only cost fifteen dollars for labor and ten dollars for the road service call. *Now, was that worth dying over? The committee was riled up. Yeah, but what's gonna happen now? She's not gonna just give up and leave town is she? We better take some precautions.* The members batted the situation around without providing any solutions or even ideas. *Worthless bunch of disjointed bums.*

I knew I needed to change the locks on the car but it would not be possible on the weekend and I didn't think she knew where I was living on base so I figured I'd go on Monday. Bad decision.

I heard the phone ring Sunday morning in the hallway of my main-side quarters and someone answered it. Usually, it was the guy closest to the phone or anyone passing by. "Pincer!" the voice yelled.

"Yes! Coming!" I had an uneasy feeling on the way to answer.

"Bobby, I have your car and if you want it back you'll have to give me a hundred bucks—CASH!"

Where the hell did she get the key? Shit! She still had a key from when we were together. "I don't have a hundred bucks cash today and why would I do that anyway? I've already reported the vandalism you did Friday night and the police are already looking for you. I can hang up and tell them you have now stolen the car and you're still in town. It's a pretty special car and I'll bet they can find it pretty quick."

"You can do that and I'll tell them you beat me up and knocked out two of my teeth. There will be a huge investigation and your precious Marine Corps career and flight school will all be down the drain."

"What the hell do you mean two missing teeth?"

"I have a bridge for two missing teeth. You never saw it because it's a great bridge and because I hid it from you. I knew it would come in handy someday, just like it has in the past with the guy who really did knock 'em out."

Doesn't leave much choice does it? The committee was quiet and depressed again.

"Okay, I'll find, beg or borrow the money and I'll take a cab to wherever you are. You will give me the car and key and you will not make a scene and you will leave me alone permanently! Clear?

"Yes."

"Where are you?"

"I'm at a bar downtown—it's called the Gold Bracelet."

"I don't know where it is but the cabby can find it."

I hung up and dialed a cabby number on the card stuck behind the phone. I'd lied about not having the money, just to try to buy time and put her off so I could figure out if I could do something else besides give in to her demand. So now I wanted to get to where she was, as quickly as possible, so she won't have time to think up any other mischief.

She was sitting at the end of the bar—no other customers this quiet Sunday afternoon. She did not appear to be missing any teeth as I walked toward her.

"You're early." She smiled and kicked out the bridge and peeled back her lips, like an exaggerated smile to show a gaping black hole where it had been.

"Nice blackmail scheme Liana but I'll tell you right now if you double cross me I will report it and I guarantee you *will* pay the consequences." I handed her five twenty-dollar bills and she handed me the key.

"Right," she smirked. "I need a ride."

"Nope! No more rides for you. You ever touch my car again, you're gonna go to jail. You've got the money now, so you take a cab to wherever it is you need to go, and I hope it's outta town." I turned smartly on my heel and marched out of the bar. *I hope that's the last time we ever see that one.*

But a week later, the car was gone again. No phone call this time. It was just gone. It wasn't there where I parked it and I knew immediately she had taken it. So as I said I would, I called the police and the insurance company and reported it stolen. I didn't have much confidence in the local police, although I didn't know them, but I knew the insurance company was a nationwide firm and would have people all over the country looking for it.

Sure enough, within a week an insurance company agent called. "We found your car."

"Really, that's great! Where is it?"

"Not really so great. It's in New Jersey and it's not in good shape."

"What's wrong?"

"Apparently, it was lit on fire and shoved over a cliff."

"Oh no!"

"Yeah, the woman who did it is in local police custody as of this morning. She says she's your wife."

"Yes, technically that's true but I've filed for divorce and we are separated and she was never on the title."

"Yeah, but she was formerly listed as an added driver for insurance purposes."

"Yes, but she was removed two months ago."

"I understand but we're only going to pay for half the cost of damages in this case because she's your wife and because she used to be on the policy. And we are not going to pay anything, unless she is prosecuted. Do you want the car back?"

"Is it repairable?"

"Well, we consider it 'totaled' but I suppose it's repairable if you want to spend the money."

"What do you mean, 'spend the money'?"

"Well, we are only going to pay half either way. If you decide not to keep the car we will pay half the loan at the bank. If you decide to keep the car we will pay for half the repairs."

"So if I choose to keep the car, it will cost me half the repair bill and I still have the whole loan to pay at the bank. If I decide not to keep the car I will still owe half the loan."

Yep. That's the story."

"Can it be driven in its current condition?"

"Yeah, the engine is okay, the drive train is okay and the brakes are good but the interior is all burned out. You would have to reupholster before you could drive it and the top is gone."

"I understand. It looks like I'll have to let it go because I can't afford the payments at the bank along with the repairs and replacements."

Well, it was a beauty while it lasted.

The Weekender

She was sitting at a high table for two, a little way away from the small dance floor at the back of the Schooner. I started the usual pitch for girls I didn't know. "Hi, you're here on vacation?" Implying the answer is yes, and before she could answer, "Are you with someone or waiting for someone?"

She smiled and looked at her feet before she turned her head up to look out of the corner of her eye from under flowing waves of golden hair and answered, "Yes, well, sort of anyway, but not a vacation actually. I'm here for a long weekend just looking for some fun."

Actually, I wouldn't have seen her even if she had been there at the same table every night for a month because Aviation Ground School and Pensacola Navy Goshawks football had pretty much put me out of action since early fall. Having arrived at the training base just a little over three months earlier, I was immediately immersed in rigorous and intense six week ground school courses. Aircraft engineering, aerodynamics, avionics, electronics, meteorology, flight regulations and procedures, flight planning and map reading, presented all at the same time, which took up most of the time available. Weekends did allow for some liberty but studies required a lot of attention and energy so visits to the beach had been rare until ground school was completed.

She was wearing a white, shirt-type blouse, unbuttoned but tied in a knot around and just below a solid green bikini top. I figured the green mini-skirt wrapped around her waist was covering a matching bikini bottom. The shirt fit snugly around firm full breasts exposing her cleavage and bare midriff down to about an inch below her deep naval crevice. Her long bare legs extended to leather, open toed, cross-wrapped sandals, exposing light pink toenails to match her fingernails. *Nicely put together, chimed in a long-standing member of my brain committee. Naturally, the committee as a whole interpreted, looking for some fun as wanting to get laid.*

I wanted to go slowly, to be sure of her intentions, so I countered, "Well, there's a keg party at our house later that should be fun and will probably last most of the weekend, if you're interested?"

Pausing just a short second, she smiled and motioned for me to sit across from her at the tall table. "I'm definitely interested but what's happening before the keg party?"

"Not much," I offered as I sat and placed my draft beer on the table. "There's probably no one at the house right now since the keg doesn't usually get delivered Friday night until around 2300. I'm in charge of ice this weekend so I'll stop by the store and get it on the way over. You wanna go with me?"

"What's 2300?" She looked puzzled.

I chuckled a little at her naiveté. "It's 11:00 p.m. on the 24-hour clock, sweetie. All of the marines and sailors around here use the 24-hour clock and all of the locals are pretty much used to it and do the same. Your visitor status is showing through." I smiled outwardly, while inwardly I burned with expectations of ravishing her lovely body.

"So which are you?" she asked.

"Which am I what?" I replied.

"Sailor, marine or local?"

"Oh, sorry. I'm a Marine Corps flight student. I just finished ground school the middle of August and then did ten weeks on the navy football team here at Pensacola. I start flight training next week."

"How did you wind up on a football team in the navy?"

"Uh, well, the coaches went through all the records of new students to find out who played in college and sent out letters asking for volunteers to play for the team. We were advised a 'request to volunteer' is not really considered a request. More like a strong suggestion and not quite an order."

"Well, I was a cheerleader at Alabama and I'm a big football fan. You know, the Crimson Tide?"

"Sure. Of course I know them. Doesn't everyone? Great team's year after year! What was your major at Alabama?"

"I graduated last spring with a bachelor of arts in education and certification to teach high school English and history in Alabama but I haven't applied for a job yet."

"Why not?"

"Because I don't know where I want to live. I know I don't want to stay in Alabama. I want to move someplace more exciting. I've thought about California, but I'd have to go back to school for another year to get certified there. So now, I'm considering Florida or someplace else where they will accept my credentials without additional school."

"Have you ever thought about the Department of Defense?"

"No, what do you mean?"

"The DOD hires teachers for schools on military bases around the world and a few here in the USA. Overseas there are DOD schools in Korea, Japan and Germany, that I know of for sure and probably a lot more I don't know about, but also U.S. territories like the Virgin Islands, Guam and so forth. Lots of opportunities for travel."

"Oh, it sounds like a great idea! I'll look into it. Thanks, and yes, I'd like to go to the keg party. Still, it's only nine o'clock so what will we do in the meantime."

"Would you like to dance?"

"Not really." She smiled.

"Do you want to shoot some pool?"

"No," she shook her head slowly without moving her eyes from mine.

"How about darts?"

"Nope." She chuckled and turned her palms up.

"Would you like another draft?"

"Yes, but maybe you can get it to go so we can take it with us?"

I cocked my head and raised an eyebrow with an inquisitive look. "Take it with us?"

"Well, I've been sitting here for two hours and I'm kinda tired of the scene. It's loud, hard to talk, and harder to hear." She paused and looked at her feet. "If it's too early to go to your house, I have a room at the Beach Inn," she grinned and looked up with a flirtatious corner peek again.

"Alone?"

"No, I have a roommate who came with me but she already hooked up with a navy flight instructor who has his own place. She won't be back until sometime tomorrow."

Well, so much for taking it slow. "Okay, it's not too early to go to the house but we would probably have more privacy at your room and we can always go to the keg party later."

I was half way to the bar before I caught Angie's eye and ordered two drafts in to-go cups and asked her to bring my check. She looked in the direction from where I came and spotted the girl for whom the second beer was intended. She raised an eyebrow, tossed me a double take and asked, "Scored early tonight, huh, Marine? What's her name?" She wasn't jealous and this wasn't the first time after we met that I'd picked up a date at the Schooner. We discussed it during our first outing after our first meeting and she was, of course, perfectly okay with whatever happened in my life. "Especially if it makes you happy, Bobby," she had said.

"I dunno, Angie. She's a weekender."

"Well, you should at least find out her name before she fucks your brains out!" She laughed. She was one of the sexiest waitresses. Older than most, she was 25, married to a sailor since she was 19 and had picked up his salty language.

"Before who fucks whose brains out?" I quipped as I laughed at her frank candor. "Besides, why do I need to know the name of a girl I will probably never see again after this weekend?"

"Because, you fool, you won't always be as young and handsome as you are now. So you should start building a rapport with ladies you can call later in life who knew you when," she said half seriously.

"Yeah, but by then they'll all be married with kids and jealous husbands."

"Since when would any of that stop you?" she said with a knowing smile and a twinkle in her eye, reminding me fondly of our times together when her husband was out to sea or off to training.

"I was just thinking of the kids and husbands," I quipped.

As I approached our table the blonde asked, "No luck on the beers?"

"Angie's bringing 'em. It's easier for her to get to the waitress station than it is for me to try to squeeze my way through at the bar and she can bring my check. Can I get your check?"

"No, I've been paying cash. Thanks."

Nice! Cheap date! I was curious. "How does a gorgeous woman sit here alone without getting picked up or at least have someone sitting here buying the drinks?"

"Oh, a few stopped by and some stayed for a little while but I've managed to dodge the ones I didn't want, and the ones I thought I might like, either didn't stop or seemed to just fade away after a while."

"Yeah, a lot of the younger cadets or recent college grad officers are shy, especially when confronting the challenge of a stunningly attractive woman. She acknowledged the compliment with a smile. The more beautiful the prize, the more painful the rejection, the greater reluctance to take a risk. Also, some just don't know how to ask or they want to build up their courage or weaken your resistance with alcohol. A few, who may not be able to afford to buy a lot of drinks, may wander off to return later when someone else's dollar might have paved the way. And some just don't ask in order to avoid the risk of rejection."

"And why are you different?" She tilted her head to one side again.

"Well . . . I'm a little older, a little more experienced maybe, at least more willing to accept the risk-reward relationship, I guess. It took me six years at three different colleges to graduate. Between classes, work at a bar, football and Marine Corps Reserves, I learned a lot." *You left out being married and divorced one of the brain committee members scolded—No need to give out too much info at this point chimed in another.* I have a philosophy, based on the premise 'Ask and ye shall receive' and the clear and obvious conclusion to be drawn is the converse 'Don't ask and you don't get.'"

Angie arrived with the beers and the check. "Nice," she said as she smiled warmly at the weekender. "Anything else for my favorite marine?" She smiled more widely as she turned toward me and stopped sharply with a clearly intentional wiggle of her hard-nipple breasts.

I don't know if I visibly blushed but my face was burning with the memory of our several times together since my arrival.

The Beach Inn was well-known to people who lived and worked in the area. Almost everyone shared living space with someone and needed a place for privacy. Navy ensign and marine second lieutenant flight students were assigned quarters with two men to a room, after ground school, and enlisted cadets, who would be commissioned upon completing flight school, were assigned to squad bays with other cadets. The girls who had come to town to find husbands usually shared bedrooms in houses or apartments, which may not contribute to private liaisons.

The Inn is a 15-unit motel consisting of small individual bungalows with green shuttered wooden windows and pine shake roofs. The floors were clean but worn, and the furniture was old but the mattresses were firm. There were small differences in each room, like torn paper shades here or there, taped with yellowing cellophane, or the curtains and bedspread were faded to a little different color.

The bathtubs were white ceramic coating over oval steel, poised on iron, lion-foot legs. The showers, obvious afterthoughts, consisted of chrome-coated flexible tubes with hand-held shower heads hanging on hooks. The water, which the wrap-around shower curtain couldn't catch, would fall into a drain in the ceramic tile floor in the center of the room.

The rooms were not air-conditioned but the windows in the front and rear could be opened for a cross-breeze from the gulf and the screens held the mosquitos at bay, if they didn't have holes, or if someone had already stuffed the holes with cotton balls. The bottom line . . . it was generally described as "affordable."

The inn was only three blocks from the bar, but we drove my car, now a beat-up '57 Chevy, because I didn't want to have to go back and get it later. *She's quiet. No chit-chatter. Quiet's good. The brain committee approved.*

"I'm feeling pretty grubby. I'd planned on getting the ice, going to the house, taking a shower and coming back to the bar, but since that didn't happen, do you mind if I take a shower?"

"Nope—not at all. It's bungalow 11," she volunteered as we pulled into the parking lot.

"Wanna join me?" I grinned.

"Wow! That's kinda forward isn't it? We haven't even kissed yet and you want me to get naked and climb into the shower with you?" She was smiling though, and I could tell the idea intrigued her.

I was smiling too and said, "Well, the key word is yet. We haven't kissed yet, so you know we will, and you know we're gonna do a lot more, cause we're not goin' to the motel to play tidily winks. You're gorgeous, you're sexy, you're adventurous and the idea of kissing your beautiful lips for the first time, pressed against your naked body in the shower, makes me hard just thinking about it."

"Oh my God," she said, as we arrived at the parking spot in front of Bungalow 11. "No one's ever talked to me like that before!"

"But you would like to do it," I said, convinced she was visualizing the scene and realizing how exciting it might be.

She sat quietly for what felt like about five minutes but was probably more like five seconds. She was still holding the two cups of draft beer. "You'll have to come around and get these beers so I can get the key out of my purse." She was looking straight ahead. Not smiling. Not moving. Not angry or mad, maybe just determined to overcome her inhibitions. Nevertheless, it seemed obvious to me she had resolved to do as I'd asked. I didn't say anything. Dad always said, "When the pitch is made, keep your mouth shut and wait for the buyer to close the sale." I clawed my lanky frame out of the car and went around to open her door.

Handing me the beers, she fished the room key out of her purse before she climbed out. Walking silently up the two wooden steps to the little porch under the eave, she opened the screen door wide so I could hold it with my hip. She turned, unlocked the door, reached in, turned on the overhead light and stepped inside. I followed her inside as she turned to take the beers from me. I closed the door and locked it. She bent to place the beers on the nightstand next to the nearest twin bed and turned on the lamp.

I turned off the overhead light after she turned to face me. She was truly beautiful standing casually in the soft light of the bedside lamp—no flaws I could see. Golden hair flowed naturally—not straight and not curly but just kinda wavy, down to her shoulders. Her eyes were wide and intensely green below slightly arched eyebrows and her nose was straight, not turned up. A noble nose I thought, shaped like an elegant Roman nose but not large. Her lips were slightly perked up in the middle toward an ascendant bow. Young, smooth, light cream skin, tinted with a little sunburn from the day on the beach, surrounded the package. She just stood there gazing at me with a kind of mysterious smile. Not like she didn't know what she was doing, rather, knowing full well I was staring, admiring and anticipating.

With my gaze on her lips, I decided to push my luck. "I want to watch you undress."

Her mouth opened and her head jerked just a tiny bit like she was getting ready to say no. Her arms rose a few degrees, as if to start a protest, and then dropped back to her side. She hesitated, only for a second—her smile faded a little and her eyes showed a slight bit of doubt—but as she raised her arms again to start untying her shirt, she smiled broadly, tilted her head down and to the side, switched her hips with her knees and said, "Only if I can watch you at the same time." She was definitely into it and I'm sure my face had a huge grin as I took a couple of steps toward her and began unbuttoning my shirt.

She stayed by the nightstand, untied her shirt and let it hang loosely. "How tall are you?" she asked.

"Six-two," I replied. "And you?"

"Five seven. What are the rest of your statistics?"

I continued to unbutton my shirt and lay it on the bed. "Chest 44 and waist 36. Let me guess? You are 36c, 22 and 30?"

"Close," she said, as she slipped out of the shirt and laid it on the bed. "You're mostly right on for the top"—as she cradled the two green cups in each hand—"and the waist is 22 but the hips are 32, not 30."

She untied the back of the bikini top and let it hang tantalizingly around her neck for a second while she untied the top strings—then took if off and put it on the bed on top of the shirt. She stood still again letting me gaze as she cupped one hand under each bare breast again and said, "These are actually between a C and D but you're right—they look better in a C. They leave a larger bra a little bit loose—not good." She smiled—not nervously, not shyly or proudly, but somewhere kind of between, more like, "So be it." They were nice and full with small pink areolas about the size of quarters and perky excited nipples standing up at attention like they were straining to be noticed.

"Perfect!" I exclaimed. "Beautiful!" Applause and cheering followed from the brain committee. *We don't like overly large breasts. C cups are perfect. D cups are good, but anything larger is not really appealing. B cups are okay, but anything smaller was not as tempting although they are not a reason for rejection, depending on the rest of the package.*

I kicked off my shoes, unbuttoned my jeans and sat on the edge of the bed near the foot to slip them off. It squeaked loudly. *The mattress will have to go on the floor later.*

She unbuttoned the side of her wrap-around skirt and tossed it on the bed near the pillow. We were still about four feet apart but I could see the tips of her short curly hair through the thin green bikini. "Are you a natural blonde?"

"I don't bleach, so you can see for yourself." She smiled again, almost brazenly now, as she rolled down the top of the bikini, exposing a small light reddish-strawberry-blonde patch.

"Very nice," I said almost breathlessly, as I stood, pulled off my under-shorts and leaned down to slip off my socks.

She wriggled her hips, slid her bikini bottoms down over her sandals and stood back up.

I moved toward her. "Let me help you with your sandals." Kneeling in front of her with my face very near the strawberry patch, I was breathing on it but not touching. She shivered a little. I spoke to her like the patch was a microphone. It smelled fresh and sweet. "I want to be inside you. I want my tongue, my fingers and my cock in you and in every opening in your body."

She shivered again.

I fumbled a bit but managed to get the sandals unbuckled and she stepped out of them backward and bumped the nightstand. My face followed her automatically and my tongue found her smooth shaved skin below the patch and then her clit as my hands moved up the back of her legs to her butt and pulled her close. She shivered again—more intensely and almost continuously.

After a while, I stood up with the tip of my erection almost touching her naval. The electricity, the stress, the tension between us, was nearly unbearable. Bending forward and reaching for her shoulders I whispered, "I can't wait for the shower. You are too beautiful, too exciting, too tempting, too absolutely delicious. I want you now!"

Her shining eyes turned up and blazed into mine. "No, she said softly. You can't build me up to a fantastic crescendo and then take away the vision. I want that first kiss in the shower like you promised."

Smiling ruefully, I let my hands slide down her arms to her hands. "Let's go then, gorgeous."

We walked hand in hand to the tub and shower like children on an adventurous trek. The bright overhead light in the bathroom made her skin glow and there were slight sunburn lines only slightly visible at the traces of the bikini top outlining her breasts and at her bottom, but no strap lines on her back or shoulders. Was she sunbathing topless on the beach?

I turned the water on in the tub and adjusted the temperature to moderately warm and pulled the lever to switch the water to the shower. After climbing in, I offered her a hand for balance as she stepped over the high-sided tub. It was not the most graceful entry for either of us but we managed.

Pulling the shower curtains all the way around wasn't necessary since the floor was tile and the floor drain looked clean. It would probably just get in the way in any case. There was a large bar of soap in a tray hanging on the side of the tub, which I rubbed briskly to form some suds. *Smells good. Not one of those stinky little motel bars.* Next, I took her shoulders, pulled her under the water and stepped around behind her. She ducked her head and let the water flow down and I soaped her back like a massage from her neck to her hips. I moved close pressed against her soapy body and reached around to soap her front. Starting with the arms and pits, I spent a lot time on and around those beautiful breasts. Back and forth I rubbed across her hard little nipples, then dragged my nails lightly, as she shivered with each stroke. I moved down and in and out of her navel and reached farther to the strawberry patch. It was nice to find she was shaved smooth on the sides between her legs below the patch. Soaping her there, I bent my knees to slide my erection between her legs, felt the tip in front with my fingers, and pressed it against her. She shivered and then quickly shivered again. I continued to move back and forth in her soapy crotch and massaged her aroused clitoris slowly with my fingers. She shuddered violently and bent forward as she convulsed involuntarily again and again. Her knees buckled and I almost lost my balance but I recovered quickly and managed to hold us up. It took every ounce of restraint I could muster to hold off while she finished.

Eventually she slowed down and pushed my hand away. I gently moved her forward under the water and turned her around. As she stood to face me, her eyes were closed with a smile on her face, as if remembering and still enjoying. I put my hands on her cheeks and gently held her face as I kissed her softly—long and deep. She wrapped her arms around my neck and gently pressed her body against mine.

The water temperature began to cool and we still needed to do a little more rinsing but I didn't want to end the moment. Finally, she whispered softly, "Oh my, God. You made me come before you even kissed me. You must think I'm an absolute slut."

"No my lovely, you're just a wonderful, beautiful, soapy little girl." I softly kissed her deep and long again and breathed her hot breath into my lungs before I turned my face and sunk my tongue as far into her throat as I could.

I leaned back and looked in her eyes again. "How was that my lovely lady?"

"I can't begin to tell you how good that was—a kiss I will never forget."

I chuckled. "Let me rinse and I'll get the towels while you finish."

"I don't want to let go," she whispered.

"Don't fret sweetheart. I've only just begun with you."

We turned around together so I was under the water. Finally, she let go and stepped back while I looked her up and down again. Quickly, she ducked her head, crossed her arms in front of herself and hid the strawberry patch with her hands.

Smiling at her sudden shyness, I stepped out and got a towel for myself and dried my hair and upper body.

She turned the water off and was ready to get out just as I reached out with two towels and offered her a hand. She stepped out more gracefully than when we got in.

"Nice," I murmured, and I looked her up and down again, as she reached for the towels. "Here's one for your hair but I want to dry you with the other." She glanced at me warily and took the towel to dry her face, and as she raised her arms to wrap it around her hair, I started patting down her underarms, breasts, and torso. I toweled her softly, covering every inch from neck to toes, and briskly fluffed the patch. I tapped the inside of her knee and she spread her legs. "Nice little filly," I whispered. She turned, looked down at me and smiled knowingly. *She probably was raised around horses or at least rides.*

When I finished drying her, she took the towel and wrapped it around her body so she could tuck it in at her cleavage. "I need a minute," she said softly.

Staring at her all the way, I backed out and bowed before closing the door. "Yes my Princess," I joked. A long sip from one of the beers on the nightstand was not as cold as I would have liked, but it was wet and helped to quench my thirst. I quickly tossed our clothes, the bed spread and top sheet from her bed onto the other twin bed, grabbed the mattress with the bottom sheet and pillow, and threw it on the floor. I lay down on my back and propped my head up with the pillow.

She came out of the bathroom still wrapped in the towels. Not saying anything, she just smiled and slowly unwrapped her hair and then her body as she walked and dragged the towel. Kneeling between my feet she pushed my legs farther apart and bent down to slide her tongue along my thighs, around my package and up slowly to the tip of my erection. It was my turn for involuntary shivers with each tantalizing lick and nibble. "Put this towel underneath so we don't mess up the sheet," she instructed.

I complied, and when I was situated again, she momentarily buried me deep in her throat, leaving me slick with saliva. Smoothly, she dragged her breasts farther up over my stomach and chest, lingering a little with her tongue on each of my nipples and onward to my lips for a long, deep kiss. When she pulled away she stared into my eyes and smiled, almost devilishly, as she spread her legs around my hips and rolled the strawberry patch over me. She straightened up and positioned her hips slightly forward, barely touching. Wet with anticipation, and shaking slightly, she slid back and forth with a little more pressure each time. Balancing herself with one hand she put me inside with the other, eased down a couple of inches and paused.

I felt heat for a moment—she was very hot inside—*and Bonnie crossed my mind.* Then suddenly hard pressure met the end of my shaft as she eased down a little more. "Oh my God, you're a virgin," I exclaimed and pulled my hips away but she pressed downward to keep me inside.

"Not for long," she said, as she adjusted her hips, straightened up a bit, and sat down hard. Her eyes squeezed shut and she yelped a little cry and I hoped it didn't hurt as much as it seemed. "Are you okay?"

"I'm fine, you just relax and let me enjoy it for the first time in my life. She eased upward again, a little bit, and hesitated, only for a couple of seconds, and eased down again slowly, all the way, spreading her legs and rolling her hips to bury me as deep as she could. I felt the bottom of her insides on my tip. It wasn't painful, although I could feel the sensation of depth at the end and the exquisite pressure at the base. She sat up straight for a time, rolling her hips forward and back, as her clitoris rubbed gently on my pelvic bone.

She tilted her head back, so I couldn't see her face but the arch of her back brought tips of her breast directly into view. Her nipples, now pointing up at the ceiling, were irresistible. I reached up to find the hard little tips to tease as I stroked and massaged her firm breasts. She leaned her upper body into my hands, and as her head came forward, her eyes opened and looked at me with hard, penetrating eyes. Smiling, she stared, a confident look, as if to say she knew how good it felt to me. She pushed my arms away as she continued to move a little faster while holding herself upright with her hands on my stomach. Her arms pressed against the sides of her breasts forcing her hard nipples to stand out even more. I watched intently as I watched her move gracefully in the soft glow of the lamp. Her eyes were shining with excitement, her teeth were clenched with lips drawn back and she was breathing heavily.

I knew she was close and I wanted to wait to release with her. I could not speak—could barely breathe. I had been hard a long time and ready since before the shower and now with the heat of her insides, the pressure on my base and her beautiful body moving rhythmically above me it was difficult to hold off. Suddenly, she leaned forward, stretched out her legs behind her, on top of mine, and let her body rest on me. Stretching to get her mouth close to my ear, she whispered, "Roll me over and come inside me, Bobby—it's okay, I planned for this and I'm on the pill."

"I've never been with a virgin and didn't know what to expect, sweetie. I don't want to hurt you. Are you okay?"

"Yes," she said breathlessly. I want to lay back and feel you on top and deep inside me."

I spread my legs, wrapped my right arm around her waist, propped up on my left elbow and spun my body around. Her hair fell around her head and her shining face glowed with a pink rush of excitement. I held myself up with my arms outstretched and looked down where I was buried, below the strawberry patch, then up past her naval, across her pink tipped breasts, to the shine in her eyes. She quivered. I stroked my hips slowly a few times, gently, watching myself go in and out but I was too far gone to hold off any longer. I wanted to be gentle, still not knowing whether she might be hiding some pain. I lowered my body but held my weight off with my elbows, except where we met at the patch. I folded my body a little to kiss her long and slow on the lips and then, her neck, while I pressed my pelvis against hers.

She convulsed involuntarily and pressed hard against me. *So much for gentle.* Our bodies shook and shuddered together violently and involuntarily. She raised her hips to meet me with gusto and my long hard strokes penetrated deep inside. The shivers ran fiercely all the way to my toes and I let go.

We lay together for a long time afterward while I kissed her dozens of times on the forehead, eyes, lips, cheeks, neck, shoulders and every place I could reach without moving, until eventually, I rolled off onto my back and nearly rolled off the narrow twin mattress.

I was about to doze off when I remembered the ice for the keg party. "It's almost 2300 and I have to get the ice. Do you still want to go?"

"Well, my hair is a mess, and I'm kinda tired, but I don't want to stay here alone. Can you give me a few minutes to fix up a little?"

"Sure, I can go pick up the ice and come back by to pick you up on the way? Or, I can deliver the ice and come back to stay here with you. We can go to the house tomorrow."

"Staying here tonight would be nice." She smiled. "And you still have some promises to keep."

Four of my Goshawks teammates and I rented a five-bedroom house on the beach during the first part of the football season. A two-story frame house with four of the bedrooms and two bathrooms on the first floor and a large master bedroom with a full bath and a separate half bath on the second floor, along with a huge family room and kitchen. The house was encircled around three sides by a balcony, with great views of the Gulf of Mexico, about 50 yards from the south side and with Santa Rosa Sound, about a quarter mile from the north side. Long views of white sandy beaches and dunes graced the southern shoreline to the east and west.

We regularly scheduled weekend keg parties where flight student buddies, and civilians we met on the beach, were invited to come and share the house. Girls were admitted free, but men were asked to chip in a dollar, or more if they could afford it, for the beer and chips and to bring their own hamburgers or hotdogs for afternoon cookouts on the charcoal broiler. We put the keg and the broiler on the second floor balcony so limiting access by only the outside staircase could control admittance. We closed off the inside staircase at the top with a couch placed crossways on the landing. It could be breached if someone were athletic enough to climb over but we figured, for a dollar, who would be crazy enough to try it and risk falling, not to mention inciting the wrath of five crazed guys.

We also liked the inside staircase to be blocked because it provided some privacy for the downstairs bedrooms and extra bathrooms. Access to the downstairs was through a small living room at the front door or by private, keyed entrances to each of the four downstairs bedrooms which we all vowed to keep locked at all times.

The girls on the beach almost all wore bikinis, hot pants or mini-skirts with minimal cover ups like bikini tops, halters or crop tops. Their exposed bodies, with few exceptions, were very good, so the shopping and selection criteria generally meant checking for what they wanted. Some came just to look and check out the party atmosphere, some were shopping for a husband but some were ready to explore the sexual freedom that the open atmosphere of the 60s afforded.

When she came out of the bathroom her hair was in a neat, tightly pulled ponytail bobbing high up on the back of her head exactly where a pony's tail would be. She wore a clean, short-sleeved blue blouse hanging loose outside. When standing straight the shirt tail hung down below the bottom of whatever she was wearing underneath so I couldn't tell whether she had on a skirt, shorts or a bikini.

"Nice," I offered, giving her the once-over. "You're very well put together I think?"

"Thanks," she said smiling, as she stepped toward the door.

"Is the shirt over a bikini?"

"Yep," she smiled again. "But I have a pair of shorts for later."

"What else you got in that beach bag, sweetie?"

"Just some makeup and girl things but I did bring a toothbrush, just in case." She swung the bag flippantly over her shoulder and winked.

"Are you hungry?"

"Yes, I'm starved."

"I can stop by the drive-in and get a burger or we can go straight to the house and raid the refrigerator."

"Raiding at the fridge is fine."

When she bent to sit in the car it looked like she might be moving a little gingerly so I asked, "You okay?"

"I'm a little sore, but I'll be fine."

Her eyes were shining and her smile seemed genuine so I figured she really was telling the truth. "Well . . . tell me, how does a beautiful college coed get to be a graduate without losing her virginity?"

"I was saving it for my fiancé. We were attending different colleges and could only see each other on holidays and semester breaks. We had really hot and heavy make-out sessions doing almost everything. Everything, except straight vaginal penetration—saving the cherry, so to speak," she continued smiling ruefully. "He'd been everywhere there was to go mouth, boobs, rear end and teasing at the front but not inside.

I turned and glanced at her just for a second, mystified at her frank and open admissions. *The brain committee was baffled.*

"Yeah, I know," she seemed to read my mind. "It seems absolutely ridiculous now when I look back on it. We agreed to wait to have sex until we were married which was supposed to happen last summer, in June, just after graduation. Last spring, I found out he'd been having sex all along with a high school girlfriend, who was attending his college, so I broke off the engagement. I was so hurt, I couldn't even think about men or sex for several months. Then, this summer, I decided to get on with my life."

"Lucky me! I'm sorry your plans didn't work out but I'm glad to be on the other end of your recovery. It was my first time with a virgin." I hope it was okay and I didn't hurt you more than was necessary?"

She smiled, a little ruefully. "No, I'm fine and it was even better than I had imagined but the long episode with him is the main reason I'm sour on Alabama. He's still there and probably will be, so I'm wanting to find somewhere else to settle. A fresh start, so to speak."

"Pensacola is a fun place to be if you're looking for adventure and future potential. A lot of flight students will do four years of obligatory time in the service and jump to the airlines for a very nice, secure, lifetime career."

"And you're not going to do that?"

"No, I'm a career marine. I'm no catch for anyone. I'll probably spend half my life overseas."

"You wouldn't like to fly for the airlines?"

"I don't think so. I wouldn't rule it out depending on what happens in flight school and the Marine Corps but flying straight and level with a belly full of passengers or cargo is not my idea of an exciting or interesting career, although the pay is good. Here's our place up there on the right."

The beachhouse was visible from the highway but the beach was not. The sand dunes near the beach obscured the water's edge from the highway and hid most of the downstairs of the house. However, the white ship-lathe siding, the green window shutters of the second story and the wrap-around balcony were clearly visible. There were no other houses for a quarter mile on either side so it was easy to direct visitors to what became known to locals and visitors alike as the Pilots' House.

I parked the car close to the outside steps to the balcony without getting off the driveway into the sand. "We'll go up the outside stairs and check in with crowd control before I show you the rest of the house."

"Around here, since all the other guys living here are navy, I'm known mostly as the marine. Insiders, mostly from football, also have a nickname for me, which carried over from college, but I don't like it. One of my college teammates showed up at football tryouts and yelled it at me across the field. I don't like to use it but it stuck. You'll probably hear it soon enough and you'll know but don't pay any attention to it or use it, okay?"

"Okay," she glanced at me curiously and fell in behind as we started up the stairs.

"Hey Pisser, you crazy son-of-a-bitch, where the fuck you been?"

That was quick. What's he doin'? Readin' my mind? "Hey, Tommy! Watch your language sailor," I replied amiably. "I've got a lady in tow on the steps behind me."

"Roger, Marine. What's her name?"

"You don't need to know Tommy. She's a weekender who's with me for the duration, so steer clear. Clear?"

"I hear you loud and *clear*, Marine," he responded cheerfully, as he nodded knowingly and smiled. Even though it was early in the day, Tommy was on duty at the head of the stairs to collect dollars from visiting men and stamp their hands. He was a Naval Academy graduate with a stocky fullback frame—about six feet tall and in the range of 220 pounds but with a small waist. His weight was contained mostly in his chest, shoulders and upper arms. "I saw you bringin' ice last night and you suddenly disappeared."

I didn't respond directly as to where I disappeared. "You have any collections from last night Tommy? I'm due some money for that ice if there's enough."

"Yeah, we have a little extra."

"Here's the receipt for $3.12 but just round it off at three bucks."

"Okay," he replied, as he reached into his shorts pocket and pulled out some dollar bills.

"Great, looks like the parties are paying off, huh?"

"Yeah, we'll have more than enough left over to start a new party next weekend and everyone who put in seed money has been paid back."

"Great! Any left overs in the fridge?"

"Yeah, there's some hamburger meat and a few hot dogs from last night and we bought some eggs, bacon, buns, bread and donuts this morning and the coffee is on."

I took the bills and headed to the kitchen, hand-in-hand with the blonde. "Tommy is one of our roommates, who is also known as Snake, so watch yourself when he's around. He's not much more likely to try to steal or "snake" a date than the others if you happened to be found unattended, although he seems to be more successful at a quickie behind your back or working his way into a multiple situation right under your nose. Suffice to say, he's earned the nickname."

"Really? He would actually have a quickie with someone else's date? She was obviously curious.

"It's relatively common around the beachhouse because some of the girls are here by invitation but not specifically "with" a guy who invited them. Others are walk-ins who would hear about the party and just show up—girls are always admitted free. Sometimes it's difficult to know if someone is here with a date or not if they appear to be unattended. And it's become pretty well-known that a girl can find just about anything they want here."

"What do you mean by a multiple situation?"

"Well, it could mean different things to different people. Sometimes, the girls who are here on vacation are really relaxed and free of inhibitions around a partying group of people where they don't know anyone, especially after a long day in the sun, followed by a few drinks. I've seen all kinds of what some people would call strange or exotic things."

"Like what, for instance?"

"Oh, I dunno . . . maybe like a girl who, over the course of an evening, would visit two of the bedrooms. Or a girl who would visit one of the bedrooms with two guys. Or other combinations like a couple of girls with one guy. It is a *very* kinky house sometimes."

"Wow!" She laughed. "Maybe you shouldn't have told the Snake to back off!"

I chuckled and raised an eyebrow while searching her face for clues about her sincerity. "I can certainly rescind the order if you're interested?"

"Not in him per se, at least not now, but I am interested in doing more this weekend."

"What do you mean more?"

"Well . . . you know. You made some promises, or at least suggestions, and since you mentioned the sometimes kinky scene here, I'm tempted to see what happens if we spend the rest of the weekend here."

"Okay, twice now you've mentioned the promises I made. What exactly are you talking about?" I turned to face her head-on.

"I remember exactly how you put it. I don't forget things like that. When we were getting undressed last night, you were taking my shoes off and you said . . . you wanted your cock in there and in every other opening in my body and I'm still waiting." She smiled a cute smirk and flirted with her eyes.

I chuckled. "And not so patiently, I see, and after that you want to stick around and see whatever kinky scenes happen—like you're ready to gang-bang the whole house."

"Well . . . no, not the whole house but possibly someone! The thought of it excites me and it's my first and maybe my last opportunity and I don't want to miss out."

"Okay, but for now, you said you were hungry, so can I fix you some bacon and eggs with toast or an egg sandwich, or an omelet?"

"Bacon and eggs would be great!"

"Okay, you make the toast and set the table. The bread is over there and the butter and jelly are in the fridge. How do you like your bacon and eggs?"

"Crisp and over medium, please."

I took the bacon out of the frying pan and set it aside to drain. "Considering our discussion, I'd like to give you my rules of the house, so to speak."

"Rules?"

"Yes, rules for as long as you're with me. Okay?"

"I guess so. I think I'll have to hear them before I agree completely."

I began cracking the eggs into the left over bacon grease in the frying pan. "All right, first, I get to tap your buns before anyone else and second you don't go with anyone else unless I approve or go with you."

"How do you mean approve or go with?" She tilted her head to one side and looked at me curiously.

"Well, I would only approve of you being alone with someone if it is one of my roommates—so no strangers—and I would only approve of a double if I were with you, so also, no strangers but I've gotten to know a few guys who've shown up here in the past few months so there should be a wider choice."

She pondered the situation for a moment, "I understand and accept the conditions, sir." She smiled and curtseyed with a little tug to the side on the bottom of the shirt. "But how about if you don't approve of someone I want to go with?"

"Sure, you can go and do that but it would be to leave the house with him and you would become his responsibility."

"Ah, I see . . . I guess that's okay too but I have no intention of doing it."

"Right. The eggs are ready." I put the eggs and bacon on the plates and set them on the kitchen table. She had already done the flatware and the toast. We ate breakfast nearly in silence. Like it was perhaps a solemn prelude to major unknown events to come. Tommy came in to get a cup of coffee and she stiffened, sat up straighter in her chair and watched him out of the corner of her eye. I smiled at her knowingly, and her face turned bright red. "You're ready for him already, huh?"

"Well, yes but not as a preference over you but just because he's attractive and different and it feels exciting."

"I know, sweetie. It's not like we have a long-term relationship or a commitment or something and besides, I'm not crazy jealous or anything. I just want us to have a great time together. Whatever happens, happens and it's all good."

"So," she asked timidly, "then a double with Tommy would be all good?"

"Of course! What could be bad about that?"

After we cleaned up the breakfast dishes we headed toward the outside stairs to go down to my room and as we passed Tommy I said, "The guard rails are down, Tommy. She's fair game!"

"Holy shit, Pisser! You've got to be kidding! Aren't you?"

"Nope. And you're up next if you want."

"If I want? Of course I want! She's beautiful! When?"

"Come to my room in about an hour for a double if you can get someone to relieve you of the door duty."

"Oh, that's already done, Pisser. My four-hour shift will be over by then, so I *will* see you there!" He was like a happy little puppy jumping to see his returning master. Excited, barking, running around in circles, not knowing which way to turn.

He turned to the gorgeous strawberry blonde, almost in disbelief, "It's true?"

She smiled broadly at his antics and said, "Sure, Tommy. Why not?" And turning to me, as we headed down the stairs, "I have to stop by the bathroom on the way, Bobby."

"Okay, the nearest one is right across from my room. I have to go too but I'll use the one down the hall and meet you back at my room."

My room was sparsely furnished with wood stick furniture from garage sales in little towns around the area. There had been lots of inexpensive but functional pieces from which to choose. I picked out a regular size bed, because it had the best mattress I could find. A dresser with a mirror, a chest of drawers and a couple of chairs completed the set. The windows on the north side, facing the far away street, were covered with Venetian blinds but no curtains.

I got back to the room first but left the door open. She came in and locked the door behind her.

"That took quite a while, gorgeous. Are you okay?"

"Yeah, well . . . I had to cleanse."

I knew what she meant. The girls I'd known before, who liked anal, always wanted to do an enema before any action.

"Nice." I smiled.

"Well, not much here," she said as she turned around to view the room. "But it's clean!" As if it were a surprise.

My laundry was folded but not put away—stacked neatly on one end of the dresser. "I am a marine, you know. Most people would expect nothing less than 'spit and polish' but I just haven't had time to put the laundry in the drawers."

"It's fine—I just meant not much furniture but very neat and functional." She turned to face me, stared into my eyes and slowly unbuttoned her shirt. When she finished she pulled it off and turned to hang it on the back of the nearest chair and bent over to slide her bikini bottoms past her ankles. *The rear view is more inviting than we could have imagined.* I was so caught up in her beauty that no part of my body had moved, since she came into the room, except for my eyeballs, but the swelling in my jeans was evident again.

I miss my valet chair—in storage in Dad's garage—strange thinking of it at a time like this the committee wondered. Her comments about the furniture I guess.

"Are you here or is your mind somewhere else, Marine?"

Geez, how do women do that? My mind wandered for only a half second and she caught it. Why does my mind wander like that?

I lied, "Well, beautiful, my body is definitely here but my mind was intent on absorbing all of your lovely attributes." *Good recovery someone else on the committee chimed in.*

I began to swiftly remove my clothes as she turned toward the bed, climbed aboard and settled herself face down but turned with one knee up and looking over her shoulder at me. I pulled the Vaseline jar out of the top drawer of the dresser and followed her to bed. Before I climbed in I pulled her hips up to expose the target between her enticing buns. The ensuing anal exploration was easy and very good which I attributed to her previous experience with her fiancé but when I touched her pelvic arch to try to enhance her experience she pulled my hand away.

"Not there now, sweetie," she whispered. It took a little longer without clitoral and vaginal manipulation but I was able to wait for her and we finished strong together.

"I'm pretty sore down there from last night, sweetie, so I don't think I can do a double. I've always thought about it and this would be a great opportunity, but I think I'm gonna have to wait for another time."

"No problem, lovely."

"What about Tommy?" She smiled bashfully. "Can I still have him?"

I laughed out loud. "Of course you can! He's on his way down anyway. We wouldn't want to disappoint him."

She laughed too at my reaction and said, "But that's probably it for this weekend, I think."

"Okay, my lovely. I'll tell Tommy to keep his mouth shut about his good fortune and we'll put the guard rails back up." I smiled at her upturned face, kissed her forehead, cheeks, lips, ears and neck and rolled her over to spoon behind her—thinking, as I dozed off, it would be our last time.

The knock on the door woke me up. "Is that you, Tommy?"

"Yes."

"It's locked. Give me a sec."

I let him in and spoke softly, "This isn't going to be the double we planned, Tommy—she's too sore. But the back door is still open, if you want it."

Of course he wants it! Why do you keep saying things like that?

His mouth was open as he stared at her lying there naked on the bed. Her back was still to him, but she rolled her shoulders and looked at him out of the corner of her eyes. "Oh my God," he whispered loud enough for her to hear.

I chuckled and said to her, "I think I'll stay and watch the show if that's okay." I knew Tommy wouldn't care.

She turned a little more at the waist and shoulders but still kept her legs rolled away. Her breasts now fully visible to Tommy, she looked directly at me and smiled. "C'mon, Tommy, and you *have* to stay, Marine—I don't want to do this alone."

She turned her shoulders away again and continued to roll onto her hands and knees and pulled a pillow below her face. "C'mere, Bobby," she whispered, glancing my direction and patting the pillow as she licked her lips and winked.

"Well, of course, if you insist," I chuckled again. "At least I'll have a good view of the action from there."

She took Tommy's assault with his oversized equipment easily and teased me with her mouth and hands while enjoying another orgasm.

Tommy was a little awkward when he finished. "I hope it was okay for you, sweetie. I realized just now that I still don't know your name. Are you okay?" He was still standing at the foot of the bed admiring her naked figure where she had immodestly rolled over on her back and exposed herself completely as she softly caressed the strawberry patch.

"You can call me anything you want, Tommy. I'm feeling perfect and if I weren't so sore in front we could do that again right now as a double."

"Well, whatever you want. You just say when and I'll be happy to oblige."

"Okay, maybe a double tomorrow night?" She glanced at me with a questioning look.

Tommy interjected, "Sure!"

I laughed and said, "Whatever you want, sweetie!"

When he left she asked, "Is Tommy a Negro or part Negro?"

"I don't know, sweetie. I never asked and it's not something that has come up. His skin is lighter than most Negros but he could be part. Does it make a difference to you?"

"Well, you know, here in the South, it's considered an unpardonable sin for a woman to be involved with a Negro—to have sex, I mean—and if anyone ever found out, I'd never be able to go home."

"I think you said you didn't want to go home anyway so I think you're safe. Some are saying that what's happening with Martin Luther King is going to make it all okay eventually anyway. Although there are many ignorant assholes who are adamantly against it."

"Wow, so you think he's really Negro or part Negro?"

"Didn't you think so when you first met him?"

"I guess I did but I didn't think much about it at the time."

"I kinda thought that might be why you were so suddenly turned on by him. No?"

"No . . . well, maybe kinda." She frowned as she pondered. "Wow, what a weekend! I lost my virginity, I've had sex in a room with two men and I've had sex with a Negro. I've really turned into a number one slut, haven't I?" She was smiling though and actually seemed quite proud of herself.

"Not only that, my lovely weekend slut, you've also just set yourself up for a double with a white guy and a Negro for tomorrow night." I laughed and teased her. "Do you want me to spank you for being a bad girl?"

"Absolutely not!" Her eyes were wide with mock fear. "I'm only being as bad as I want to be and I'm not going to feel guilty about it. It's way too good and way too much fun to feel guilty about."

She did do the double on Sunday night and was happy to let Tommy introduce a girlfriend to the mix, which removed all doubt as to his race, and I had my first black woman, which also eventually became a double with Tommy.

The crew of roommates, at the beachhouse, all noticed the *togetherness* of the *foursome* that weekend, of course, and would often remember and ask, "When is the *Weekender* coming back?" She was long gone though. Destined to become a special memory as the legendary *Pensacola Weekender*.

Third Time's A Charm

As friends, long before we "dated," Jamila and I had discussed the separation aspect of being married to military men. She was there, in Pensacola, looking for a husband, or maybe I should say hoping to fall in love with a pilot, who would have a good future in the military followed by a career as a commercial pilot or other aviation orientation.

When we first met she was living with three other girls in a three bedroom, one story house on the beach. All four girls had good jobs but lived together to be able to afford a nice house on the beach rather than a less crowded ordinary house in town. One was an airline stewardess, two worked for rental car agencies and one was a legal secretary. I was dating the airline stewardess at the time. She was a nice looking, freckle faced, fair skinned, blue eyed, natural redhead. My part of the rental agreement included sharing my redhead's bedroom for half of her rent so I could stay there on weekends even when she was out of town on an overnight flight.

The redhead and I often joked about the agency girls as "rent-a-girls" because of the way they often went out, and came home with, rental car customers. All of the girls also dated student pilots who, due to their training schedules, were usually available only on weekends.

The fourth to move into the house, Jamila was relegated to the fold out, hide-a-bed couch, in the living room, where she would sometimes be sitting up in bed reading, when the redhead and I got home. Not shy—to say the least—she always wore a see-through nightgown which clearly displayed her splendid, braless breasts.

"She really pisses me off when she flirts and shows off like that! I wish she'd cover up when we come in and wipe that grin off her face," the agitated redhead hissed through clenched teeth. "I know you'd like to fuck her, if you haven't already."

I didn't say anything, but she'd guessed it already. I had, more than a few times at that point. The first was just shortly after we'd met when the redhead left early one morning for a flight. She came into the bedroom in one of her spectacular nightgown outfits, exposing herself from nose to toes, including a large, thick, black, neatly trimmed bush showing through the panties. She stood there posing and looked at me with wide gorgeous brown eyes and a titillating grin.

"You got all you wanted last night," she teased?

"Well, that was last night." I smiled and lifted the covers off my naked body, motioning with my other hand, inviting her to join me in the bed.

She stood there for a few seconds before she closed the door—obviously proud of the way she looked. Her skin was a smooth natural brown, garnered from her father's middle-eastern genes, and her dark hair hung straight down to the middle of her back, held with a clip at the nape of her neck. Her breasts, dark nipples and areolas were clearly visible through the sheer outfit. "I don't want to mess this up," she whispered as she turned her back on me and slipped out of the baby dolls.

I lifted the sheet again as she slid in next to me like she'd done it a dozen times before—it seemed entirely normal—no stress, no over-excited-first-time rush—just a smooth, natural, loving, caring, closeness. She smelled fresh lying there on her side pressing her body against mine, wiggling to get as near as she could. Did she get up and shower and put her baby dolls back on to come and seduce me?

She stroked my back and kissed my chest and neck and felt to see if I was hard or maybe to check my size. She licked my nipples with her tongue and noticed how I reacted with a shiver and an arch in my back. *How did she know I would love that?* It wasn't all she knew either as she spent the next half hour demonstrating. I just lay there on my back wallowing in my good luck and drinking in her beauty rising above me as she mounted me with the hottest insides I'd felt in a long time. Her pelvis ground into mine as she rolled her hips over my thighs and her breasts bounced up and down and waved side to side as she put all of her energy into the action.

Afterward, I asked, "How old are you?" I was sitting with my back against the headboard and she was sitting up in the middle of the bed, facing me, with her legs crossed Indian style. I loved the way she sat there completely exposed. Maybe even enjoying my stare.

"19," she said off-handedly. "Why?"

"Well, you seem so at ease and experienced and yet, you're so young. You were very much at ease and knew very well what to do for me and for yourself. How do you know so much at your age?"

"It's not a bad thing, is it?" She looked at me almost sadly with wide brown eyes, as if looking out of a burka and asking not to be punished.

"Oh no! I think you're wonderful. I think you are the best I've ever had . . . *The brain committee pondered the veracity of the compliment.* "I was just curious, that's all. Jamila is such an unusual and pretty name. Where does it come from?"

She was quiet for a minute, got up and leisurely stretched her sumptuous naked body. She had the smallest waist I'd ever seen. She watched me drinking in her beauty and flashed her familiar wickedly playful smile. "I'll be right back. I want to get a cigarette and an ash tray. Then we can talk."

When she came back she lit two and handed me one of the cigarettes. "Jamila is an Arabic name meaning beautiful. My father is from Syria and he named me. He told me later that he knew when I was born that I would be beautiful and that I should always be proud of being beautiful but then he went back to Syria when I was sixteen and I haven't seen or heard from him since."

She looked at me seriously for a minute or so and finally said, "I learned all I know about sex from an older man—not old but older, about 30 when we started. He was a neighbor and friend of the family and I loved him from the moment we met. I was 17. I had sex with him the first time, a few months later, after I turned 18. Yes, he was my first and I seduced him. He didn't rape me or force me or even come on to me in any sordid way. I used to stop by his house on the way home from school just to be with him. He was single. His wife died in a car accident. He enjoyed my company and I loved him and I thought we would get married someday."

"What happened? I was genuinely interested and a little concerned at this point.

"To make a long story short, he was an incredible lover. He somehow knew everything I wanted to feel. He knew every sensitive spot, every crevice, every way to touch and feel, everything to say and do. He took my body with his tongue, hands and fingers and made me come several times whenever we were together. He also taught me all the ways to please a man. I can use my body to make you come without you even moving a muscle. He taught me to love sex and how to please myself with sex or without, and to love men in a way that's more exciting than anything else."

"Unbelievable! How long did this go on? What happened?"

"It lasted a little less than a year. Then his company transferred him to New York. There seemed to be no way for me to tell my mother about us and go away with him. I suggested it but he wouldn't have anything to do with it. Once, he came back to see me, on a pretext to see my mother and I snuck out to meet him. We lost touch after that and I haven't seen him since. I've realized I was infatuated and not necessarily in love, so at least, I've rationalized it away."

"Wow! You've developed a tremendous level of maturity for being so young."

"That's a compliment, right?"

I nodded. "Of course, but as long as we're being totally honest with one another, I have to answer your first question about last night. I'm not fucking the redhead."

"What! You're sleeping with her and really sleeping and not doing anything else?"

"Well, not exactly. It's a mutual satisfaction arrangement with no actual intercourse. She's allergic to the pill and petrified of getting pregnant by a broken condom."

"So what do you do?"

"Well, different things, depending on the mood—I do oral for her, or oral and fingers, but it's difficult for me to get off with her doing oral for me. I do tap her butt once in a while. She doesn't like it much, so I don't insist."

"What do you mean oral is difficult for you?"

"I like oral as foreplay but I enjoy some kind of penetration or skin on skin for orgasm, except I can get off just about any other way if there is a tongue or lips on my nipple."

"What does 'any other way' mean?"

"Like between your breasts, between the cheeks of your butt, rubbing on your stomach or between your thighs—just about any way, anywhere."

"Anywhere but in the mouth, huh?"

"Not exactly, but for me, it's more a matter of when it occurs. A beautiful mouth on a beautiful face is a great place to come after you've fucked everywhere else. Doing it in the mouth is okay as foreplay but if that's all there is it just takes too long since a lot of girls don't know how—they're nibblers."

"Nibblers?"

"Yeah, the guys joke about that sometimes. Trying to tell, by looking at a face and lips, whether she would be a gobbler and swallower or a nibbler and spitter or a crossover."

"A crossover?"

"Yeah, a kind of unusual combination of nibbler and swallower or gobbler and spitter."

"Aaaah, I see. And what do you think I am?"

"You, my sweet, are definitely a gobbler but we'll have to wait to see if you are a swallower or a spitter."

She laughed and was quiet for a moment again. "We're friends, right." She was making a statement—not asking a question. "This is not going to be a serious long term relationship, right?" This was not really a question either but she paused, still sitting there naked, smoking and looking at me like she expected me to define everything about us.

"Right, I agree, at least for now. I'm dating your roommate and you're dating other guys but I love what just happened and would like to do it again as often as circumstances permit, if you like it and want it also."

"You mean like booty buddies, when it's convenient?" She was inquisitive—asking a sincere question, I thought.

"Yes, you could put it that way if you want. I'm not ready to have a serious relationship, at least not 'til I'm closer to graduating from flight school. I know you're looking and expecting to find a husband

and I'm sure you will, but you're still very young. You have a lot of time before you will be considered an old maid." I chuckled.

"Well, that's what I mean. I know I have time to look but I like the idea of having a booty buddy. I know you're sleeping with a roommate. I didn't know you weren't having sex but I know you've had sex with the other two roommates on at least one occasion each. I heard you one Saturday afternoon with Cindy when you two thought no one else was in the house and you were in Beverly's room just a couple of weeks ago when I got up early to go to work. You were quiet with her but I know you weren't just sleeping in there."

"Okay, sweetie, all that's true but what's your point?"

"Well, I know I'm operating in the dark here, but do you have a booty buddy relationship with either of the other girls?"

I chuckled at the frankness of her question. "No, I only have a relationship with the redhead and it's not exclusive and the incidents with Cindy and Beverly were just the one time each, so far, although I don't plan on turning them down if another occasion arises. Cindy was sunbathing topless in the backyard between the house and the sand dunes when I came in the front and saw her through the back patio doors. She saw me through the glass and waved and I opened the door to talk to her. 'I'll get my suit on and join you!' I yelled. 'You might need some suntan oil on those beauties,' I remember saying, nodding toward her bare breasts. She smiled and said, 'Don't bother, I'm ready to come inside anyway.' I told her, 'Okay, just my bad luck. I'll see you later then.' I had just sat down on the couch when she came in, still topless, and waved her hand at me to follow as she went toward her room. 'Come this way, if you like what you see, Marine.' She smiled and gave me an extra wiggle of her hips as she walked by."

"I didn't realize we left the door to the bedroom open but anyone in the house would have known anyway. It was a rather noisy and wild afternoon."

"Yes," Jamila said. "I heard you before I saw you." She laughed, and I knew she wasn't angry or jealous.

"You saw us?" *Incredible! How did that happen?* The committee was excited but confused.

She ducked her head and looked out the corner of her eyes. "Yep, I peeked in and watched for a couple minutes. It was the first time I ever watched anyone and I liked it."

"Wow, good to know!" I chuckled at the prospects that knowledge could include.

"And what about Beverly?"

"Beverly and I just ran into each other at the Schooner one night when I stopped in for a beer. The redhead was on a flight and wouldn't be back that night and neither of us had anything or anyone else going on, so we just wound up enjoying each other's company. It was all fun but nothing special and there is no arrangement, as such, with either of them.

Jamila smiled again and began, "Well, I understand but here's the thing. Have you noticed I don't bring men here to the house?"

"Sure, it would be kinda obvious, out there on the fold-out, if you did."

"Of course, that's why I don't. At least not now but I used to."

I guess I looked kind of surprised. "Really!"

"Really, not out there on the couch but in this room, before you started sleeping here. I used to have the use of this room whenever she was on an overnight flight."

"Aaaah, so what do you now propose, you gorgeous creature?"

"Well, I've never seen you bring a girl here to the house—do you?"

"No, I didn't think that would be quite kosher. I usually go to their place or to a motel."

"So if you don't have a date and I don't have a date, we could sleep here together and I wouldn't have to be on the couch—just as friends on a booty buddy basis," she added quickly.

"Wonderful! Sounds like a great deal to me. Win, win . . . uh, what's the catch?"

"Well, the catch is, if the redhead's not home and I have a date . . . would you sleep out there on the fold-out and let me have the bedroom?"

"So you'd leave me out there on the couch to listen to you having fun in here?"

"I'm sleepin' out there listening to you when you're in here, doing whatever it is you do—but maybe, Cindy or Beverly would take pity on you and invite you to their room," she added as she laughed.

"Aaaha, such a deal." I laughed out loud. "Maybe you can intervene with the girls for me—you could say, 'Cindy, I need to bring my date here tonight. So could you please fuck Bobby, so I can have the bedroom?' I'm paying half the redhead's rent for that bed, you know?"

"I know but would it hurt if once in a while you could sleep out there on the couch so I could have some occasional privacy?" She almost pouted a little bit and flirted with her dark eyelashes. It was very cute.

"Privacy? Why couldn't I just stay in here and participate—like a double?"

She laughed and surprised me again. "I'll tell you what, I'm not a virgin there but I haven't had a double yet. But if I decide to do it, while we're booty buddies, I'll let you be the first."

"Ha, I'll hold you to that deal." I laughed out loud again. "But tell me, what happens if it turns out you have a date every time she's out of town, so I never get to have the benefits of your beautiful, sexy body."

"Okay . . . that's not likely but it could happen, I guess, but if it does, I'll do you anyway."

"When?"

"Well, at the first opportunity—same night after my date leaves, if he leaves early enough, or the next morning before I go to work."

"Seems like a lot of work—it might wear you out. It could be more fun to do it all at once," I joked about the double again.

"That's enough," she said chuckling. Is it a deal or not?"

"Sure, it's a deal, sweetie, and talking about it has made me very horny again, so we can seal it right now and I'll take your awesome bubble butt as confirmation. Come 'ere, booty buddy!"

She laughed and happily surrendered her gorgeous butt.

She was true to her word from the very first and lived up to her bargain in every way. She truly loved sex and was not shy about expressing her desires. Sometimes, after her date left, she would wake me in the middle of the night or early in the morning for what she cheerfully called her duty fuck and would come and make me come in less than five minutes. Yes, she was that good. Other times when neither of us had a date she would take her time and come caressing and teasing and making me hold off for half an hour or more or get me up for seconds while she had multiple orgasms and then we'd come together.

The arrangement lasted longer than I thought it would. We had a great time on a steady basis for the better part of six months until she got engaged and moved in with a marine flight student about to get his wings.

We met again, a couple months later, at the officer's club at Pensacola Naval Air Station after a Friday night happy hour. The bar and lounge area were packed and I didn't see her at first.

She ran across the room, threw herself into my arms, gave me a big hug and kiss and asked, "Are you alone?"

"Yep, just out trolling to see what I can catch," I joked. "Where's your fiancé?"

"He got his wings and was transferred to California a month ago."

"And you didn't go with him?"

"I was getting ready to move to California three weeks ago when he was suddenly transferred to Okinawa. Now, I don't know what's gonna happen."

She looked more beautiful, fresher and younger than ever in a tight fitting red sweater and striped red, white and blue hot pants. "So you're also out trolling by yourself, huh?"

"Not if you're ready to go." She laughed. "Where are you living now?" She knew the redhead had moved on and therefore, I wasn't at her former beachhouse anymore.

"Back at the big house on the beach but with different roommates. All the old guys have gone on to the jet pipeline or graduated in helicopters."

"Well, okay then, let's go there!" She laughed and wiggled her body from nose to toes, and I was instantly aroused.

As we lay there smoking a cigarette afterward, she said, by way of explaining herself, "I'm not married, you know, just engaged. We are not committed to celibacy until we're actually married, and probably not even then, when he's deployed. Besides, we may not even be getting married."

"Well, my old friend and booty buddy, you keep me informed of your status because I'm gonna get my wings in the spring next year, if I get through this football season in one piece and you can go to California with me, if you want."

"If I commit to go to California with anyone else, it's gonna be after a wedding. I still have time. I'm still two years younger than most of the graduating flight students."

"And four years younger than me, since I'm two years older than the average flight student. So I guess I'm an old man."

"Not too old my friend. I'd make you a good wife and booty buddy if you want."

I ignored the wife suggestion. I smiled and looked into her huge brown eyes, put my arm around her tiny waist and pulled her close. "I'll take the booty buddy offer for now, gorgeous."

She kissed me again softly and pulled back slowly with a big grin. "I'm always ready for you, Bobby."

She stayed with me for the weekend and the next few days, coming out to the beach after work, and we discussed marriage.

"I wanna have kids," she said. "I want to have a normal married life, except I don't want to sit around on my butt and wait for a man to come home from a long deployment or maybe never come home from a war."

I hedged, "I don't really want kids, although I wouldn't mind kids, if you can take the responsibility of raising them. I know how you feel about sex and I wouldn't hold you to a celibacy commitment when I'm deployed, but what happens if the marriage doesn't work out in the long run?" The brain committee was doubtful. *How did we get into this kind of discussion again?*

"I wouldn't hold you to a lifetime commitment either, and really, it's not what I want from you anyway since you're a career marine. So if we get married, we should plan to split someday and when we do, you should agree to help out with child support until I can make other arrangements."

"You mean like a prenuptial agreement?"

"Yeah, sorta. Only we don't have to do a formal contract or anything. We know each other well enough. Our likes and dislikes, wants and desires. If it works out for a long term marriage, it works out. If it doesn't work out, then we each go on in our own happy separate way." *Deja vu? Isn't this the same crap we just got free of with Liana? Maybe so but this one we know much better and at least she's not crazy.*

The relationship with Bonnie had killed any of the forever-love-type-feelings I'd ever had and I was sure they would never occur for me again. Marriage vows were meaningless. Just a technicality, really. But I did have a special attraction to Jamila. Her special dark, middle-eastern beauty and carefree open sexuality lit a ravenous fire of desire unrivaled by previous relationships.

We were married just a few weeks later, and two weeks after the knot was tied, she made it clear what kind of relationship it would be. She was supposed to work until 1800 and probably be home around 1830. I called the office at the rental car agency where she worked at 2000. "She left at 1800," the agent said.

"Did she say where she was going?"

"No, she didn't say anything. I assumed she was going home."

"Okay, if you hear from her, ask her to call home please."

"Sure, I will."

When she didn't show by 2100, I went looking for her, stopping by the rental car agency. "Have you heard from Jamila?"

"No," the guy behind the desk replied. "And I don't expect that I will." He seemed a bit edgy.

"What does that mean?"

"Well, she never has called in or come back here after she leaves at the end of her shift and I don't expect her to do so tonight. That's all."

I called home to see if she was there yet and then drove by Trader Jon's but didn't see her car in the lot. I cruised the main drag downtown and out to another night club and dance hall where the local girls usually hung out with servicemen. No car there either. I gave up and went home. I was exhausted and went to bed.

I woke up in a fog when she came to bed, "Where've ya been," I yawned?

"I'm really tired now, Bobby. We'll talk about it tomorrow." She kissed me, smiled, said goodnight and turned out the light.

The next morning, she woke me up with her tongue on my starter button and her naked body snuggled up next to mine. Shortly after I became conscious, she climbed on me like she was settling into a saddle on a pony. She licked her thumbs and forefingers and teased my start and come buttons while she rocked herself back and forth on my pelvic mound. I tightened my butt cheeks, pushed up against her and pulled her hips down with my hands around her tiny waist. Her nipples pointed out at me from her gorgeous breasts as I looked past them to her face. Her eyes were fixated on mine and we both came almost immediately. Yes, she was still that good! She lay down on me, until her breathing returned to normal and then rolled off to the side.

She fixed breakfast for the two of us and sat down at the kitchen table before she said anything. "I was with a man last night, Bobby."

I guess I must have looked a little shocked because she flinched and straightened her back. "I kinda figured that, when I couldn't find you anywhere and considering how your associate at the agency was acting, but how the hell does it happen just two weeks after we were married?"

"It was almost like an accident, Bobby. I'd been going out with him, a customer at the agency, and he came in last night expecting that I would go out with him, like I always had. When I told him I was married he got really upset—almost like angry and insisted that we go out and talk about it. I didn't want to make a scene at the agency so I agreed to meet him for dinner."

"You had dinner? Until 0130 in the morning?"

"Well, no, but yes, wait a minute. We had dinner in the room at his hotel like we had been lately since I moved out of the house on the beach."

"That's convenient," I said sarcastically.

"Anyway, during dinner he began to talk about our times together and I began to think about taking him to the beachhouse and remembered being with him in the bedroom while you were on the sofa bed. And then I remembered the double."

"The double?"

"I hope you didn't forget the double at the beachhouse. My first one. The virgin one I promised to you? Do you remember it was Kenneth?"

"Of course, I especially remember the double but I'm not sure I remembered the name of the guy until you just said it."

"Well, it was Kenneth I was with last night."

"Really?"

"Yes, and we called you about 2100 to see if you wanted to come to the hotel for a repeat but you weren't home."

"So you just decided to fuck him anyway?"

"Well, actually, at that point, I already had. Remembering and talking about the double made us horny again and since you weren't home, we decided to do it again and call you later to see if you wanted to come over."

"I was home later though. Did I miss your call? I may have been asleep already."

"No, we didn't call again. It got late and I was tired and decided to just come on home."

"So now what?" I was a little perplexed at the status of our relationship.

"Well . . . I thought you would understand or at least be okay with it."

"How do you mean 'be okay with it'?"

"We were booty buddies for nearly a year before we got married and we've already said we don't expect each other to be celibate when you're deployed. It's obvious the relationship hasn't been exclusive in the past and it isn't expected to be exclusive in the future. Is it so different for us to be open now considering the existing past and the obvious plans for the future?"

"No, not if it's what you want, sweetheart. Is that why I got the duty fuck this morning?"

"It is." She smiled at the reference to our previous relationship and looked almost shy about it. "But I really enjoyed it, didn't you?"

I stared at the remainder of dried yellow of the eggs she had made for breakfast and contemplated my answer. "Sure, you can wake me up like that almost anytime. One thing though—just call me if you're not gonna be home so I don't go nuts with worry trying to figure out where you are."

"Okay, it's a deal."

"Is Kenneth still in town?"

"Yes, for the rest of the weekend."

"Do you have any plans with him?"

"No, except we did have a conversation about you."

"And what was that?"

"He said, if you were okay with it, the three of us could get together tonight."

"Was that his idea or yours?" I smiled and crossed my arms in a mockingly defensive posture.

"I told him I wouldn't see him again unless it was also with you."

"What did he say to that idea?"

"He was happy about the idea but sad that we wouldn't be seeing each other again separately."

"Well, of course he was, but are you okay with not seeing him alone again?

"Yes, really, it was my idea. You know I like doubles and it doesn't appear we would get too many opportunities as a married couple unless you would bring me home a gift sometimes." She smiled and seemed to almost blush again at the suggestion.

"I'm happy about your decision. In fact, I would like for us to make a commitment to an exclusive arrangement." *Oh, that again? The brain committee remembered previous circumstances.*

"Ok, like what?" She looked puzzled.

"Like we will not have separate single relationships with anyone, except when we are separated by unavoidable circumstances such as deployments or combat."

"Like geographic singles?"

"Exactly, when we're together, we're together, and when we're not together, singles are okay. I'm not a pilot yet but pilots are infamous for acting single when they are out of the local area control zone."

"What is a control zone?"

"Technically, it is an area around an airfield, on the ground and up to certain altitudes where the aircraft in that area come under the management of the tower or ground control, to provide aircraft spatial separation and safety. When an aircraft is outside a local area control zone, the pilot may be considered free of local air traffic controls and other conventional controls such as marriage vows and so forth. Most pilots do not extend the same or similar privileges to their spouses, although I've known a few wives who have taken liberties in spite of the lack of a formal agreement."

She smiled slyly. "I understand conventional controls, Bobby, but what about unconventional controls?" she asked, eyeing me with a little humorous suspicion.

"Well . . . we've both been doing all kinds of things together and apart ever since we met and I really enjoyed those exciting and interesting activities, but we should maybe be more discreet. I don't mean we shouldn't participate at all in orgies or toga parties like we used to but swapping with another couple or a small party might be more appropriate.

She seemed to ponder the situation as she lit a cigarette. I'm okay with whatever you want to do as a couple as long as we do it together"

"Good, but if we do anything you'd have to be the one setting it up because I just won't have time."

"Fine, I'm not saying we would actually do anything, other than what I've already done and I don't have anyone in mind right now other than Kenneth but I wanted to know how you feel about it."

"Fine, how does this fit in with your plans to have kids? You're still on the pill for now, I know."

"When we're ready to have children, I'll have to go off the pill and any extracurricular activities would have to stop until I get pregnant. Don't worry. I'll take care of it when the time comes and since you brought it up, how does next month sound?" She looked at me sternly, as if to say, "Trust me and don't argue."

Helicopter Transition

Danny Schumaker became a marine aviator by choosing his path upon graduation from the Naval Academy in the spring of 1963. About my same height at six feet two inches, but of slightly smaller build, he was a swimmer at the Academy. He was in good shape but looked older than our contemporaries because of his thin hair and receding hair line. Actually, he was a little older than most in our aviator class because of a delay getting into the Academy and the extra year he spent in prep school before his freshman year. Also, he spent his first six months on active duty at Quantico, Virginia attending the Marine Corps Basic School (TBS)—a training regime for new marine officers—while most of the rest of the marine flight students came directly from college because of completing Officer Candidate School (OCS) during summers in college.

When Danny reported to flight school he was a few months behind me but caught up by the end of T-28 carrier qualifications because of my delay in training to participate in two seasons of football. I met Danny at happy hour when we were both celebrating the completion of carrier qualifications or "hitting the boat" as it was called.

Actually, I met his wife first. She was sitting at the bar drinking a coca cola with a cherry while two young naval aviation cadets were obviously trying to impress her but without any success at all. She looked to be several months pregnant and her wedding rings were clearly visible. A beautiful woman in her early twenties, she had straight dark hair parted in the middle above her high forehead which hung down to well below her shoulders. Her softly angled face supported a Roman nose of obvious Italian descent, between wide, shining dark eyes and a great smile.

"Where's your husband, gorgeous?" I asked.

"He's in the back shooting craps." A separate room in the back of the building was furnished with a table against a wall for craps along with a couple of high tables for cards.

"What a shame he's left his beautiful woman to suffer at the hands of these loose sailors," I joked nodding at the cadets and turning back to her, "My name's, Robert, call me Bobby."

"I'm Jeri—no, it's not short for anything, just Jeri. He's celebrating 'hitting the boat' with two of his favorite addictions—drinking and gambling."

"Me too, I hit the boat Wednesday evening. "Aaaah, but only two of his addictions—indicating he has others?"

"Well, yes, also airplanes and women—and he . . . smokes."

She was smiling still, but I could tell she was a little bit less than jovial about the addictions. The look in her eye had changed, and she tensed just a little as she looked directly into mine as she said "women" and paused before she said "smokes."

The two young sailors quietly slipped away.

"Sounds like a typical aviator to me," I said laughing again. And then, feigning concern, but smiling, I asked, "He hasn't been unfaithful, has he?"

"Oh no!" She laughed and loosened up again. "He hasn't had the opportunity since we've been married. He went to the Basic School as a second lieutenant right after we came back from our honeymoon and we've been together the whole time since, but I've heard stories about you pilots and your escapades."

"Well, first, we are not pilots yet, Jeri. And second, all of the stories don't fit all of the pilots. And third of all, and most important, not that I profess to be one, there are good, honest, homebody, faithful pilots out there who are committed to their marriage and their family."

"I know . . . and speaking of addictions, here's mine now."

He kissed her on the cheek and then looked at me.

"Danny, this is Bobby," she said. He hit the boat this week too."

"Did you really?" His genuine interest caught me a little off guard. "Isn't it great? How come I haven't met you?" He reached across and shook my hand.

"I dunno. Probably Goshawks football and odd training cycles. But yeah, hitting the boat is really something! Nothing I've ever experienced even comes close! Especially, coming around after the day landings, as the lights on the ship are getting brighter against the dusk." I circled an arc in the air with my hand simulating the aircraft in the approach to the landing. "I was thinking I'd love to have a photo of the approach with the meatball and carrier flight deck cut out against the gold rimmed horizon just after sunset."

He seemed to finish my sentence. "Yeah, and right after that it gets so dark you really can't tell the difference between the ship and the ocean except for the lights on the ship's deck."

And I finished his: "It's almost like flying on instruments with that big ole yellow ball showing the way."

"Yep—let me buy you a drink," he offered.

"Sure," I said.

I'd been talking to his wife and thought there might be some tension when he came up but there wasn't an ounce of jealousy in his demeanor. He was self-assured, poised, intelligent and at ease with himself and his bride.

"When did you decide you wanted to fly, Bobby?"

We were off and running about our first love. Flying was what we were all about and we knew it. Any other subject would be a distant second on our horizons. Our desire to fly and to be good at it, if not the best, were all we really cared about except we were marines first, and marine pilots were even more dedicated to be the best support we could be for our fighting men on the ground.

"My folks tell stories about, before I could walk, I crawled onto a floor furnace and burned my arm pretty badly." I lifted my left arm to show the scars which were now barely visible. "The only way they could get me to quit crying was to take me to the airport and let me watch the airplanes."

"Wow, that's really early!" He laughed.

"Yeah, I don't remember the incident itself, of course, but I remembered the stories later and I think it made an early impression. I used to watch birds fly when I was very young and wish I could join them. I would imagine I had wings and imitate the birds spreading their wings and gliding and slowing their descent by lowering their outstretched tails."

"Like flaps or speed brakes," he offered.

"Sure, but I didn't know it at the time."

"Did you fly or learn to fly before you came to flight school?

"No, I only flew on a commercial airplane as a passenger from Oklahoma City to DC and from Albuquerque to DC when I went to PLC training at Quantico and Jump School at Ft. Benning, Georgia. I never actually flew an airplane until I climbed into a T-34 for my first hop at Saufley. How about you, Danny?"

"I came to Pensacola during summer vacation my junior year at the Naval Academy. We did a ground school orientation and flew a couple of demo flights with an instructor."

"How was it? Did it make a difference in your choice of career path out of the Academy?

"It was nice and it was fun but it didn't really give an impression of the intensity and depth of the training. I'd already made up my mind to ask for flight school anyway, before I even came to the orientation."

"Were you in Marine Flight Section 18 at Saufley Field?"

"Yes, weren't you?"

"No, I was originally slated to go there when I finished ground school but I was diverted to play football, and after the season was over, the powers that be decided I should go to Flight 13, which was all navy students except me."

"Why was that I wonder?"

"I'm not sure exactly. I finished first in my ground school class and I've had about three years extra training with the Marine Corps Reserves so maybe they figured I didn't need any more Marine Corps oversight right now."

"Whaddaya mean, extra training?" He set his beer glass down hard on the wooden bar.

"Well, most of the guys sign up for PLC (A) and they just go to the summer 12-week OCS training at Quantico. So they show up here at flight school with just that minimum exposure to the Marine Corps. I already had two years of ROTC when I signed up for the program and decided to get as much military and Marine Corps training as

I could, so I also signed up for the Marine Corps Reserve. I trained regularly, went to Jump School and other schools and made corporal in the Fifth Force Recon Company and would have made sergeant if I hadn't graduated from college and been commissioned."

"Really!"

"Well, probably. I was on the list to be promoted to sergeant but my active duty staff sergeant on the Inspector and Instructor Staff said I was too dumb to be a sergeant so they were going to make me a second lieutenant."

He laughed at the takeoff on the old joke about how dumb second lieutenants are thought to be. Danny and I became immediate friends and established Friday night happy hour traditions from day one, finishing up that night back at his house sitting around the kitchen table after Jeri went to bed.

A few days later, Danny and I found out we would be continuing in flight school along the Helicopter Track. It became the topic of the discussion of the day at our usual happy hour gathering at the Officers Club. I knew he, like most of the flight students, was hoping for the Jet Pipeline but such was not to be the case for him.

Although he was disappointed, he said, "Well, Bobby, it just means I'll be workin' closer to the real Green Machine."

Danny always had a positive outlook and I understood the reference immediately. Green Machines with the Green Marines. I had come to flight school from the Green Marines in the Fifth Force Recon Reserve Unit. Marine helicopters are painted camouflage green because they work mostly at low altitude or on the ground in close proximity to marines in the field. Jet planes are painted light gray to better camouflage them against the sky. I had always thought "Either way I'm glad to still be in the mix for wings of any kind. I don't want to wind up going to Quantico for Basic School and doing a tour as a grunt lieutenant."

"Not much chance of that happening now my friend. You're far enough along you shouldn't have any problem with the transition from fixed wing to rotary wing. It's not supposed to be much more difficult."

"Easy for you to say. I've had difficulty from day one, including a down, and I don't expect it will get much better now!"

"Aw, c'mon. Whaddaya mean day one you got an actual down? How can you fail what is essentially a demo ride?"

"Yes, actually, day one. I got a down on my first flight in the T-34 basic trainer at Saufley."

"No way! How'd that happen? Nobody can get a down on their first hop. Mine wasn't much more than a ride-along.

"Well, it happened and yes, it's supposed to be pretty much an orientation flight to see and become familiar with the area and the airplane but my instructor didn't approach it that way at all."

"Whaddaya mean? What did he do?"

"He took off and flew to the training area and then said, 'You've got it,' and let go of the stick. I looked in the rear view mirrors and saw him holding up his hands and I grabbed for the stick. Of course, as soon as I grabbed it the aircraft started moving around, and I began shoving the stick and overcorrecting and he started yelling."

"Yelling? Yelling what?"

"'Trim, trim, trim! Maintain 1,200 feet! Trim! Maintain altitude. Trim!' I didn't have a clue how to trim and was trying to maintain altitude by holding the nose level with the stick—stupid, I know, but I didn't know better at the time. I'd never even been in an airplane before, except as an airline passenger, much less flown one. He kept trimming the aircraft so I would have to use more and more pressure to try to keep the nose down so we wound up in pretty much a steady climb. I couldn't stop it, and when he threw his knee board at me, I gave up and yelled into the mike, 'You've got it,' and let the stick go."

"What happened then?"

"Well the aircraft was trimmed so far nose up that when I suddenly let go, the stick flipped back toward my lap and we went almost straight up. The aircraft shuddered and fell off to one side."

"Wow! You're lucky it didn't stall and spin."

"Oh, I'm pretty sure it stalled but by the time I let go we were almost up to 4,000 feet so he had time to recover, even if it had spun."

"And so, after all of that, you're still in the program?" He laughed heartily and made a motion with his hand like an aircraft stalling and spinning out of control.

"Yea, I was afraid I was gonna be gone without even completing my first flight. He flew back to Saufley, landed, shut down and beat it out of the airplane so fast I didn't know where he had gone when I climbed down. Looking under the airplane I saw his skinny ass on his bony little frame in his baggy flight suit beating feet so fast his body seemed unable to keep up with his stride. I followed at a quick pace but not wanting to catch up with him until maybe he would have a chance to cool down a bit.

"When I got to the ready room, I could hear him yelling in the flight commander's office—telling the story of the flight. I stopped just outside the open hatch to the office, about six feet behind and raised my arm to throw his knee board at him."

"Jesus, Pisser, you didn't hit him with it did you?"

"No, the flight commander, looking past the instructor, raised his hand to halt the action and said to me, 'Hold it, Lieutenant.' Luckily, I stopped in time but my instructor turned around to see me looking at him with as much hate as I could, still poised to throw. I think the little shit was so afraid I was gonna kill him he couldn't move. His eyes were wide open and his mouth was flopping open and shut like a fish gasping for water. I walked straight at him, staring hard into his scared bulging eyes and stopped when we were nearly toe to toe. He was looking up, like out of a pit with his face about two feet below mine. I brought the knee-board down quickly in front of his face and the motion caused him to jump back and bump his ass on the desk. I said, with all the sarcasm I could muster, 'Here, Lieutenant, you're lucky you missed me.'"

"The commander said, 'That's enough, Pincer. You're dismissed for the day. Be here in my office at 0800 tomorrow.' So I smartly did an about face and marched out. The next day I noticed on the Squadron Readiness Board my instructor was on leave and when I reported to the commander's office he explained he was going to be my instructor. He said, 'You will have to do a lot of off-wing flights with other smaller instructors because the aircraft is underpowered for aerobatics with two big people.' He was about my size so together we probably weighed close to 500 pounds with all of our gear."

"But you got through it okay after that?" Danny shifted his weight from one foot on the bar rail to the other and took a long swig on his beer.

"Yeah, the commander was a super patient instructor. He started just talking about flying. He could not believe I had never even been in a small aircraft before and wanted to know, how in the world would I know I wanted to be a pilot if I had never flown before."

"How didja answer that one?"

"I told him I don't know. I've just always known I wanted to fly. I told him the story my parents told about taking me to the airport to stop me from crying."

"What about the rest of the syllabus? Didja get any more downs?"

"Yep. I got through T-28 basics, aerobatics and formation okay but then another season of football came around when I was ready to start instrument training. In order to continue flight training and football at the same time, the squadron scheduled flights to mainside, near our season quarters, to pick up three students at a time and go fly a 4.5-hour hop with 1.5 hours of flight time under the bag for each student. It worked okay for those who were already in the midst of the syllabus, but for me, starting with the initial flight, it didn't work so good. The flights were few and far between, and while I made it through a few of them, I eventually got a down for flying a landing pattern backward."

"Hello, marines!" She had gone to the lady's room and splendidly reintroduced herself as she came sauntering back. She leaned back, threw her arms around him, kissed him long and sweet and then flashed her eyes at me. "What am I interrupting? Because I know I'm interrupting something."

Danny offered. "Bobby was explaining to me how he got a down on one of his training flights in the SNB."

"What's a down?" She asked sounding puzzled.

He responded, "The opposite of an up!" He laughed and continued, "No, really, an up means the student demonstrated the ability to perform the maneuvers required by the curriculum and a down means you didn't. You probably don't know about downs because I never got one. When you get a down you have to repeat the flight until you get an up. If you get two downs on the same flight or you get too many downs, you might be dropped out of the program."

"So, Bobby, continue. Backward? How the hell did you do that?"

"Well, it's easy if you know how!" I joked and laughed at the painful experience, and he laughed with me. Jeri still looked a little confused but laughed anyway. "I was the last of three student pilots on the SNB that day. I'd spent three hours dozing in the back while the other students flew their hops and when I finally got my hands on the yoke I was a little groggy. Here I am flying an airplane with a yoke. Something else I had never done. The thing is though, I flew the pattern perfectly, according to the debrief and write-up, but I turned the wrong way at the initial point and flew the whole route backward, out over the water. When the instructor said, 'Pop your hood,' I knew I was in trouble when I saw nothing but open sea instead of a runway."

"So you got another down and how didja get outa that one?"

"Well, right afterward I broke my hand in a football game so I wasn't able to fly anymore of those flights and when I reported to Whiting Field, to the instrument training squadron, I was informed it was shutting down. The syllabus was to be flown in the T-28 and I would have to start over."

"What a bummer?" Danny shook his head in empathetically.

"Well, it didn't turn out so bad. In fact, I really lucked out."

"Whadaya mean?"

"I met a marine major when I first came to Pensacola who was the XO of the instrument training squadron. I had seen him several times since we met and when I was there, standing at the operations office counter, he overheard the conversation and recognized me. 'How much of the syllabus did you manage to complete before you broke your hand Pincer?' He didn't act like he knew me or offer to shake my hand so I just replied formally and told him about half way. He asked when I was going to get the cast off my hand and I told him I was supposed to go to see about it that afternoon and they would probably take it off. He said, 'Okay, if you get your cast off today, call to let me know and then go home, pack a bag for four days and be here at 0600 tomorrow.' As it all turned out, we flew the entire remaining instrument training syllabus in four days. We flew about eight or nine hours a day on Friday, Saturday, Sunday and Monday on a Florida cross-country to MacDill AFB, Jacksonville Navy Base and Homestead AFB and landed back here at Whiting Field late Monday."

"Wow, what a break!"

"Hey, Danny, you were commissioned as a regular marine because of graduating from the academy, right?'

"Yep, why?"

"I applied for augmentation a few months ago and it just came through so I'm a regular marine now."

"Well, congratulations! Augmented to the regular Marine Corps and promoted to first lieutenant in the same month."

"That's not all the news though. We just found out Jamila is pregnant."

"Well, Papa, congratulations again! When is the baby due?"

"In late June or early July."

"Well, we should have our wings and be at our first Fleet Marine Corps assignments by then."

"First, we gotta learn to fly helicopters?"

Danny was right, the little TH-13M helicopter was easy to fly and all we had to do was take off, air taxi and fly some low-level patterns, air taxi back to our spot and land. I breezed through the syllabus and soloed without a problem and the check ride for advancement to the H-34D Sikorsky was routine.

Flying had become nearly second nature by this time and learning to fly another type of helicopter used all of the same muscles and memory as the previous training. I still managed to almost get bounced out because I got vertigo on two separate occasions on the final instrument check ride. I didn't have any problem with actually flying on instruments in weather that required it. Taking off and landing in fog was relatively easy, but most of the training and the check rides were conducted under a "bag," which simulated instrument conditions when the aircraft was flying above the clouds. The flicker of the sunlight reflection off the rotor blades coming into the side of the "bag" caused me to get vertigo and I simply could not fly through the disorientation. Two downs on the final check rides caused concern at a higher level of command so I had to face an evaluation board to determine if I would get another chance at passing the final check ride and get my wings.

As it turns out, the "Board Members" were more concerned with whether I was intentionally trying to flunk out at the end of the training or if I had a physical defect which would cause vertigo. After answering some questions and going through a new physical, the board scheduled a recheck which I passed with ease since it was an actual IFR day without flicker vertigo conditions.

Danny got his wings and orders to California a month ahead of me, although I entered the helicopter syllabus only a week behind him.

Jeri was there at a happy hour celebration with his Naval Academy contemporaries and other students in his class where she pinned on his wings. When I finally finished the 18-month syllabus, 22 and a half months after I reported, none of the students I had started with were still around. There were a few who didn't make it for one reason or another but most had simply finished the 18-month syllabus in 18 months or less. There were actually some who could not fly—which I found to be incredible, considering my own inabilities but apparently, there are those who just cannot handle the pressure or who do not have the coordination or talent. In any case, there were no old friends with which to celebrate.

When I went to check out, the clerk in the operations division handed me my logbooks, a large brown envelope that contained my orders and a small brown envelope that contained the naval aviator wings. I went to the head, took off my shirt and pinned them on myself. It was April 1965. I would be 26 in another month. Three years older than most of my contemporaries.

The trek to the cherished golden wings included two football seasons, several downs and reflights or rechecks, augmentation to the regular Marine Corps, a promotion to first lieutenant, a divorce, dozens of keg parties, too many women to count and unbelievably another wife—the third, and pregnant—a new car stolen and another new car bought. Oh yeah, when I finally got the MG paid off, I bought a new Pontiac GTO hardtop. The beat up interim 57 Chevy saw me through most of flight school and got me back the same $300 I paid for it, which was enough for the down payment on the new one.

Flight school continued without unusual incidents but Kenneth was in town on two occasions and felt obligated to bring a girlfriend to contribute to the fun. Not the same one each time but both were definitely foxes. Neither could hold a candle to Jamila but it was fun. It didn't last long because when football season was over Jamila decided to get pregnant and went off the pill.

The spring of '65 brought graduation from flight school, naval aviator wings and orders to the Fleet Marine Force in California.

"Did you get your orders," she asked with excited anticipation?

"Yep, pack your bags, my sweet, we're goin' to California."

"Our bags are already packed, Marine. Let's get the hell outa here!" Her smile was huge, her eyes were shining and her nearly seven-month pregnant body was bouncing with joy at the prospect of the new adventure.

Embarkation

Danny and I wound up in the same Air Group but different squadrons after graduation from flight school along with several other friends who had preceded us and shortly afterward, we all embarked on our first deployment to combat in the Fleet Marine Force. The FMF is the active force deployed or ready to deploy anywhere in the world upon very short notice. Much of the FMF is constantly deployed aboard ships in the Far East, the Mediterranean Sea and the Atlantic Ocean as large Marine Expeditionary Forces or smaller Marine Expeditionary Units.

The air field in Tustin, California, was built during World War II as a blimp field. The huge blimp hangars are visible for miles around. They were in use, in 1965, as Marine Corps helicopter squadron facilities and group headquarters for the west coast Helicopter Air Group.

Danny rushed into the pilots Ready Room, "Hey, Pisser, did you know the whole group is gonna ship out for South Vietnam sometime in August?" He was more than a little excited.

"No! When did you find out? How do you know?"

"I overheard the group executive officer talking to the operations officer. They were talking about who they were going to tap to be the group embark officer."

My first FMF squadron was scheduled to embark sometime in late July or early August on the USS *Princeton*, a helicopter aircraft carrier. The deployment was to be a routine rotational replacement of a sister squadron already in South Vietnam as a result of the earlier Gulf of Tonkin incident. However, because of increased enemy activity, President Johnson ordered an even bigger and faster build-up of forces than had already been anticipated.

Our group commander immediately pushed for and eventually received orders for the entire air group to embark on the *Princeton* instead of only our squadron.

"How the hell are we gonna get some 70 odd helicopters, all the motorized support equipment, jeeps, trucks and supplies stored in these huge hangers on one ship plus nearly 500 marines?" I was more than a little perplexed because the USS *Princeton* was a small WWII Essex or Boxer-class aircraft carrier that had been converted to carry one squadron of 20 to 24 helicopters and operate off shore in support of troops on the ground.

"We'll have to squeeze," Danny replied and took a long sip on his coffee. His Naval Academy training had included a lot of background on the capabilities of different kinds of ships and I had virtually none, beyond recognition schooling. The closest I'd come to being on a ship was when I made the six daylight and two night arrested landings on an aircraft carrier, in the T-28, in the training command. The Ready Room began to fill up with pilots coming in for the morning briefing and we took a seat in the back.

"So how do you squeeze three medium helicopter squadrons, a heavy lift squadron, a maintenance squadron, group headquarters, a support squadron and supply personnel with all the equipment and other support into a space usually considered adequate for just one squadron?" I thought maybe Danny had a clearer understanding of the situation.

"Well, we probably won't be operating until we offload, so some of the flight deck and most of the hangar deck can be used for storage of aircraft and equipment, and as for personnel, we'll all have to double or triple up for the trip."

"How long does it take to cross the Pacific?"

"Usually, about three weeks with planned stops for refueling and provisions." It could be done a few days faster by refueling at sea but it wouldn't be necessary unless we were under extraordinary emergency circumstances."

"Wow! Looks like we've got our work cut out for us."

Generally speaking, I love marines. And I love the Marine Corps. That is not to say my love for marines or the Marine Corps is all encompassing. There is a difference. The Marine Corps, as such, sometimes includes some disturbing aspects and attracts a few very nasty, narcissistic and cruel individuals.

Mostly, when I speak of marines, I am referring to the enlisted men and women of the Corps as the individuals who make up the heart of the Marine Corps and the noncommissioned officers—sergeants, staff sergeants and so forth, who along with company grade officers, including aviators, are actually responsible for the daily functioning, operating and fighting of the Marine Corps. I served as an enlisted marine and as a noncommissioned officer in the Marine Corps Reserves with the Fifth Force Reconnaissance Company and as a reserve commissioned officer on active duty until I augmented to the Regular Marine Corps during flight training in the Naval Aviation Flight School.

During my career in the Marine Corps, in the reserves and on active duty, from 1959 to 1981, I served with only three individuals who did not fulfill my expectations of marines, and none of these were enlisted men, noncommissioned officers or junior officers.

I believe a conscientious marine's biggest fear is not being able to live up to the expectations of fellow marines. I know this was my biggest fear when I served as a captain of marines, my favorite rank, or for that matter, as a corporal, lieutenant or major of marines, especially while serving as a commanding officer of a squadron or as an officer in charge of a detachment. In such cases, I told my marines, "Your number one responsibility is to take care of yourselves and each other because if you are wounded or dead you are not able to do your jobs. Following this, it is your duty to do your job to accomplish our mission to the best of your ability while serving our country and our Corps with the utmost loyalty. My job, in addition to being responsible for the accomplishment of our mission, is to take care of you and to see that you have everything you need within reason and every opportunity to do your job well with the least amount of exposure to danger or interference from any outside influence. Anything, other than the enemy, that interferes with the accomplishment of your mission is my responsibility and I will spare no effort to neutralize, or at the very least minimize, the consequence of any such interference."

My marines knew what I meant. If you don't know, you've probably never experienced such things as a shortage of food or water and ammo or to a lesser extent, aircraft parts, truck parts, a warm, dry place to sleep and sometimes to a greater extent, unnecessary and sometimes ridiculous requirements of self-aggrandizing senior officers, or wanna-bees, who may never have experienced an actual day of combat. The latter of these problems is more commonly known as "the shit rolling downhill."

There were major going away parties during the first few days of August 1965, most of which I don't remember but one stood out. A junior officers' party, mostly second lieutenants who had been marine cadets in flight school and junior first lieutenants, like me, who were second lieutenants in flight school and most of whom were still single. It was at a squadron member's beautiful two-story house in Laguna Beach and lasted all one Saturday night. There was no public sex or even much public nakedness although, considering the California beachhouse nature of the location, topless was not really considered nudity and panties are just as good as bikini bottoms, aren't they? There were several instances of girls in skirts flashing above the thigh fur without panties and there were a few girls, including a few wives, who disappeared into upstairs bedrooms, closets and bathrooms for periods of time much longer than necessary to powder their noses. Sometimes their husbands were too drunk to notice or others who maybe didn't care because they were also participating in extra-curricular activities. I recognized one girl and a few pilots, who had participated in similar activities at the "pilot's house" on the beach in Pensacola. I suppose for them, as it was for me, a goodbye party that might be our last goodbye party ever and we didn't want to leave anything on the table, so to speak.

On the loading platform at the docks in Long Beach, on the day of our departure, one of the girls pulled me aside and whispered in my ear. "You're gonna fuck me at the goin' away party and not even kiss me goodbye today?"

I pulled away a little so I could see her face better.

She leaned back, smiled and winked. "Don't tell me you don't remember?"

"Well, honestly, I don't. I had a lot to drink. Are you sure it was me?"

"Yes, I'm sure, you jerk." She chuckled and slugged me in the shoulder. "I sampled a couple of pilots that night but I was very selective about which ones." She chuckled again.

Nicely dressed in a crop top and short skirt, she was at least a 3-T, maybe a 4-T. "Tits, Toned, Tanned and maybe Talented" as the good old boys used to say. Tits firm, and not too big, nice shape with good muscle Tone, smooth, nicely Tanned skin and possibly Talented. All the prerequisites of a perfect beach bunny. *Was she a Pensacola girl who'd been dragged to California just to be left all alone out here during the deployment?*

"Wow, sweetie, I'm not happy I don't remember, but listen, don't wear it out while we're gone. I'd like to come back and try it again sober, so I can remember it."

"Well, that's part of the whole scenario. Isn't it? I did it because, first, you guys probably, or at least maybe, won't come back and secondly, if you do come back, you might not be stationed here in California. And lastly, I wouldn't do it sober."

"Aaaah . . . but you were sober enough to remember what you were doing and who you were doing it with."

"Yes, but I had enough drinks to loosen up my inhibitions and besides, I was into the mind-set of the party, thinking we probably wouldn't ever see you guys again."

"You might be surprised. Marines sometimes have a way of surviving when you least expect it, and of course, we all think we're invincible."

"Okay then, I'll save some just for you, Marine—if you get back you can count on it."

"Great! I'll hold you to it then." She was a great package. I did notice her wedding rings. I wish I could remember whose wife she was and what it was like to be with her at the party, if it was really me. *Will I be one of the ones to come home? Will I ever see her again? If I do, will she still be with the same man, widowed or divorced?*

"So kiss me good-bye, Marine!" she yelled. She threw herself at me and locked her arms around my neck and her lips around my tongue and I thought she was going to suck it out.

Jamila finished saying goodbye to someone else and came back to me. She'd lost all the baby fat and regained her tiny waist in just six weeks. She looked fabulous and the sting of leaving her was very strong. She gave me a little box and said, "It's just a card, a nude Polaroid and some panties." Think of me out looking for doubles when you masturbate." She laughed wickedly.

"Ooooh, you are the devil! I'm so jealous it cramps my stomach. You be careful, darlin'."

"I'll be careful. I went back on the pill before the party last week. You're the one who needs to be careful and make sure you come back to me."

"That's not what I meant, but I'm glad to hear it, considering what I saw at that party. You just be careful who you meet up with."

"So you were watching me?" She smiled.

"Of course, I'm always watching you. You're beautiful in action even when I'm not the one doin' it."

"You're getting me excited talkin' like that, Bobby. You're not jealous?"

"I'm jealous now that I'm leaving because you're gonna probably get all you want any time you want it while I'm gone but I wasn't jealous at the party—I was also busy—apparently busier than I even remember and you're not jealous?"

"No, of course I'm not jealous! We're both doin' what we like to do. I'm a big girl, Bobby. You know I prefer marines, so how bad could it be?"

"Marines can be just as crazy as anyone else, if not worse, Jamila. Just look at me!"

"Well, I love my crazy marine and I want him back. Promise me you'll be careful."

It was the first time she had ever even mentioned love. "I promise I'll do my job the best I can and do my best to come home. I love you too, Jamila, my beauty, and our little girl." *I supposed there might be a spot of unbroken heart with room to love. Not a big enough spot to allow hope for the permanent kind of love that goes along with "until death do us part," but a spot for love like puppy love or love of life or love of a beautiful woman or of a baby . . . the committee contemplated.*

Transpac

As it turned out, loading into the tight quarters on the *Princeton* wasn't as tough as we thought it might be. A second lieutenant, who was a former enlisted, embarkation NCO, had been assigned as the embarkation officer for our squadron and was tapped to become the officer in charge of the task for the whole group. Although there were doubts all the way from the lowest to the highest, the ship's captain, our group CO, and an experienced former NCO got the job done. In fact, when all was said and done there was room enough for the aircraft elevator to operate, limited flight operations on the flight deck and a volleyball court on the hanger deck.

I wound up with two other junior officers in quarters, which would usually have been for one senior officer or two junior officers, but we had plenty of space. Our cabin was all the way forward on the starboard side, just below the anchor chain housing and had a port hole that looked almost straight down at the wake peeling off the starboard bow. The space contained two racks in a bunk bed stacked on the inboard side of the room and a single rack built-in on the curved outboard side. There was a small locker on the forward bulkhead by the entry hatch where a few items could be hung and a set of six built-in drawers on the rear bulkhead. A steel sink with a mirror above provided a shaving station.

I arrived at the room first and threw my bag on the single rack next to a port hole which caused a fight with Sammy when he arrived.

"What the hell you mean you'll take that rack? What makes you feel entitled?"

"Nothing, Sammy. I was just thinking I fit it better. The top rack on the other side is close to the ceiling and looks really small for my size and the bottom rack is also a little short as well."

"Bullshit! I'm senior and I'm takin' that rack and you can find other quarters if you don't like it."

First day, first hour, first minute in close quarters. This might be a long voyage. He tried to reach around me to pull my bag off the rack but I stepped up and blocked him from getting to the bag. Sammy's wiry build with tight muscles on a smaller frame made him quick and troublesome to manage but his lighter weight limited his ability to control a fighting situation. He tried again to push past me so I shoved him across the room.

"Sammy, cut it out! Knock it off! You're no match for me and you're gonna get hurt if you don't stop!"

He lunged at me across the room flailing his arms. I stepped in, blocked the wild swings and he lost his balance. I tried to catch him but his head hid the corner of the bulk head at the built-in drawers. His knees buckled and he crumpled down and went out immediately.

Harvey, our other roommate, as well as my former roommate during part of Flight School, entered the quarters right at the end of the fray. "What the devil is going on here?"

"He wanted to fight over the bunk by the port hole," I explained motioning to the lump on the deck with his head leaning against the wall and my leg.

"Not very smart." He smiled. "He's bleeding, you know."

"I know, wet the towel by the sink and hand it to me will ya, Harvey? I'll hold him so he doesn't fall farther down and hurt himself more than he already has."

"Okay." Harvey wiped the cut with the wet towel and wiped away the blood dripping down his cheek. "He's probably gonna need stitches on this eyebrow."

"Yep, I'll take him to Sickbay when he wakes up. Throw a cup of water on his face and see if he comes around."

"Hey, what the fuck!" Sammy awoke confused by the water and his position on the floor.

"Take it easy Sammy. You've fallen and hit your head. We're gonna take you to Sickbay. You're probably gonna need some stitches."

"What happened?" he demanded.

"Well, you were angry and wanted to try to take this bunk away from me. You lunged across the room at me, fell, hit your head and knocked yourself out. C'mon now, get up and we'll get you to Sickbay."

The rest of the transpacific trip was mostly uneventful. We stopped in Hawaii for about six hours for the ship's supply replenishment so we headed for Waikiki Beach to hit the bars with the intent of getting totally wacked out drunk as quickly as possible. Danny and I ordered two double rum and Cokes each, and the waitress commented, "You two are in a pretty big hurry?"

"Yep," Danny replied. "There's no booze allowed on the ship and we're not sure where we're going next or how long it will be before we'll be able to hook up with our next drink."

"You're off the *Princeton*?" The question was more rhetorical than quizzical.

"How'd you know?" I jumped in, surprised.

She smiled knowingly. "We know about all of the ships coming in and out of the harbor. You'll need to be getting back pretty soon."

I went to take some photos of the beach for "cruise book memories" and when I returned the four drinks were on the table. Danny had already drunk half of his first one. Our waitress came back to the table with another waitress and they each had a Lei which they presented to us—light green petals that smelled really fresh and strong and felt more like thick leaves than flowers.

"We know where you're going and what you'll be doing. God bless you for serving our country. These are for good luck on your voyage," she said. She put the string of strong sweet smelling green leaf flowers around Danny's neck and leaned over to kiss him and her companion did the same to me. It was not a little peck on the cheek. No, it was a full on surprise like a hot lover's kiss of hello and goodbye. Standing back then, she looked from him to me, and back again and said in a shaky emotional voice. "These Leis should be tossed on the ocean from the boat after you leave the harbor. If they float to shore it means you will return to Hawaii someday. If you see them sink you will not return." A tear formed in the corner of her eye and dripped slowly down her cheek. She wiped it quickly and turned abruptly away.

While I am not one to believe in this kind of fable, when the ship pulled out of the harbor, Danny and I went to the fantail and offered our Leis to the ocean and watched them float as long as we could as the day faded to night behind us and we sailed west into the sun setting over the Far East.

While en route to the Philippines, we found out our landing site and airfield at Ky Ha, South Vietnam, would not be ready for us by the end of August, as our commander had planned. The Seabees were there starting to build it but very little had been completed. The landing site would be fully graded but there would only be time enough to lay about half the steel matting. Also, the marine ground units in the area did not have enough men to carry out their operations and provide security for us. Our aircraft, equipment and our personnel would be at the mercy of the enemy and the elements.

"That's pretty scary shit, Captain." I was called to the admin office and informed I would be assigned as a platoon commander for our perimeter defense company. What I originally thought would be a benefit to my career, my training with the Fifth Force Recon Company Reserves, turned out to be a thorn in my side. Not only was I not going to fly, but I would be assigned to a position for which I felt mostly unprepared.

Nonetheless, I resigned myself to do the best job I could and began by meeting with the temporary officer in charge of the company. He was temporary, because after we landed in Ky Ha, a captain from the combat ground unit in the area who would be reporting to his regular ground force's chain of command would replace him. Our platoon and two other platoons formed by our sister squadrons would be formed as a company and assigned to a larger force.

It was decreed so and so it would be. Our group CO had taken each challenge in stride and provided solutions to them all. When the navy said, "We don't have transport for your entire air group to go to Vietnam." He said, "We'll all fit on the transport available." When the Navy Seabees said, "We can't have your airfield finished, your hardback tents erected, your mess hall ready or even your outhouses built by the time you're planning to be here," he said, "We'll build it ourselves. We'll live in our own tents, cook our own meals, dig our own trenches and fox holes and fill our own sand bags." When the Marine Corps combat commander said, "We can't provide security for your base. He said, "We'll provide our own defense." When the I Corps administration headquarters said, "We can't provide security screening for indigenous personnel to work on your base. He said,

"We don't need indigenous personnel to work on our base. In fact, no indigenous personnel will be allowed on our base ever, as long as I am in command. We'll cook our own meals, wash our own pots and pans, utensils, plates and cups, wash and dry our own laundry and cut our own hair."

My platoon sergeant, a staff sergeant from our squadron Maintenance Section, somehow came up with an M-1 Carbine as my personal weapon. The TO, Table of Organization, called for my weapon, as a platoon commander, to be a .45-caliber semiautomatic pistol, but none were available. Thank God. I couldn't hit anything with a .45 and the TO .38-caliber pistol I'd been issued as a pilot was a joke.

The sergeant and I spent the better part of our first week together going over the records of the men we were assigned and interviewing each one. We were able to get to know them a little and swap out a few. A couple we thought might not be totally suited for the job and we were asked to give a couple back to the squadron because they were shorthanded in their specialty in the maintenance department.

My platoon was mentally prepared, if not physically trained, to lead a practice assault landing on a beach in Okinawa. Yes, because I was deemed to be the "most experienced platoon commander" my platoon would comprise the first assault wave. Thankfully, by the time we got to Okinawa, Japan the practice assault was cancelled. The ground commander in Vietnam convinced our CO it wouldn't be necessary. He assured us the area was secure and our landing would be unopposed. However, even though the landing was supposed to be unopposed, the assault order didn't change and we were told to be prepared, in case there were any *surprises*. The new scenario didn't do much to alleviate the anxiety of sitting on the boat for two more weeks waiting.

Debarkation

As the sun rose behind us off the coast of South Vietnam on the 30th of August 1965, my platoon loaded onto eight of our squadron's helicopters for transport to the beach. The aircraft would land in a mostly flat area about four hundred yards wide located just west of steep cliffs 60 to 80 feet above the shoreline and 75 to 100 yards from the irregular beach. The area between the beach and the cliffs was overgrown with dense brush and trees. The ocean lapped at the edge of the white sandy beach about 30 yards from the tree line as we crossed.

"Feet dry!" Our crew chief yelled, as if we couldn't see out the open hatch. The pilot had already started to slow for the approach to a straight in landing onto the big open field.

Beautiful! Is it high or low tide? The marine amphibious landing at Tarawa crossed my mind where thousands of marines died in an assault because the tide was low and the amphibious assault vehicles got stuck hundreds of yards from the shoreline. The marines had to wade to the shore in chest high water and mud. I dismissed it. Then came to mind a helicopter assault last spring by our sister squadron into a valley which was thoroughly bombarded by artillery and air to ground attack aircraft which seemed to have had very little effect judging by the intense fire and loss of aircraft in the initial landings. Iwo Jima also came to mind but was again quickly dismissed—this landing was supposed to be in a friendly, secure area. We anticipated very little, if any resistance. *Yeah, right. The brain committee was restless and nervous.*

West of the landing area a dirt road traversed the site from south to north toward a peninsula running northeasterly with a river on the northerly side and the ocean on the southerly and easterly perimeters. The tip of the peninsula was occupied and secured by a Navy Construction Battalion, Seabees. West of the dirt road the terrain rose at about a 20-degree angle to a soft ridge line on which a large radar site was located to the south. This would be part of the support for the fixed-wing marine air base at Chi Lai, farther south, which should also have been secure. The marine ground unit with which we would hook up was located west of the ridge line, and the nearby village of Ky Ha would be included within the area of responsibility. Pertaining to the makeup of the villagers, an intelligence briefing did not seem to be available, but as a matter of deduction, the only area that was not determined to be secured by friendly forces would be the cliffs east of our landing area and the overgrown area between the cliffs and the shoreline.

As a result of site and situation analysis our plan was to set up a perimeter line of defense along the top of the cliffs looking eastward out to sea across the dense vegetation below. Hopefully, we would be able to connect with other defense forces in the area—the Seabees on our northeastern flank, the Chu Lai support group on our southern flank and the marine ground units would protect our rear on the other side of the ridge line to our west. What none of us recognized—not even the most senior warrior among us—was the mobile aspect of this new kind of warfare.

There was no one there to greet us when we landed. Not even a friendly face, let alone an enemy. It was like we were landing in a wheat field at home. The choppers landed. We jumped out into the knee length wavy grass and moved away from the rotors. The choppers left to return to the ship for other loads as the rest of the air group personnel, equipment and supplies would all be moved ship to shore all day.

The noisy helicopters left a silence in the landing zone which was broken only by the distant lap of small waves on the sandy beach about a hundred yards to the east. No enemy, at least no enemy small arms fire. That was great news! But maybe they were watching? If the area was secure, why wasn't there someone here to meet us and point out where we should set the north and south ends of our perimeter?

My platoon was supposed to be on the northern end of the line in close proximity to the Seabees. Where the hell were they?

Nervously, I began to move my marines into a ragged line along the ridge at the top of the cliffs and set up interlocking fields of fire overlooking the thick brush and trees directly below and out toward the shoreline. The irregularity of the cliffs caused some of the lines of fire to overlap friendly positions, so we drove stakes at the limits by the foxholes so we wouldn't shoot at each other at night. The second wave of our assault landed and the Second Platoon, as it was now known, joined up on our flank to the south and we coordinated our lines of fire with them. We each had three M-60 machine gun crews so we set ours within each of the three squads. We needed to get ourselves into a good defensive position and dig in before nightfall.

All marines are riflemen first, and it was obvious our marines had not forgotten this basic premise. They efficiently dug in, filled their sandbags, fortified their foxholes and cut down brush to clear their fields of fire. They dug their own latrines, ate when we brought the C-rations from the continuing stream of aircraft arriving, pitched their shelter-halves two by two, took breaks, smoked, sent some men for water—all on their own. Basic guidance was all they needed. Set your line here, coordinate there, get it done before nightfall. They were all specifically trained to repair hydraulics, electronics, engines, transmissions, rotor heads, avionics and sheet metal—virtually everything that could possibly require their specialties, but they accepted their fate, albeit sometimes grudgingly, to be the safety net for the rest of the group.

I set my own half of a shelter with the open side facing the ocean and dug a small foxhole on the open side—to fight from if necessary but also in case of a mortar attacks. By sundown it was all done. I inspected the perimeter the troops had built and made a few small adjustments to more safely prevent the overlap of firing lines. First nights can be precarious—first time in a combat situation, first night in a strange environment, a lot of firsts. It would be a moonless night and we were just as likely to shoot each other as we were to have to defend ourselves against an enemy. I wanted them to relax as much as possible and not be nervous or trigger happy.

"You are professional marines," I said. "You have remembered your skills as basic marines like you just got out of the Infantry

Training Regiment." They had done an excellent job, and as I watched the ships anchored off shore from where we had come, I felt a great sense of pride in my marines, and I was proud to be their leader. I hope I don't have to write condolence letters home for any them.

The next few weeks we diligently maintained our perimeter defense but began to leave only skeleton squads on duty during the day so we could rotate into the work sections in the squadrons. However, my marines were allocated to aircraft maintenance duty with our sister squadrons since the rest of our squadron was sent to billet at Da Nang Air Base. Our CO tried to squirrel us away from perimeter defense duty altogether and take us to Da Nang but was not successful until the squadron was later detached to work for the army farther south in Qui Nhon.

Our company commander, the grunt captain, who shall remain nameless, only because I can't remember it, wanted us to do night patrols in the bushes between our cliffs and the beach to preempt surprise attacks.

"Captain, I know such maneuvers are perfectly within the capability of my marines but it is beyond my comfort level. They've had no training for several years while we were all in school for and practicing our aviation specialties and I've had essentially none other than Officer Candidate School at Quantico."

"What about the Fifth Force Recon?"

Another one who had perused my qualification jacket. "It was in the reserves, Captain, and other than Jump School, it was mostly classroom work about what to look for on a reconnaissance mission and learning the ability to subsist behind enemy lines for long periods of time without being discovered. There was some training in controlling and spotting for artillery and air support but mostly, the weekend training was about discipline—close order drill, uniform maintenance, personal conduct, weapons knowledge and marksmanship. I don't recall any training in scouting or patrolling. I don't feel adequately trained to lead a patrol myself or to provide training for my marines."

"Why do you keep calling them your marines, Lieutenant?"

"Because I am responsible for them, sir. If they get wounded or killed, I'm the one who has to write the letters home. I hope I don't ever have to, but I will if eventually I must, but I will do my best to resist ordering them to risk doing something I feel is not necessary, or they are not prepared to properly accomplish or, as in this case, both."

"What do you mean both?" He looked at me quizzically.

"Well, I believe it is not necessary and won't accomplish anything worth the risk and I feel we are not professionally ready for such a mission."

"Okay, but what if I feel it is necessary and order the patrols?" He had not ceased the direct eye contact and I held his steady gaze as the anger welled up in my gut.

"Sir, I would then respectfully request, since the captain believes there may be enemy troops there, we should have daylight anti-mine sweeps of the area, by an experienced, operational mine sweeping unit, before we go night patrolling."

"Fine, you draw up the map overlay for a patrol route in front of the perimeter and I'll see about getting a mine sweep of the area," he said, turning his head away and shrugging slightly.

"Yes, sir. Does the captain require an overlay for the area east of the entire perimeter or just in front of my platoon?"

"Do the whole perimeter in front of all three platoons and we'll rotate each platoon over the whole area."

"Yes, sir. Has the captain spoken to the other platoon commanders already?" I could tell I was testing his patience.

"No, I'll inform them later he said emphatically. We'll have a meeting with the officers and staff. Your group headquarters is providing me with an executive officer and a first sergeant tomorrow."

"A first sergeant?"

"Well, a senior staff NCO to act as first sergeant." He appeared impatient again.

I recognized, as if I hadn't suspected all along, this captain was an "Empire Builder." He wasn't satisfied with being the commander of a perimeter defense company. He had to have a staff and be planning and executing and making waves for the purpose of stirring the pot and being noticed.

Thus came about my first face to face personal meeting with the group CO. Known affectionately as King William, he was a colonel and a commander who took great interest in the wellbeing of his junior officers and men. The day after the meeting with my company commander, I inquired of the group administrative officer, who was a lieutenant colonel doing admin work, while waiting for a squadron CO position.

"Good morning, sir. Is the colonel busy?"

"I'm always busy, Lieutenant," he said pleasantly. "But what can I do for you?"

"Sir, I'm the CO of the First Platoon on perimeter defense and I was wondering, will the XO and first sergeant for the Perimeter Defense Company come from one of the squadrons or from the group headquarters?"

He looked at me like I had more than a few screws loose. "What the fuck are you talkin' about, Lieutenant?"

"The grunt CO, the captain, said the group was going to provide his staff, which would include an XO, probably a senior first lieutenant or a junior captain and a senior staff NCO to be his acting first sergeant."

"Well, this is the first I've heard of it."

"Oh shit! I guess I'm out of bounds, Colonel. Forget I said anything, and if there's any discussion, please leave me out of it."

"Okay, I'll leave you out of it but I'm glad for the heads up. I can be prepared to protect my own assets from being squirreled away."

"Speaking of assets, does the colonel know if the captain has spoken to the CO or operations officer about sending our perimeter defense troops out on night patrols?"

"Night patrols! Is he nuts? Night patrols with greenhorn pilots and aviation mechanics? He must be out of his fucking mind."

"I've asked for him to get the grunts to do a daylight mine sweep of the trails out there before we go traipsing around in the dark, sir."

"Holy fucking cow! What the hell are you thinking, Lieutenant?"

"Sir, I'm thinking, my platoon is assigned to his company—we're working under his orders. He's directed me to draw up map overlays for night patrols in front of our defense perimeter, and if he orders my platoon to conduct those night patrols, then I suppose we'll be conducting night patrols. Some of these men haven't even been on a training patrol since they were just out of boot camp, which may have been two or three years ago, before they were school-trained for aviation jobs. I don't want my marines out on combat night patrols without any recent training so I'll be taking them out myself."

The colonel seemed to slow down and consider what was happening. "Lieutenant . . . wait here! I'll see if the CO wants to hear about this now."

The brain committee panicked, Oh shit! What have we done?

A few minutes later, the group CO came rolling slowly out of his office like a wary bulldog cagily checking the surroundings for danger. "What's your name, Lieutenant?" He put both hands on his hips, raised one bushy eyebrow high into his wrinkled forehead and stared inquisitively in my direction.

"Pincer, sir. First Platoon commander in the Perimeter Defense Company, sir."

"What's this I'm hearing from the XO? You've been ordered to do night patrols beyond our perimeter?"

"Not yet, sir, but that's what's in the works for the near future. The company CO has directed me to do some map overlays for night patrol routes."

"You people are on perimeter defense and you will man defensive positions on the perimeter only, unless you hear otherwise from this headquarters. Is that understood, Lieutenant?"

"Yes, sir."

I chuckled inwardly as I strolled back down the hill to my cozy little shelter half on the cliff. I had a good view of the woods and thick brush between the beach and us. It would be nice to know if the area was secure. It would be a great beach for swimming and sunbathing.

The officer's meeting with the grunt CO was cancelled. All I know is when the other platoon commanders and I showed up at the captain's tent, as scheduled, he wasn't there. The general purpose tent served as his office and his living quarters, but no one was there. No CO. No new XO. No new first sergeant. Just an empty tent. A sergeant, in a supply tent a few yards away, said, "He was called to his grunt CO's headquarters. A jeep came to pick him up early this morning. He said he'll be back later today."

Apparently, King William had become concerned about risking his aviation assets. No one mentioned night patrols again while I was with the Perimeter Defense Company, but our platoon was pulled out a few weeks later when our squadron was detached to go to Qui Nhon to support the 101st Air Cavalry and the Korean army.

Qui Nhon

When our perimeter defense platoon rejoined our squadron in Da Nang I was more than ready to become reacquainted with my oversize footlocker—a large steamer trunk donated by a kind old lady in Santa Ana. It was black like most of the other trunks but I painted a big red ribbon around it and a red bow on top so I could recognize it among the hundreds to be off-loaded and here it was. The last time I'd seen it was when I finally found it in the ships storage hold so I could put away the box Jamila had given me at the loading dock. It appeared like magic in my assigned space alongside a cot in an open concrete bay with about 13 other cots. I silently gave thanks to my loyal contemporaries who'd looked out for me and made sure my gear didn't get lost. Sleeping on a cot would be a whole lot better than sleeping on the ground under half a pup tent on the cliffs overlooking the beach in Ky Ha.

"Don't unpack." The greeting came from the bunk next to mine. "We're leaving for Qui Nhon in two days."

"Where the hell is Qui Nhon?"

"It's down the coast to the south—about 45 miles south of Ky Ha. Maybe about 85 miles from here. It's in II Corps."

Our new quarters or "hooch," as it was called in those days, was framed with two-by-four studs covered halfway up the outside with sheets of newly cut, fresh-smelling plywood. The remainder of the wall, between the plywood and the roofline, had a steel-gray screen wire, which provided ventilation, but there were plywood covers on hinges, which could be closed when it rained.

It rained often year round but almost incessantly during the monsoon season. The corrugated tin roof roared like a drum during a downpour. We joked about our "vaulted silver ceilings" referring to the open space between the beams and the roof. The sandy colored plywood floors creaked under the strain of our steps and we sometimes tripped on the uneven seams, especially if we had been at the bar too long.

Both ends of the building contained heavy, wood framed, screen doors with heavy springs to keep them shut without having to latch them. We rigged hooks so we could lock the war out when we wanted. A futile effort of course, since the concertina wire separating us from the war at large was only 30 feet from our north door. Between the doors was an open bay which had become our home for the foreseeable future and we took some pride in making it so.

There were ten of us neatly arranged and spaced with left over World War II "army" cots. Half of the "racks" were pushed head-in against each of the long side walls, creating about four feet of aisle space, between the feet. Green air mattresses, nicknamed "rubber ladies," provided a comfortable, although usually hot, cushion. There were even sheets between our often sweaty bodies and the rubber ladies. The final touch on top was a brand-new dark green, blanket with USMC printed in black in the middle of one end. This logo went at the foot of the rack because the head would be folded down just below the pillow showing the traditional four inches of sheet. Yes, there were even pillows. *Someone must have thought we were in the air force.* I felt very guilty about our "real" marines being out there in the jungles and mud.

Since we embarked on a ship rather than by air, we had been allowed to bring along a foot locker in addition to our duffle bag and flight bag. The duffle and flight bags were easily folded uniformly and stowed properly beneath the cots but the foot lockers, of many varied types and origins, presented unique opportunities for decor. Since we were not issued official foot lockers we went on last minute scrounge missions to gather up as many travel trunks or fruit crates as we could find in Southern California in the summer of '65. Many people, when they found out we were headed for combat, and supporting the war at the time, gave us their old travel trunks. These treasured gifts were arranged in a variety of ways between the cots which provided for unique settings and personality quirks in our now semi permanent quarters.

Each pilot could claim about three feet between his cot and the cot next to him. Only three feet on just one side of the rack but we made the most of it. I was on the end of the row so I shoved out a few inches more. I stood my huge trunk on end with the lid open to the right side at about a 45-degree angle and put my shaving gear and books on top. Ironically, as it turned out, "Catch 22" was among them. The trunk was so large it looked almost like a regular locker when turned on end. The spray painted big red bow on its aged ebony skin provided a colorful and practical addition to my space. I could hang up my uniform shirt inside and it barely touched the bottom. I was very proud of my neat and matchless space and immediately proceeded to the officers' bar to toast my accomplishment.

Most of us had pictures of girlfriends or wives and some had young kids. Some were in frames on top of orange crates or the make-shift foot lockers and some were pinned or taped to the walls. On one end of the room we put up a plywood "Beaver Board" covered mostly with cutouts of *Playboy* centerfolds, but our girlfriends were also encouraged to send nudes or semi nudes. They sent sultry topless bikini shots and a few exceptionally sensual negligees or nudes. It was the '60s sexual revolution, after all. Those who made the grade were honored with anonymous special notice and accolades. In the box Jamila had given me when we left was a nearly nude Polaroid photo that showed her face, so I didn't put it on the Beaver Board. However, she did send a "Boobs and Beaver Only" shot just for that purpose and it was anonymously posted to great applause and celebration.

My cot was on the other end of the building from the infamous beavers next to Tom Byrd on my right and Noah Kraft at my feet across the aisle. It was comfortable to have them there. We were all first lieutenants and helicopter pilots and knew each other from flight school although Noah and T-Byrd were a few months ahead of me. Most of the students were 21 or 22 years old when they started flight school but I was two and a half years older, having spent an extra two years in college and an extra six months in flight school because of football schedules.

We were all from different parts of the country and all different types of colleges and two were from the Naval Academy. Most were reserves, two were regulars but all were volunteers for the Marine Corps and most were volunteers for combat. We had all been through the same 12-week Officer Candidate School at Quantico, Virginia but at different times and through various commissioning programs and some went through the six-month Basic School, also located at Quantico, although I didn't.

Noah was the only Jewish marine I knew, or at least that I knew I knew, and I thought Noah was a nickname. "It must be," I thought. *"Who in the modern world would name a baby Noah?"* His demeanor was studious and serious but he always had a smile and a pleasant greeting for everyone. We kept our hair very short in accordance with regulations but Noah's curly black hair and dark eyebrows formed distinctive outlines around his angular face and kind, brown eyes.

The drab tan color of our flight suits was supposed to be a camouflage of sorts and was absolutely less noticeable than the bright "rescue orange" we had worn back in the world in training. The color would blend well with the dry rice paddies or the sandy beaches but was not very adaptable to jungle green. It came in the usual sizes, 36, 38, 40 and so forth, according to chest size, with adjustable Velcro waist tabs and in small, medium and long. Noah's flight suit hung as if on a hanger, loose on his boney frame. A little too long, it draped over the arches of his flight boots as well.

Noah didn't drink but would hang out at the officers' bar for happy hour and sometimes join in conversations if the guys were still sober enough and if the subjects were interesting or important enough. He didn't say much, but when he weighed in, it was usually with an opinion grounded in astute knowledge. Most of the time his faraway look seemed to reveal he was thinking of someone, something, or somewhere else. Maybe we were all somewhere a little out of our bodies, but I noticed it more with Noah.

T-Bird was a livelier entity. His fervor for life was more extroverted but he was not overbearing or unpleasant. His demeanor was pleasant and he took his responsibilities seriously, as did we all, when it came to our primary duty as pilots. His flight suit was the same size as Noah's but he filled it out more fully in the shoulders and hips and being a little taller, it wasn't too long for his height. He and Noah often flew together as HAC (helicopter aircraft commander/pilot and

H2P, helicopter second pilot) although they swapped roles as HAC or H2P according to the designation in the daily flight schedule.

On my left next to the north wall, which we called the back door, was an open space reserved for our maid, La'nh Tien, meaning Gentle Spirit or Gentle Angel. We shortened her name to Lan, without the accent, which literally meant *orchid*, but we thought it meant *angel*. It seemed she didn't mind when we incorrectly spoke, as she responded quietly, and in near perfect English. She spoke with a slight accent, probably learned from the French nuns, who had remained in the country following World War II.

"Good morning, sir." She smiled sweetly, turning her smooth, luminous, unvarnished face away while still engaging our eyes directly with her tantalizing almond-brown orbs. Her youthful shyness turned us geographic bachelors to butter.

Her long black hair usually hung straight down, except, while she was working, she pinned up in a swirl—with what looked like a painted chop stick with colorful little beads and decorative glass. I thought to myself, if she wore it in a ponytail, my favorite hair style, it would be longer than any I'd ever seen.

Lan's traditional *ao ba ba* clothes consisted of a pair of long white silk pants fitted at the waist and hips and flowing outward from the knees into billowed bottoms just below her ankles, exposing her tiny feet and leather thongs. The top, worn over a white silk backless camisole, was a fitted, embroidered, long sleeved jacket also made of white silk. It buttoned down the front to the waist of her small, thin, not quite frail body, and flared out slightly just over and beyond her hips. She wore almost the same thing every day, although the jacket was lighter, more like a shirt, in warmer weather, but in any case, it was always spotless and wrinkle-free.

We gave her a wooden crate we scrounged from the mess hall, which she stood on one end, in the corner, where she kept her iron and cleaning equipment. She covered the front with some kind of white cloth—almost like cheese cloth. A large nail, stuck in a two by four stud, above the crate, made a hook where she hung her ao ba ba jacket while she worked.

If she were there when we were off duty or when we were allowed to sleep late, after night flying, she would be in her space, kneeling beside a long wooden box, ironing our sheets, or rolling our socks and folding our skivvies, t-shirts and flight suits. She swept and scrubbed the floors and made the beds as neat as any marine barracks squad bay. We only described her regular duties once and never had to mention them again. She was vigilant and punctual and we knew we could depend on her.

She didn't have to iron our uniforms very often because we only wore them for R & R, which happened only once for each pilot during a normal thirteen-month tour but if we needed her for ironing or other favors she would gladly oblige with a little bow and a sweet smile . . . for a few extra Piasters. She was the keeper of our home away from home, the meat of our fantasies and often the subject of our dreams as well.

As I left for *Rest and Recuperation*, in Taiwan, I yelled and waved at T-Bird, Noah and Captain Matt Lucas, who were throwing a football between the north side of the building and the perimeter fence, "See ya later!"

Rest And Recuperation

Taiwan was a bustling Island in 1966. It had been recently opened up to Rest & Recuperation for troops in Vietnam and the city of Taipei was replete with servicemen of every stripe and congested with every product, service or game imaginable with the primary goal of parting visitor and money. The streets were full of vendors and the bars were full of women. It was a party atmosphere everywhere I turned and all I wanted was some peace and quiet times with a bottle of American bourbon, some good old American Coca-Cola and a sensuous woman.

I barely knew my traveling partner because he had joined the squadron while I was on perimeter defense. We made a simple plan on the way on the commercial chartered plane. Get drunk, get laid and take whatever comes from there. As it turned out, it was not as simple as it sounded. The newly opened city was overwhelmed with the arrival of many more visitors than the facilities could handle. We found several bars that had plenty of booze, of course, and American bourbon was available but expensive and standing room only. There were plenty of women, needless to say, and beautiful but there were almost no hotel rooms available for overnight stays. One or two hours was possible but expensive, and the girls were also expensive. Not so expensive that we would pass up the opportunity but more than we could afford on a daily basis for the duration of the trip. We finally found a two room suite with twin beds in the bedroom with a couch in the living room that we could afford so we could have at least a little separate space.

Charlie and I were both pretty big guys and the Chinese girls were so tiny it seemed like the mismatch would be way too much for them to handle. Not so, however; it turns out the tiny little girls were tight but plenty big enough inside to handle us and probably whatever else came down the pike. My lady had an American hairstyle with soft black curls that hung down past her shoulders. She was wearing silk, as were all of the other girls. She was very pretty and cute but I picked her mostly because of her great smile. She reminded me of Lan. She spoke very little English and I didn't speak a word of Chinese but that night was one I'd looked forward to for a long time and verbal communications were almost totally unnecessary.

We knew we couldn't afford to stay in the city so the next morning as we headed out we began looking for alternatives. The English speaking hostess at the hotel said, "A relatively inexpensive taxi ride or an even less expensive bus ride would get you to a quiet resort area known as Peitou. It's in a valley surrounded on three sides by mountains and has a natural hot springs stream running through it. It has several hotels along the winding road up the hill, which are priced based on the distance from the hot water stream and the view of the valley, with the lowest prices at the bottom of the hill and the higher prices toward the top."

"Like what can we expect to find as a range?

"It's less expensive than it is here because of the demand, and as you might expect, as you move up the hill, the amenities are also more expensive but the range for a nice size two-bedroom suite about halfway up the hill would probably be around twenty-five dollars American each, for all of the amenities, including the women."

"Including the women? That's incredible!"

"Yes, and you wouldn't be allowed to bring outside women in there, like you did here."

Charlie chimed in, "Wow! Are there other amenities included?"

She chuckled. "Breakfast, dinner, beer, rice wine and soft drinks are all included but if you want hard liquor you have to buy it here and take it with you."

"The price is very good, but are the accommodations good? We're coming from tents or wood shacks with tin roofs, so we're not gonna be real picky, but would it be clean? And," in a softer voice I asked, "the quality of the women?"

She chuckled again quietly and also blushed a little. "Yes, of course, I wouldn't recommend it otherwise. It was built by the Japanese when they took over the Island of Formosa, as it was called then. They built it back in the late 1800's and early 1900's and upgraded it before and during World War II for R & R for the Japanese pilots. The locals have kept it up since and turned it into a really nice resort area. If you like hot tubs, sauna and massage they are the best and uh . . . well . . . the women there are very pretty, maybe even prettier than here in the city and more controlled by the hotel owners. And much more likely to be free of disease," she added quickly.

Charlie was already nodding his head like there was no question in his mind and there certainly wasn't in mine. "We should get a cab, hit the package store, grab some booze and head for Peitou," I suggested.

"Of course," he agreed, as if there is no doubt and no discussion required.

A taxi driver that spoke a little English, two bottles of bourbon and a small duffle bag in hand found us about half way up the hill just off Guangming Road overlooking the steamy valley of Peitou. We could see the vapor rising from the stream as it wound its way down between the lush green foliage and the meandering rock waterfalls that were obviously introduced to control and form the shape and speed of the water. The cabdriver had recommended the small, maybe ten-room hotel because, "The rooms are large and very clean, the food is great, the mama-san speaks English and is very nice and the women are beautiful!"

"Are you related? I queried.

"No, No," he quickly replied, shaking his head. "I'm not related but I know them well. I live nearby and I've known them all my life. They are good people! They will treat you very, very good. I promise!"

"Okay"—I smiled and nodded—"we'll check it out."

"If you don't like it, I will take you wherever you want to go for free. Okay?

"Sure, with that kind of recommendation, how can we refuse?"

The Japanese influence on the culture of the little Chinese resort community was evident not only in the slang of the language but everywhere we looked. The architectural style, miniature gardens with tiny trees, colorful and finely trimmed flowers enriched the exterior of the property and the landscape. Colorful art enhanced the walls, printed rice paper art and other wall décor and design all pointed to the heritage of the invaders.

He was right. The place could not have been more perfect. The price was right and Mama-san was very nice. She showed us to a large suite with comfortable living room furniture, polished bamboo floors, a huge lazy Susan table and four chairs for dinner. Separate bedrooms with queen size beds and separate baths on either side of the main room made the perfect setup for our vacation but the women would be the clincher.

The details were just as the hostess at the hotel and the cabdriver had said. We tipped him well and told him we would try it for one night and if we liked it we would stay for the week.

Mama-san brought ice and soda and American Coca-Cola and I began an intense effort to enjoy my favorite drink and relax. I fell asleep after a couple of hours.

She brought five women to our room about 1700. "Two of these ladies will serve your dinner and stay the rest of the evening for as long as you want for whatever you wish. All you have to do is choose."

They were all dressed in see through lingerie' and had long black hair. The hotel hostess was right again. They were just as pretty as the city girls but they all had better figures. They were obviously fed better in the country and it showed. They were all tiny, of course, but they all had nice breasts and nicely rounded hips, butts, thighs and calves, as opposed to the mostly stick formed city girls. I wondered if they were mixed Chinese & Japanese. Would they be the daughters of the Japanese pilots that were here on R & R in World War II. It ended in 1945, about 21 years ago and these girls were all in their early to midtwenties, as were we, the sons of American World War II veterans. I wondered if the Mama-san could be the mother of one of the girls. Of course, they were all beautiful and choosing among them is nearly impossible so I did my usual default and picked the best smile.

All of the girls left and the two Charlie and I picked came back in about half an hour dressed in kimonos and carrying trays with soup, rice, steak, chicken, fish, noodles, vegetables and bread which they put on the lazy Susan and began to serve us. I introduced myself as did Charlie, and we tried to get them to sit and eat with us, but they would not. They just smiled politely, shook their heads no and continued to serve. Neither seemed to speak any English. After a while she touched my shoulder, nodded toward my bedroom and waved her hand gracefully toward the door, and said, "Bobby?" She was obviously asking if it was my room.

"Yes," I nodded and started to get up.

She raised her hand off my shoulder to stop me with the palm in my direction, shook her head no and left to go into the room. I guess she needed to go to the bathroom.

When we finished eating, my lady took my hand, nodded toward the bedroom and led me gently there. Inside, she closed the door and went to the bathroom where the water was running in the sunken tub and motioned me to follow. She stopped at the tubs edge and turned to undress me. When she finished undressing me and hanging my clothes on a chair, she took off her kimono and completely bared her naked body which caused an immediate erection. She smiled and washed my entire body from head to toe with washcloth and soap and spent a little extra time with soap and hands on my shaft and balls and didn't miss my ass, then sponged me off with a loofah. She rinsed me off with the shower head hanging from the ceiling and motioned for me to get into the tub.

The tub was about three feet deep and curved concave at the back down to a seat near the bottom and long enough so I could extend my legs most of the way out. It was hot and I could see that she must have come to the room during dinner to fill it with the fresh hot stream water. It stayed hot because the water continuously flowed from the faucet on the end by my feet to the neck high drains by my shoulders. It was very soothing and relaxing and I made a note to the brain committee: *We need to figure out a way to have this kind of treatment more often. Of course, that set off a storm of discussion.*

She went to a corner of the bathroom where the traditional hole in the floor Japanese toilet could be surrounded by a curtain. There was also another shower head hanging from the wall and a bidet and it was obvious she was using all of the equipment to cleanse herself thoroughly. When she finished washing, she dried and wrapped herself up with an oversize terry cloth towel tucked between her breasts and pinned her hair up in a bun with chopsticks. She then spent some time at the sink brushing her teeth, taking her makeup off and washing her face. It was very comfortable. Kinda like we were an old married couple just getting ready for bed. Matter-of-fact doing our daily chores and so on.

She finished and turned toward me, spread her arms down, one open palm pointing at me and the other at the door to the bedroom. I think I'd never seen a woman so calm and in command of herself and the situation than she was at that moment and she was beautiful. She smiled, tilted her head at the door and asked, "Bobby?"

I laughed and said, "Bobby, yes!" I clawed my lanky frame out of the tub in a pretty ungraceful manner but managed to get upright as she came toward me, unwrapping her body and wrapping mine. She dried me briskly, waking my skin and me with quick motions up and down and back and forth until I was dry and she smoothly and softly dried my package as if it were precious.

She took my hand and led me to the bed and pointed with her open hand again, "Bobby," she said softly. I thought I knew what that meant and I immediately jumped in and rolled over on my back but she said, "No," and motioned with both her hands rotating, I should roll over on my stomach. She followed me and spread her legs to either side of mine and began to press on my back with her hands. I think she massaged every muscle in my body for the next hour or maybe more. She squeezed and pinched and rolled her palms into every muscle. Sometimes it hurt a little but when she finished it felt so good I could hardly believe it.

She pulled on my arm to turn me over sat near my fully flaccid package while she massaged my chest and shoulders. It wasn't flaccid long with the heat of her sitting there moving closely over me, but she turned to sit beside me and massage my thighs and stomach. I raised my head to watch her and put a pillow behind to hold it there. She was gorgeous and talented and I was instantly rock hard. Finally, she touched my balls and moved to put my shaft in her mouth—just the head in and she paused. *She's so little. How's she gonna get that fat fucker in her tiny mouth.* And then she swallowed the whole thing right down to the base and held it there squeezing my balls and holding it in her throat. *Wow! That's never happened before!* She held it longer that I thought would be possible and when she came up she took a deep breath and did it again. *Oh my God she's good. We just got laid and came twice last night in Taipei and we're having to work on holding off.* When she came up again she stayed up and turned to sit with her hot pelvic arch hovering over me again and dragged herself several times back and forth, just barely touching with her pubic curls.

I started to rise toward her, but she put her hands gently on my chest, shook her head and said quietly, "No, Bobby."

I didn't know if she was teasing me or teasing herself but she shivered and lowered herself a little more so I could feel how wet she was as she continued to move slowly back and forth. *She has to be into it if she's wet. Right? Do prostitutes ever really get into it and come or is it all just for show.* She rose and reached down to put me inside and sat down slowly and smoothly to the full bottom without stopping. She was small and tight inside but was also wet. She sat still and squeezed her insides more than I ever knew was possible and I couldn't hold off anymore so I pumped her quick a few times and came. It was violent for me and when I came, she came, or pretended to come. *Oh hell. Who cares whether she came or she faked it. It felt great!*

She relaxed and stretched her legs out behind with her tiny body stretched out on top of me. She couldn't weigh a hundred pounds. She's so little but what a great figure. Every muscle and bone in my body was so relaxed I didn't want to move. I stroked her back and bottom and realized I had not touched any part of her until then, except her hand when she led me to the tub and to bed. I came partially awake sometime during the night and felt her spooning, snuggled next to my back. When I moved a little she pulled her upper body away and began to stroke my back and shoulders until I went back to sleep.

Coffee, Danish and scrambled eggs were on the lazy Susan when I awoke and she was there setting the table as I came in from the bedroom. She was wearing an all-white robe, well more like a kimono than a robe, with a high stiff collar that cupped around the back of her hair which was in a bun again. I motioned for her to sit and refused to sit down until she finally relented smiling shyly. I took a plate from the lazy Susan, served her eggs and a Danish and offered coffee, but she waved her hand and shook her head to refuse. She smiled and bowed her head and put her hands together, as if praying, but pointed them toward me. No words were necessary. I smiled and repeated the gesture toward her before I sat down and served myself.

She finished her breakfast and went to stand by the bedroom door as she had the night before. When I turned toward her she gestured again with her outstretched arms and palms one pointing to me and the other to the door. "Bobby?" She tilted her head and flashed the smile for which she was chosen.

Of course I went. I almost jumped out of my chair.

This scenario repeated four times except that when Mama-san showed up with five new girls from which to choose I always asked for "Number 1." She said no until the last day she when she brought only one girl and said, "Okay, Bobby, you can have Number 1 again now if you still want."

"I do want Mama-san."

She brought four new girls for Charlie that we had not seen before.

When I returned to the squadron, Noah and T-Bird were gone. It was as if they'd been erased. Only their racks remained. Neatly made up. Not a speck of dust or a wrinkle to be found. The photos, the foot lockers and boots were just gone.

There was a big assault while I was gone. A super gaggle they called it. We were tasked to support the U.S. Army 101st Airborne Division who were in-country but had not yet received all of their new UH-1E (Huey) helicopters. The 101st had just enough birds and just enough pilots, with minimum training, to fly daylight, visual flight regulation (VFR) flights only, and therefore flew only "day VFR" medevac, or emergency resupply flights. No flights in the rain or clouds and no night flights.

T-Bird and Noah had been flying together, as pilot and copilot, in a formation with several other aircraft, when their aircraft apparently caught a large-caliber round or a rocket-propelled grenade somewhere in the drive train. The transmission is a particularly sensitive area of the H-34D aircraft because it is the only connection to the rotor head, which provides not only power but directional force. There was not enough left of the aircraft to determine the exact cause but a single large-caliber round or rocket-propelled grenade apparently disconnected the rotor head from the controls which rendered the aircraft completely at the mercy of freewheeling rotor blades and gravity. Pilots and crew in the formation witnessed what looked like leading edge blade stall, wing over type maneuver and a spiraling, flailing, uncontrollable heap falling helplessly to earth for several seconds. Tough way to go—rather catch a round between the eyes and go suddenly than have to know it's coming and watch it happen. *The brain committee was unanimous on this point.*

Another change resulted in my assignment to a crew on one particular aircraft which meant I would fly only with that crew whenever the aircraft was on the schedule to fly. It was a concept which our older commanding officer, which we nicknamed Deputy Dog because he looked so much like the familiar cartoon character, pulled from the WWII squadron organization style. It's okay but not the modern random flight and crew organization that most of the younger commanders preferred.

The aircraft to which I was assigned, along with Captain Mark Hastings, was down for parts for a couple of weeks so I was assigned to little do nothing jobs like standing the duty as the ODO, officer of the day, which was an administrative job consisted of sitting near a desk and answering a combat type land line which never rang. All of the important information such as operation orders or flight schedule requirements came by tactical radio or messenger on classified messenger equipment to the Operations Department.

I was ordered one night to kill a dog hanging around our camp that may have had some kind of disease that caused his head to shake but I didn't want to do it so I fired a shot into the air and he ran off. The shot was a tracer, of course, from my totally inadequate pilot's .38-caliber pistol. The sound of the shot totally disrupted the otherwise peaceful evening with immediate lights out, diving under the tables at the bars and under the cots in the hooches and is still remembered today at reunions as "The Deputy Dog Attack.

A big flight supporting the Korean army was my first flight with my new aircraft and crew. It was a huge gaggle consisting of all of our flyable aircraft and was going into a hot landing zone. My part of the team effort was to preflight the aircraft and have it ready to start when the helicopter aircraft commander, or HAC, arrives after the flight briefing. Then during the flight, I would essentially do nothing unless the HAC were to be wounded and unable to fly. Although, I was carrying a "grease gun," named such because of its black color and design resemblance to an actual grease gun tool used to grease cars and trucks, which I was supposed to fire out my cockpit window if there were enemy firing at us or approaching my side of the aircraft. I had never fired a "grease gun" before and only knew that if I flipped off the safety, pointed it out the window and pulled the trigger, it would fire and maybe hit something.

As it turned out I did have something to shoot on the approach into the landing zone. We were well back in the gaggle and the approach into the zone was high and slow. This was a big mistake since it leaves the back part of the flight sitting nearly motionless in the sky like a big target. Toward the bottom of the approach I saw a man in traditional Vietnam "black pajamas" firing at us from a rice paddy dike. I felt the bullets hitting the aircraft behind me, but it appeared that our window gunner had shot him, and by that time, we were past the point where I could have fired at him anyway. Shortly afterward, when we landed in the zone I saw another man, dressed in a similar manner and armed with a similar weapon stand up and aim directly at me. I had already flipped the safety off on the "grease gun" at the previous sighting so I whipped it up and pointed out the open hatch and fired. I missed by quite a lot I guess because I had no idea of the range or accuracy of the weapon I was firing. However, as I started firing I noticed the man turn away from me and start firing in the dirt of the dry rice paddy right in front of our aircraft. Shortly after that someone, probably one of the other window gunners in our flight hit him and took him out. It wasn't our window gunner because I learned later that he had been fatally wounded by the first attacker.

When the firing began across our immediate front, Captain Hastings, knowing our aircraft was wounded and seeing the firing in front of us, made an immediate lift and hard turn to the right rear. Apparently, the enemy had been taught to aim slightly in front of an aircraft and let the plane fly into the projectiles. I guess he didn't know the difference between a sitting duck and a flying truck and certainly didn't know we could fly backward but he was probably dead before we split anyway.

Night Medevac

As briefed, our pilot, the experienced Captain Hastings, called the ground contact on the FM radio. "Delta 14 this is Zulu Seven Dash One, at 1,500 feet estimating two miles south. Over."

"Roger, Zulu Seven Dash One, I read you loud and clear and hear you coming. We've not had any hostile fire for about an hour but we know they're nearby. We have two wounded earlier tonight, who probably won't make it 'til morning, and one KIA (killed in action). Over."

Contact was clearly established and with no other radio traffic to interfere, the captain dispensed with formal radio protocol. "What's the direction and distance of your last hostile fire, Delta?"

"Zulu Seven, we last received fire from the northeast up the hill. We moved a little farther south, down the hill, to get to this zone, so we're about 250 yards away from their last known position. Over."

"Roger, Delta, we'll make our final approach from the south keeping the low ground behind. Pop a smoke for me now."

"Roger . . . smoking now."

"I've got green smoke, Delta. Confirm." Often, the enemy monitors our radios and pops a smoke to try to lure the helicopters into a trap. Hopefully, we don't get two smokes of the same color but if we do, we just do it again until we get positive identification of the friendly zone.

The ground radioman now dispensed with most protocols also, "Affirmative Zulu. Green smoke is our LZ (landing zone)."

"How tight is your LZ, Delta?"

"Zulu, the LZ is just barely large enough, about 35 to 40 yards across, but there are tall trees on the northern and southern perimeters and it slopes slightly to the south. There is no wind in the zone, and with contact to the north, it might be better if you angle in from the southeast or southwest."

"How far spread out are your men?"

"We're all within about 50 yards from the edge of the LZ in a half circle on the east side. You're cleared to return fire anywhere outside 50 yards and to suppress fire anywhere outside 100 yards."

"Roger that. We'll approach from the southwest and land heading east."

On the ICS, the Internal Communications System, the captain said, "Corporal, you copy the enemy position up the hill on your side, on final?"

The window gunner, on the left side of the aircraft replied, "Roger, Captain."

On the UHF radio, he said, "Dash Two, hold here." Our wingman had been briefed to hold over the landing zone, monitor the AM and FM radios, watch for and call the direction and distance of any incoming fire at the descending aircraft and be ready to come into the zone to pick up additional medevacs, or to get us out if we got shot down or crashed. In some cases of heavy hostile fire, Dash Two might be asked to make a gun run to return fire while lead is getting into or out of the zone.

"Running lights off," he said as he started a descending right turn, back to the south, away from the landing zone, so we wouldn't overfly the enemy position.

"Roger, running lights off," I responded, as I flipped the switch.

"Stand by the gages and landing light," he reminded as he started the descent.

"Aye, aye Skipper," I replied. I enjoyed calling marine captains by their traditional nickname and using the "aye, aye" response instead of yes sir, especially when it referred also to the captain of a mission like this one with all of our lives so obviously and so precariously in his hands.

As the lesser experienced second pilot, my job was to monitor the gages for the engine and rotor speed revolutions per minute (RPM), and to a lesser degree, engine oil pressure and temperature, watch for and call incoming hostile fire, and be ready to fly the aircraft if the aircraft commander is hit. I was armed with the usual .45-caliber automatic weapon called a "grease gun." Releasing the safety, I laid it back against my stomach hanging from the strap around my neck and pointing to the left out my open window hatch. On high approach to the zone, at about 600 feet above ground, just as the nose of the aircraft was turning back to the north, I yelled excitedly into the ICS, "Incoming!" I saw the tracers off to my left side through the open cockpit hatch as they passed by harmlessly outside the rotor tips. The tracers formed an optical illusion, appearing to be going down, while they burnt out and slowed down, as they actually passed by, going up.

"I guess that answers the question whether the zone is hot," I offered.

He didn't reply. The helicopter aircraft commander was busy but responded calmly on the intercom, "The fire is on your side, Corporal. You see it?"

The window gunner responded, "Yes, sir. Right now they don't know where we are or which direction we're headed, so I don't want to telegraph our position too soon. They're aiming at the exhaust pipes, not leading us well, and we're turning away so they're missing wide left. I'll get on 'em in a few seconds when they come broadside on final."

The timing of our machine gun fire is more critical than one might imagine. If we open fire too soon and put out our tracers for the enemy to see and follow we could catch a lot more incoming rounds than if we open up at closer range and give them less time to respond. A rat and cat game, for sure.

Inside the H-34D helicopter, affectionately known as the "Dog," the red lights on the instrument panel glowed softly in a moonless night like the inside of a very dark cave. Six hundred pounds of aviation gasoline in our magnesium skinned belly would explode into a very bright, very large, white ball, like a star burst if we were hit with a rocket propelled grenade or large-caliber tracer. No stars above, no horizon ahead and no lights below until we asked the ground unit to "pop a smoke" to light it up. Only the faint red glow from the cockpit instrument lights and the blue and orange flames of our fiery exhaust would be visible to those on the ground but our butts would be thirteen feet up in the air, six feet above the fiery exhausts, when we're sitting in the zone. *Maybe the trees on the north side of the zone would be tall enough so the enemy can't see us or have a direct line of fire.*

Night flight on instruments in a fast, tight, spiraling descent is about as disorienting as it can get. If the pilot tries to look in and out of the cockpit, he can get vertigo switching from lights on the ground and back to lights on the instrument panels. As a result, most of the approach is flown by hearing and feeling the aircraft with hands, feet and body while the pilot's eyes remain mostly outside on the LZ. The second pilot backs up the approach by watching the instruments and calling out any unusual conditions.

We were descending nearly as fast as a rock falling out of the sky and we would need all our power and residual "windmill" rotor speed to make a quick stop over the site and land or hover. There would be no hover if the captain could see the ground—just a quick approach all the way to touchdown, requiring last minute perfect coordination, culminating in zero airspeed and zero rate of descent at the same time the landing gear touch the ground. Sometimes the high angle of attack, required to stop the aircraft quickly, results in a broken tail wheel as the first part of the aircraft to strike the ground.

Suddenly, my seat began to shake as the machine gun, mounted in the cabin window, behind and below me, started banging out bursts of fire when we turned on final. I noticed we were passing through 250 feet above ground level on the radar altimeter. Sitting on the left side, just in front and forward of the left window gunner, I had a good view of the fight. Our gunner was all over the enemy, nailing them with short bursts of pinpoint accuracy. The incoming tracers slowed, then stopped, as the tops of the trees became visible below. Our window gunner stopped firing as well just as the light of the smoke grenade and flare in the zone burned out. The "Dog" was not shaking, the engine was idling, the rotor blades were flat and gliding smoothly without lift pressure. I noticed we were passing through 75 feet above ground level as I scanned the instruments. The quiet lull produced an almost tranquil, quixotic moment in the dark but it didn't last long.

Less than maybe two seconds later, the captain pulled the nose up sharply into a big flare as we passed the treetops near the bottom of the approach. "Landing light on, at my call," he said.

I reached for the switch and waited for his call as he smoothly rotated the aircraft out of the flare toward level flight.

"Now!" he said forcefully as he rolled the nose down and added power. The landing light lit up the zone as the dust and leaf fodder began to enfold us. The engine roared and shook the whole aircraft, increasing to full power as it pounded its massive exhaust through three oversize, glowing pipes about seven feet from my left ear. *Why couldn't Sikorsky have designed an exhaust route to the bottom of the airframe instead of to a lighted target four feet below my butt?* I scanned the left side of the LZ. Dark, shaking trees stared back at me as the rotor wash consumed them. Not a sound from our window gunner. The corporal would be mostly watching our rear quarter since our ground marines would be to his center and right protecting the front of the aircraft. The pilot's sense of timing and feel for the aircraft resulted in a near perfect partial hover over a slightly sloping site. Since the right side was downhill, he had to hold the right landing gear off the ground slightly to keep the aircraft level and to keep the rotor blades above the heads of the troops carrying their wounded and dead. On the intercom he said, "Landing light off, now!"

My finger was still on the switch and I flipped it off instantly. It had only been on for about four or five seconds but the illumination would mark the zone for everyone in the vicinity. If we sat there very long, we knew we could expect incoming mortars, rocket grenades or machine gun fire. Nestled below the tree line the engine methodically rumbled and the rotor blade noise whipped rhythmic and steady slashes of dark air as time seemed to pause.

"Get 'em in, get 'em in, get 'em in, Delta," the pilot urged on the FM radio.

We could see dark forms emerging from the tree line ahead in the shadows of light from our exhaust. The wounded and KIA were being carried into the zone toward the nose of the aircraft. I lost sight of them as they came closer to the right side but the pilot, leaning out of the open hatch on his side, could see them all the way to the open bay and would react accordingly when they finished their task.

I scanned the tree line again while my hands rested nervously on the grease gun. Apparently, we were safe from a direct line of fire. Suddenly, the engine roared and we leapt into the air, rotating right, in a sharp, backward lifting, right turn, swinging around to the exit the way we had come. As we cleared the tree line the crew chief laid down suppressing fire to the north of the zone, just in case any wise guys had ideas about challenging us again.

"We're out Dash Two," the captain said on the UHF. Running lights coming on, now, and as he looked at me and nodded, I flipped the switch.

"You got us Dash Two?"

"Tally ho lead! We gotcha comin' up below us. Great job! We're on your starboard, about two o'clock, at 1,500 feet headed south."

Fall in loose at six o'clock Dash Two. We're goin' straight to Charlie Med.

On the ICS he asked, "Any damage?"

The Crew Chief reported, "None comin' in on my side, sir."

The window gunner reported, "One hole on my side—probably .30 caliber. Looks like it went through and out the other side but I don't know where or if it hit any wires or tubes. Nothing is leaking and everything seems to be working okay."

I took a deep breath and tried to relax a bit as I realized how fast my heart was beating, how hard I was breathing, and how tense I had been. As good as it felt to successfully get the wounded out, carrying a dead marine made the mood somber.

"Good night, Delta. Keep your heads down," our captain said to the marines on the ground.

"Good night Zulu. Thanks a million times over! We love you guys."

"Anytime, marines. Semper fi."

The moves from Ky Ha perimeter defense duty to Da Nang, to Qui Nhon caused a long lag in my mail delivery. There were a few letters trickling through once in a while but Jamila said she was writing every day so I knew there were more to come. It finally caught up with me in a big box full of letters and care packages. It was great to be able to sit and relax catching up on the news and eating the canned sardines and clams but the most recent letter carried some news I'm thinking most of the pilots would not want to hear.

> "I know this won't bother you because of our arrangement," she wrote. "But I wanted you to hear it straight from me rather than second hand. There was

a party for the squadron officer's wives but several young studs were also there. Some, but not all, were obviously marines. I don't know where the hostess knew them from or what was her intent, but the result was a hell of a party. It was wildly sexual and just as blatantly open as the going away party before you guys left but it was interrupted when the police showed up. The neighbors had complained about the noise. They arrested everyone but they eventually let us all go with no charges, except the hostess, and they only charged her with disturbing the peace. It made the Santa Ana Register newspaper so everyone here knows about it and I suppose everyone there will soon know too, if they don't already."

"Hey Skipper, I suppose you already heard about the party?"

The captain looked a little more down than usual. "Yeah, I did and I know your wife and my wife were there but I don't wanna talk about it. Did you go on R & R yet?

"Yes, sir. I went already before we swapped squadrons."

"Where'd ya go?"

"Taiwan, Skipper. It was beautiful but the city of Taipei was crowded and expensive. I recommend the resort town of Peitou if you get there. I got my first hotsie bath, first professional massage and first deep throat there in a very comfortable hotel for a very reasonable price."

"Did the captain get to go yet?"

"Nope and I won't be going on R & R 'cause I'm goin' home early." Apparently, he had gotten a similar letter about the party from his wife and used it to justify immediate emergency leave. It had something to do with divorce and taking care of his kids, according to the unofficial squadron scuttlebutt. I didn't say anything to anyone, although I knew that at least a few of them knew just as much as I did.

Paladin

While we were working in the southern part of I Corps and II Corps our friend Paladin was working in northern I Corps near the Demilitarized Zone with North Vietnam. Paladin is shorter than an average marine but with slightly larger shoulders and a rounded form sort of like a muscular bell pepper with legs. Black wavy hair, dark brown eyes, heavy dark eyebrows and a pleasant round face seem to both belie and endorse his Italian heritage.

We first met in Pensacola, Florida at the Naval Aviation Flight School when we were students.

He was an enlisted candidate, known as a MARCAD (Marine Corps Aviation Cadet) who would be commissioned upon completion of flight school and I was a second lieutenant, going through flight school as an officer, having been commissioned upon graduation from college. He swears we met when I threw him out of a keg party at our beachhouse on Santa Rosa Island. The story may be true, but I honestly do not remember, and if true, it was probably because he crashed the party. Enlisted cadets, navy and marine flight students, were doing the exact same job the officers were but were existing on much lower pay and were known to be very brazen about crashing parties or hanging around bars hustling drinks at pool tables or confiscating a pitcher of beer off an empty table while the patrons were dancing. Large parties, like our keg parties, where crowd control would naturally be a problem were usually easy targets.

We had a pretty good system at our house though—the keg and food were kept on the second floor balcony and the first floor was locked to outside entry and blocked off from the second by a couch at the top of the inside stairs. The only way into the party was by the outside staircase and we always had an entry "guard" stationed there to collect a dollar from the guys who wanted to come in even though they might have been invited by one of the residents. Of course, girls came for free and didn't need to have an invitation. When the guys paid their entry fee, the back of their hand was rubber stamped with ink in a design that changed from one day to the next. I had been a bouncer, bartender and manager at a bar in college so I was asked to design the entry/security system and my roommates most often tapped me to be the "bouncer" at high traffic times.

I ran into Paladin again and became friends, when he was a marine second lieutenant, with naval aviator wings serving in Vietnam.

Paladin was one of the most decorated pilots of the Vietnam War era. He wound up with six Distinguished Flying Crosses and so many Air Medals it's nearly impossible to imagine. Although there were circumstances when Air Medals were awarded for exceptional single missions, most were awarded on a numbers basis. Twenty combat missions or sorties flown would entitle the pilot and copilot to one Air Medal, although if a sortie received fire, it would count as two sorties. A sortie was a takeoff and flight into a combat zone to perform a task. Headquarters Marine Corps eventually decreased the number of Air Medals awarded to all helicopter pilots by an arbitrary amount because they were so far above their fixed wing contemporaries. Helicopter pilots were sometimes flying dozens of sorties per day for periods of anywhere from four hours to twelve or even fourteen hours while fixed wing missions were usually one mission or sortie per flight for an hour and a half to two hours duration and usually only one or two flights per day. The exceptions were fixed wing A-6 Intruders who could stay up for nearly three times as long as other fixed wing close air support aircraft and carry much more ordinance.

We heard the first story about Paladin while he was stationed in Hue/Phu Bai and was assigned to a mission called Search and Rescue (SAR) North. He was flying an H-34D as a wingman in a two plane flight. SAR North was a standby mission located at Quang Tri, South Vietnam near the DMZ between North and South Vietnam. The purpose of the mission was to standby to launch and search for fixed wing attack pilots who were shot down in the southern part of North Vietnam.

The mission was launched and the downed pilot was eventually located through communication on his hand-held rescue radio and by visual identification of his parachute lying out on top of the jungle canopy. The rest of the story is legendary among Marine Corps helicopter pilots. The flight leader is Dash One and Paladin is Dash Two in the following story:

"Knight One, this is Ugly Angel Dash One, we see your parachute spread out on the tree tops. What's your status? Are you ready for pick-up?"

"Ugly Angel, this is Knight One. I see you approaching from the south. I've not heard any enemy activity in the area. I'm detached from the chute and ready for pick-up. I'm about a hundred feet above ground level in the top of the canopy and I'm ready to get the hell outa here."

"Dash Two, is your hook working?"

Here the lead aircraft pilot is referring to an electrical wench on the right side of the aircraft, adjacent to the side door opening, which is operated by the crew chief. The hook is at the end of a wire cable on the wench, which can be lowered to haul up wounded or other passengers or cargo when the aircraft would not be able to land. In this case a rescue loop is attached to the hook and the downed pilot would stick his arms through the loop to be hauled out.

"Affirmative, Dash One, my hook is good to go."

"Looks like you're gonna have to get him, Dash Two. Our hook is down."

"Roger, Dash One. We'll pick him up."

Paladin had been holding in an orbit off to the side and above the rescue scene and, at this point, began a slow descent down to near the top of the jungle canopy to a position above and to the side of the downed pilot.

"Dash Two, commencing approach"

"Dash One, roger."

As Paladin's aircraft came into a hover about fifty feet above and to the side of the downed pilot, he realized there was not enough power available to stop the descent and hold the hover. The thinner air at a higher altitude above sea level and a lack of ground effect to support the hover combined to create a situation where the rotor blade angle of attack was too high for the engine to maintain rotor speed. While at maximum power he milked the collective power arm down and up trying to keep the rotor head speed from deteriorating but the effort was fruitless. The altitude could not be maintained with the power available.

"Looks like you're gonna join me, Angel," the downed pilot remarked.

"Not if I can help it, Knight One!" Still sinking slowly, he kicked right rudder to alleviate some of the necessity for power to maintain heading and slipped away farther down the hillside.

"You can't land here, Paladin!" His copilot was obviously having an exciting ride.

The aircraft continued to slip down into the top of the jungle canopy.

"You can't land here!" the copilot said a little more excitedly and a lot more emphatically.

The aircraft continued to sink and the rotor head began to cut into the top of the jungle canopy like blender blades chopping lettuce.

"Da Nang DASC, this is Ugly Angel Dash One on a Search and Rescue Mission for Knight One."

Paladin's aircraft descended below the heavy overgrowth into the tall trees and became invisible from above. He deftly maneuvered left and right and continued to fly down the hillside underneath the canopy, cutting down the small trees with the rotor blades, dodging the big trees and occasionally bouncing against the side of the hill with his main landing gear or tail wheel.

"Ugly Angel Dash One, this is Da Nang DASC, go ahead."

"We've located the downed pilot but my wingman has crashed while trying to extract him from the jungle. I don't have a working hook so we are going to need another mission to extract the downed pilot and any surviving members of my wingman's crew."

"You can't land here, Paladin!" the copilot screamed again as the aircraft descended below the upper canopy of the jungle.

"Does it look like I'm trying to land?" Paladin was exasperated.

"Ugly Angel Dash One do you have the location of the crash site?"

"Da Nang DASC, Ugly Angel Dash One, Negative. We have the position where they entered the jungle but I do not have any fire or wreckage at this time."

"Ugly Angel Dash One, what is the nearest known position to the crash?"

"Da Nang DASC, Ugly Angel Dash One, those coordinates are the same as the location we reported earlier for the downed pilot, Knight One."

"Roger, Ugly Angel Dash One. Your new SAR mission has been ordered."

"Knight One, we have another flight on the way to get you out. We'll stay with you until they arrive."

"Knight One, roger."

"Da Nang DASC, Ugly Angel Dash One."

"Go ahead, Ugly Angel Dash One."

"Da Nang DASC, Ugly Angel Dash One has Ugly Angel Dash Two in sight. He came flying out from under the jungle canopy about a mile and half southeast of where he went in. It looks like he's headed for Hue Phu Bai."

Paladin's radios were not working. The clam shell doors on the front of the aircraft, covering the engine housing, were gone, the bare engine hung out below the craft like a naked pregnancy bump, both windshields were broken out, the right main landing gear was broken off and gone, the tail wheel was gone, the aircraft was shaking violently from damage to the rotor blades and leaking fluids stained the magnesium skin like muddy rain.

As badly damaged as the aircraft was, he was able to fly to the airfield at Hue Phu Bai where his squadron was stationed and hovered while the maintenance crew rigged up a cart with sandbags. He landed the side of the belly on the sand bags on the cart where the main gear was gone and on the remaining main gear on the other side.

His commanding officer didn't know whether to give him a "Letter of Reprimand" for incompetence, for going down in the first place, or to recommend him for a Distinguished Flying Cross for flying well enough to get the aircraft and the crew home safely. They settled on a verbal reprimand and a Single Mission Air Medal, which was the first of his many personal awards.

The sixth and last of Paladin's Distinguished Flying Crosses caught up with him at his reserve unit in Santa Ana, California, which he joined after having completed two thirteen month tours in Vietnam, but he didn't show up for the parade. He was not impressed by his own bravery and was particularly unimpressed by people who over emphasized the importance of medals, referring to them as "politically motivated, social climbing, brown nosing, assholes."

The Princeton Again

Shortly after we got really settled in at Qui Nhon, the air wing commander decided there needed to be a rotation of pilots and crew among the squadrons so that we wouldn't all be going home at the same time. It was confusing because our three squadrons had all arrived at the same time, so how could swapping crews among ourselves solve the problem? It didn't, but we did the swap anyway, and in the mix I was offered helicopter aircraft commander papers if I would volunteer to transfer. I hadn't flown much and didn't really have the flight hours or experience, but I was interested in the deal. I found out one of our sister squadrons was scheduled to go aboard ship shortly after I would join them and that clinched it for me. Who would turn down three months of convenient hot showers, a comfortable bunk in a stateroom and great shipboard navy chow? So soon after Deputy Dog and crew moved out to Ky Ha, I left almost immediately to go aboard the USS *Princeton* to work off shore in support of marines in the Marine Expeditionary Force afloat and the marines already in country.

Of course, the first thing we had to do after going aboard was to head to port to replenish supplies because the *Princeton* had been at sea for several weeks in support of the squadron we replaced.

A couple of days before the ship was due to arrive in port we flew several aircraft ahead for "fresh water washing" as the excuse for getting to port early and head to the bar.

The Officers Club at Futenma Marine Corps Air Station was alive with dozens of young people on a warm Friday night. Not just marines or even just sailors, airmen or soldiers but also civilian contractors, schoolteachers and civil service employees. It was the most popular club on the island and was swarming with bodies.

I don't know how or why such coincidences occur but sometimes they just do. I yelled at her over the loud music and when she came toward me I threw my arms open to hug her. "What the hell are you doing here my gorgeous Weekender?"

"Hey, Bobby! I took your advice and looked into teaching in the Overseas Military School System and here I am. I'm teaching high school at the American school on the air force base but I often come over here to party with the marines. That's also your fault, Marine! What are you doing here?"

"Our ship is here for a replenishing stop over. Just here for a short time really. So you're still single and partying with the marines, huh?"

"You bet I am! I'm having the time of my life. We, my teacher friends and I, are essentially the only single American women within several hundred miles and there are literally hundreds if not thousands of single men stationed here or passing through. What more could I ask for."

"I seem to recall a girl who was on a revenge fling for a wild weekend and then you were going to settle down and look for a new life with a husband and family."

"I've had several offers to do just that Bobby but they are all coming from soldiers, marines, sailors or airmen headed for Vietnam. Not much promise of a future in that kind of situation so I'm holding off for now."

"Good luck for me maybe? I raised an eyebrow and studied her face.

She threw me a practiced coy smile, tilted her head to the side, shook her strawberry blonde hair and cut her beautiful blue eyes to the corner directly into mine and said, "Besides that, Marine, it can be a hell of a lotta fun being a single woman among a cluster of handsome muscles and stored up energy."

"You know, you're pretty famous as the "Pensacola Weekender" but we left your name anonymous so I still don't know it now."

"And you don't need to know it now either Bobby. I've dreamed of you and that weekend so often you wouldn't believe it and now I want some more."

"Really?" *How lucky can we get?*

"Yep, I have a car and a place and I'll take you to your boat when it's time for you to go." She swung her tilted head over her shoulder toward the door and suggested, "Shall we go, Marine?"

"But of course, my darling. Lead on! How's that little strawberry patch of yours?"

She laughed. "No one's ever called it that except you. It's still there and still red or orange as you described it but a little bushier. I trimmed it really short early last summer but it grew back twice as thick."

"Wonderful, I love thick. You should never trim it so short. It's a beautiful color and I love stroking and talking to it," I joked.

She laughed again. "Yes, I remember the 'talking' you were doing down there."

The drive to Kadena Air Force Base, where her quarters were located, passed quickly. As we passed by she showed me the school where she taught, the gym where she worked out and the Air Force Officers Club where she liked to eat lunch almost daily and dinner sometimes when she was tired and going to bed early. Being with her was like being with an old friend—familiar, comfortable, easy going.

She had been a virgin when we met in Pensacola and chose me to take her. *Take her—hell, she practically raped you, Bobby. You had no choice once she decided you were the one.* The committee laughed and joked and pointed fingers at each other.

She brought a different level of experience to this occasion but was again obviously in control from the minute she spotted me in the club. It was less than 30 minutes total since we met and she was standing by her bed looking at me and undressing. I didn't have to ask. She just smiled and smoothly removed one piece after another until she stood there before me in the soft light like the goddess she was.

I willingly surrendered as I began to revel in her beauty. I was already hard before she even got her blouse off and I was aching to touch her and kiss her all over again. She was just as stunning as I remembered in the distant fog of that weekend three years ago. I moved to hold her in my arms and she came to me hugging me close and we rolled onto the bed. Her naked skin next to mine was so warm and tantalizing I came almost immediately. *It's been a long time since R & R in Taiwan.*

"I don't mind Bobby. It happens most of the time. Well, maybe not most but at least a lot. Some of the guys are so sexually deprived that when they finally get it they have an air burst, rim fire or, at best, last only a few minutes." She smiled warmly and stared at me with soft eyes. "How long have you been in combat, Bobby? When do you go home?"

"Seven months down and six to go. We'll be on the ship for at least another three months and then we'll be back in country 'til the end of our tour."

"Will you be back here in Okinawa again?"

"I have no idea. We didn't know about this port call until two days before it happened. I think the ship usually ports in Subic Bay in the Philippine Islands but it's up to the navy to arrange the port calls in order to get supplies. We're just along for the ride, so to speak, until we get on station and join the war. At that point the ship goes where we need it to be in order to support our operations."

"When do you have to be back on your ship."

"Well, I don't know exactly. We have a few aircraft here that we'll fly back aboard the ship after it leaves port. They'll notify us when it's leaving and we'll have several hours to launch and catch up with her."

"So you won't have to leave tomorrow?"

"Probably not but we could get orders tomorrow and leave tomorrow night. We are on standby liberty but with no way to contact us so we have to check in tomorrow before 1000 to find out our status. If we check in and get orders to go, we go, and if not then our Operations Department gives us a new time to report—usually the same time the next day."

"Okay, we can handle that for this weekend but when Monday rolls around you'll have to be on your own, Marine."

I chuckled and pulled her close to snuggle a while and then turned around for a long conversation with the strawberry patch and the surrounding territory. She came twice, and I came once again at the same time as her second one.

We were together for three magical nights and got out of bed only to go check in at the squadron operations office and get something to eat. She left early Monday morning before I woke but left a note "In case you leave today Bobby—call me if you get back here again." She left her phone number and signed it . . . "Love ya, Cindy."

The Princeton didn't make it back to Okinawa but maybe I'll see her again someday. *Who knows?* The Philippines, Subic Bay, Cubi Point and the town of Olongapo just outside the gate of the base became our regular ports-of-call for the rest of the cruise.

We finished the three-month cruise with no shipboard accidents and no one killed in action. Of course our aircraft picked up many new holes and one of our aircraft commanders collected a .30-caliber round in his right shoulder and was sent to the USS *Repose*, a medical ship, for surgery and then he went on home early. Sooner than we liked we were back in the red Ky Ha mud but our wooden quarters were finally built. Not nearly as nice as the army quarters in Qui Nhon but certainly much better than the GP tents and dirt floors we had left behind.

Routine Mission

Flying is often said to be 99 percent boredom and 1 percent sheer terror. The terror occurs when an engine quits or there's a fire or some lesser airborne emergency, like an electrical or hydraulic failure. Otherwise, it's like driving a car, only safer, because there aren't any airborne idiots cluttering up the airspace like there are on the highway. Combat, in an aircraft, can be similar but with more variables; the percentages can be more toward the terror side of the equation depending on the intensity and type of the operation. The transfer to the new squadron gained helicopter aircraft commander for me, but all the pilots in the squadron were also designated, so it really didn't provide any real advantage except that I occasionally got to sign out the aircraft and fly in the pilot's seat. It was a good feeling, but I soon found out that I'd been so long in the copilot seat, I was more comfortable there.

"What's the schedule look like today, DC?" I asked, as I strolled into the Operations tent.

"Routine resupply and admin and we're together again," he replied.

"Who's the boss?"

He laughed. "I am. You get to observe and take notes."

DC and I held the same rank, as first lieutenants, with the same length of time "in country," or in combat, but he had more flight time in the H-34D and was more often assigned as helicopter aircraft commander. DC was assigned as HAC today, as was usually the case and our mission assignment consisted of carrying ammunition and food to remote outposts and bringing back passengers for routine medical attention, rotation stateside or R & R or for other transfers. We often flew together and no matter who was the HAC we usually shared flight time, landings, and takeoffs pretty much half and half.

Combat helicopter operations can be filled with up to fourteen hours of routine takeoffs and landings but can be interrupted by a few seconds of unexpected small arms fire while sitting in a thirteen-foot high cockpit in a quiet, "secure" zone. An ice cream run, interrupted by a hole in the carburetor, can ruin your whole day.

Routine operations are set up on a daily flight schedule, which included the resupply "milk runs" and standby missions such as medevac and quick strike forces. Quick strike forces usually consist of four to six aircraft designated for standby to insert or withdraw troops to or from an active battle. The most mundane of the routine are administration flights, those scheduled to pick up and deliver mail or supplies between secure areas like the airbases and headquarters in Da Nang and Marble Mountain, Ky Ha and Chu Lai, to the marine regimental headquarters in a relatively secure area like Tam Ky, or the army headquarters in Qui Nhon. However, even these flights, unless they are carrying VIP passengers, could be diverted to an emergency medevac or for troop extraction requirements.

On a clear, sunny day in I Corps, South Vietnam, south of Da Nang, DC and I were assigned to fly wing on Captain Dick Wilson. He was the maintenance officer for our squadron of H-34D Sikorsky Helicopters and was generally known as a good guy, an accomplished pilot and a great leader. But was also known as "Tricky Dick," for his tendency to manipulate a situation to his own advantage. As a result, the most routine of routine days could suddenly turn into a shit sandwich on a moment's notice whenever the opportunity presented itself. His "gung ho" attitude and competence produced a skillful combination, which seemed more fearless than his peers. Being on his wing for a long day in the field would probably mean we would be called upon to do more than a usual routine mission.

Our squadron was well-known in Marine Corps ground units for out positive attitude about being of service to them, but we were also world famous we'd served with naval and marine forces afloat around the world and were well-known for our actions in combat and support of disaster events, as well as our infamous characters.

All of the squadrons had nicknames or mascots and mottos for morale building and esprit de corps. Our motto was "Give a Shit," as an encouragement and a positive response to the typical negative rhetoric of the time and place, as in "I don't give a shit" we responded "we do give a shit!" On this day, our two plane section was assigned to routine resupply and administrative support of marines working in a battlefield in the foothills west of the provincial capital, Tam Ky.

Each ground unit that we were to resupply would set up a perimeter around a clear area on a ridge line, hilltop, or dry rice paddy for us to use as a landing zone. Sometimes, the term "landing zone," was a contradiction because the area would be so steep, narrow or rocky we couldn't actually land and would instead, hover as close to the ground as we could, and the crew chief would kick out the supplies. In these cases, if there were medevacs, we would hoist them out with a cable and electric pulley system, which we called the "hook," which referred to the heavy clip attached to the end of the cable.

After about half a dozen or so resupply trips our routine day began to get a bit squirrely. We caught two or three rounds of automatic weapons fire in the lower front of the aircraft in the area of the engine, as we were climbing out of a supposedly secure zone. We heard the noise of the rounds hitting the aircraft and didn't know if anything vital had been hit until soon after, the oil pressure began to slowly drop. This was not an immediate failure emergency because, even though the H-34D has only one engine, it is very hardy, although there are a few critical points. The engine is massive, with nine huge air cooled cylinder heads which can also serve as a barrier to small arms fire from below the front. However, it has only one carburetor and one oil cooler. It would run, although rough, if one or two of the cylinders were shot up but the silence following a round in the carburetor, would indicated the next stop to be immediately below the current position.

The "pucker factor" for an oil cooler hit is nowhere near as tight as it is for a carburetor failure and the emergency flight procedures are a great deal less intense. As the oil pressure drops and the oil temperature rises, the engine would begin to run rougher and rougher, until it overheats to the point it eventually quits. The idea is to get the aircraft on the ground safely, in as safe and secure area as is available, considering the time constraints before the engine failure—maybe ten to twenty minutes depending on the severity of the leak.

"Oil pressure dropping and oil temp climbing slowly, DC," I said calmly into the ICS. We were in no immediate danger as he continued to climb out toward the eastern coast and the dry rice paddies of the coastal farming area. Because of the flatland, visibility would be good for miles around at a good landing site if we get that far and I was spotting landing zones along our route if the engine quit early.

"Roger that," he replied to me and to the crew. "Check for damage below." And then on the FM radio, Echo Five Dash One this is, Echo Five Dash Two, over."

"Roger, Dash Two, go ahead."

"Looks like we've picked up a couple of rounds in the oil cooler, Dash One. We're climbing out toward the coast looking for a secure area to set down, over."

"Roger, Dash Two, you have the lead, we're comin' around to get on your six—we'll come in from behind and below to check you for leaks and smoke."

"Roger, Dash One. I have the lead."

"No visible damage on the starboard side or the bottom but we have some oil steaks going back from the bottom of the clam shell doors," came a report on the ICS from the crew chief.

"No visible damage on the port side," came the report from the window gunner.

DC replied on the ICS, "Roger, no damage visible. Get your gear, guns and ammo ready to transfer to the other aircraft when we land and shut down."

"Roger, Lieutenant," replied the crew chief.

"Oil pressure down by about half and oil temp up but not yet redlined," I reported.

DC replied, "Roger," on the ICS. And then on the FM, "Dash One, I see dry rice paddies ahead and a clear area for at least five miles around so I'm gonna set her down."

"Roger, Dash Two. We've got your six and will give you gun cover on your approach and circle your position before we land."

The standard procedure would require our lead aircraft to land and pick us up. We would transfer all of our gear to his aircraft and get out of the zone as soon as possible. He may have already called for a recovery mission with a maintenance crew and a new oil cooler on board. In any case, he would pick us up and stay airborne in the immediate vicinity to provide security for the downed bird until a quick response team could get to the site.

DC began a precautionary auto rotation, so if the engine quit during the descent, we could land without power by using the inertia created by the spinning rotor blades and retained by the wind coming up through the blades as we glided down.

Lowering the collective and rolling off power with the motorcycle grip in his left hand, he simultaneously rolled the nose down with the stick in his right hand and pushed the rudders with his feet to keep the aircraft balanced. He turned to the right so he could see better out his side to pick out the landing spot and set up the spiral approach with precision. Near the bottom of the flight path he gently rolled the nose up into a slight flare and added just enough power to ease the wheels softly onto the dry ground with a short roll and came to a stop.

I was ready with the shutdown checklist, but he was way ahead of me. He shut off the fuel, magneto power switch and hit the rotor brake in a flurry of motions demonstrating familiar knowledge of the aircraft and the requirements for shutting down and getting out quick. All I had to do was unbuckle my seatbelt and shoulder straps, unhook my helmet from the radio wires and climb out the hatch on my side.

As I was climbing down the side of our aircraft I heard our leader landing behind us on our left and I hit the ground running toward it. The crew chief and window gunner were ahead of me and threw their guns, ammo and gear into the open bay and jumped in after them. DC was right behind me, but as I reached the open bay, I noticed Captain Wilson out of the cockpit and climbing down the side.

"Holy shit! What's wrong," I yelled at the crew chief in the lead aircraft?

"I don't know, sir, the captain wants to take a look at your bird."

"Wow!" I turned to our crew chief and motioned him to get back off. "Get out and set a perimeter defense behind the rice paddy dikes at the inland north and south corners of the rice paddy dikes," I yelled over the engine and rotor blade noise.

Captain Wilson and DC crossed paths as the captain waived the lieutenant on toward the operating aircraft. I caught up with the captain as he was opening the clam shell doors around the engine of our downed aircraft. "What was the oil temp and pressure when you shut down, Lieutenant?"

"I don't know exactly, Captain. The temp was rising and the pressure was dropping but neither were in the red when I scanned just before touchdown."

"It doesn't look like it's leaking much."

Maybe not a lot left to leak at this point? The brain committee was obviously nervous.

"Get in. I want to start it up and see what it looks like."

"Yes, sir." I scrambled up the left side and back into my seat.

As he climbed in, he handed me his chrome-plated Thompson submachine gun—his unauthorized personal weapon and moniker. "Here, hold on to this." He immediately started the engine without a checklist and began to stare at the instruments.

Thank God the oil temp and pressure were still about where I'd said they were. He began to strap in, plugged in his helmet and motioned I should do the same. When I plugged in my helmet I heard him on the FM radio in the middle of a conversation with his original copilot . . . "Put DC in the pilot seat, grab the crew off the perimeter and follow me. You're call sign is still dash one."

I must have been shaking my head because he looked at me and said on the ICS, "If you don't want to ride with me, you're cleared to get out and ride with them."

He's my boss and one of my heroes. He's also the maintenance officer, and I work for him in the maintenance division. What do I do now? I've already been in one precautionary landing in this bird today. Do I want to ride it down again with even better odds of an engine failure? I must have hesitated a bit too long because he continued, "Well, make up your mind, I don't wanna sit here all day wasting whatever oil we have left."

I shrugged my shoulders, waved my hand in circle to indicate turning the rotor blades and said on the ICS, as enthusiastically as I could muster, "Sure, let's go, Skipper."

The captain released the brake on the rotor head and waited for it to come up to speed while closely monitoring the engine gages. There had been no noticeable change since he started the engine. He increased power slightly and lifted, gently and softly, toward a short rolling takeoff, into translational lift, the space in which additional energy from air compression between the rotor blades and the earth creates buoyancy. Eventually, slowly, he coaxed the bird gingerly into a smooth continuous climb where the lift created by increased airspeed replaces the ground effect of translational lift into the "dead man's curve" where, if the engine quits, a helicopter is flying too low and too slow for the pilot to have time to react and perform an auto-rotation to create a successful landing. The soft touch of the experienced pilot coaxing the wounded bird to fly was inspiring. It seemed more than physical, as if he were connected emotionally—willing the cripple to overcome its limitations.

I was in awe of his superb ability but found myself praying for his success, probably, for my own preservation but also for the accomplishment of the mission. We transitioned smoothly through the "dead man's curve" at about one hundred feet above ground level (AGL) and eventually reached an even safer altitude as we passed through 1,000 feet AGL. "Oil temp rising, pressure down, Skipper, both a little in the red."

"Roger. Keep watching 'em close," he said calmly, as he continued the climb toward home base.

Our wingman reported on the FM radio, "Dash One airborne with six souls and all gear on board."

The engine shuddered and miss-fired occasionally under the strain of increased temperatures and lack of lubrication but continued to run.

"Dash One, switch to Ky Ha tower FM."

"Dash One, roger."

I noticed his scan also included the all-important oil-related instruments more often now than usual. Outside, inside, all around the town. Airspeed, altitude, heading, ball, oil temp, oil pressure, fuel, RPM, outside: left, front, right, up, down. Inside: oil, temp, oil pressure, airspeed, altitude, heading, etc. The automatic scan continued as his head and eyes never stopped even when he talked. "Dash One, trail and hold over the field until we've landed."

"Dash One, roger."

The captain leveled off at 1,500 feet above sea level, as indicated on the pressure altimeter, which is about 1,400 feet AGL on the radar altimeter at Ky Ha, since it is on the coast on a flat shelf about 80 feet above the shoreline. "Ky Ha tower, Yankee Kilo 24 is five miles north, inbound with a rough runner, declaring an emergency, two souls on board, requesting an auto-rotation final."

"Roger, Yankee Kilo 24, wind zero-nine-zero at ten knots, no local traffic in sight, cleared as requested. Notify tower one mile out."

"Yankee Kilo 24, roger . . . Yankee Kilo 24, one mile out."

"Roger, Kilo 24. Cleared for approach. Call commencing."

"Oil temp at max, Skipper and the pressure's dropped all the way down." I hoped the tension didn't show in my voice.

"Roger, buckle up." I was already "buckled up" but I knew what he meant—hang on for the ride.

Directly over the landing pad he called the tower for the last time on the FM, "Yankee Kilo 24 commencing approach." And to me, on the ICS, "Call airspeed and altitude."

"Roger, Yankee Kilo 24, cleared to land."

Reducing engine power to idle, he started a sweeping right turn into a descending spiral which would wind up at the bottom at the landing pad with enough room to flare and use the rotor blade inertia and whatever engine power we had left to stop the descent and roll gently onto the pad. We practice this type approach almost every day as we sweep into outlying landing zones. It is not only the fastest way down but if we are without engine power, it is the only way to get down safely. It requires precision timing and a feel for how the aircraft is gliding on the rotor blades as it's essentially falling out of the sky.

My anxiety increased since I was now even more of a spectator. No need to monitor anything but what he ordered. "At 1,200 feet, 70 knots . . . 1,000 feet, 70 knots." The turn continued until he was lined up in an easterly direction, into the light breeze coming off the water. "500 feet, 70 knots . . . 200 feet, 70 knots . . . watch the wires . . . 100 feet, 70 knots."

As he added power to change the glide path, to stay above the wires, the engine coughed, then backfired mightily and shook angrily as the aircraft continued on its original path through the electric wires. "Shit," he yelled, loud enough to hear in the cockpit, without ICS.

The Seabees won't be happy about this! Well, we've been trying to get 'em moved farther from the pad anyway. Maybe now they would be inclined to be more cooperative while repairing the mess.

Adjusting quickly, automatically, to the situation, the flare at the bottom of the approach was nearly perfect, in spite of the wires, resulting in a landing only slightly harder than normal.

With a dead engine we didn't have any power to ground taxi, so the captain just let the aircraft roll forward off the landing pad and onto the taxiway. He shut off the gas and electrical switches to the dead engine, hit the brake for the rotor head and said, "You could have called the wires sooner."

"Right, Skipper—my view was blocked by the right turn until we rolled out on final. I called 'em as soon as I saw 'em—but I don't think the engine had much left to give anyway." I felt it was necessary to remind him of his responsibility for clearing the flight path when we were turning toward his side. *You tell him, Bobby! The brain committee approved of my defensive attitude.*

"Obviously," He scoffed as he unbuckled his safety harness. "Check the transmission deck, rotor head and blades for any visible damage and get a report from the crew chief if there is any structural damage." He climbed out and headed for the line shack.

"Yes, sir." I waited with the broken bird for our wingman to land and the crew chief to come and inspect it. I lit a cigarette, even though I was within the prohibited 50-foot radius of the aircraft, and willed myself to stop the internal shaking that had started only after the incident.

Crew chiefs are assigned permanently to an aircraft. They believe they are the owners and they are only loaning their aircraft to the pilots for short periods of time when they are "signed out" to them. The have a great deal of "pride of ownership" and they get really pissed when someone breaks one of their aircraft. After about an hour of inspecting the skin and frame, opening and closing hatches and pointing a flashlight in all of the dark corners, he inspected the bird from the rotor head, transmission and deck, to engine mounts, drive shaft and tail rotor and rotor blades to landing gear, he confirmed, "No other visible damage, sir. Just three holes, maybe .30 caliber in the bottom of the starboard clam shell door, and three holes in the oil cooler. But now, we not only have an oil cooler to change but an engine to rebuild as well."

Ah, but Captain "Tricky Dick" was the maintenance officer, and this would be seen as a major coup because we didn't have to send out rescue planes and security troops or endanger a maintenance crew to change the oil cooler in the field. Routine mission day. Pucker factor seven on a scale of ten—times two. *Whew!* The brain committee was ready for a breather and a drink.

Happy Hour

Traditional happy hour at Marine Corps officers clubs is from 1630 to 1800 on Friday nights. The translation is 4:30 p.m. to 6:00 p.m. for pogey-bait civilians. Pogey-bait consists of candy, potato chips, peanuts and similar snacks upon which civilians are known to over indulge. Are you getting this yet?

In combat, happy hour is celebrated anytime the bar is open and the flight schedule doesn't have your name on it. Sometime during our first tour in Vietnam, after our squadron spent a three-month tour on our old familiar aircraft carrier, the USS *Princeton*, our air group commander decided we should occasionally have a day off from flight duties. Up until then, before the cruise on the ship, we had been flying seven days a week, and some of those days were very long and were often followed by nighttime scrambles to react to the urgent needs of marines in the field for emergency resupply, reinforcements, extraction or medevacs.

Apparently, according to reports from field medical officers and senior staff officers, who had studied the situation, the number of aircraft accidents and incidents due to pilot error could be correlated directly to the number of days and hours since the pilot had been on crew rest—not to be confused with Rest and Recuperation (R&R) which is a vacation period out of combat and out of the country for seven days.

Crew rest for marine combat pilots and air crew does not mean you get the day off from your regular duties. It just means you don't fly on a particular day or night—just a simple day off from flight duty. Sort of like a Sunday at home but with chores on the honey do-list.

The new Air Group instructions were for the three H-34D squadrons to rotate so each squadron would stand down from flight operations for a full day and night every seven days. We would perform our additional duties during the normal work day and "stand-down" from all flight duty. At night we were completely off duty, but if an emergency arose or in the case of a big combined operation, requiring the entire air group's support, the regular day off would be rescheduled. *Yea, right! Rescheduled to the next regularly scheduled day off!*

The routine of a stand-down day off provided for all officers and men to report to their regular duty stations. All marines are basic riflemen but all marines, who are not directly assigned as riflemen in a platoon, company and battalion, also have additional Military Occupational Specialties. This list of specialties consists of several dozen job titles like basic pilot, basic infantryman, artillery specialist and more specialized personnel, including in the aviation fields, hydraulics, avionics, engines, metal smith and so forth.

On our day off, as soon as we finished with our duties in the maintenance department, operations, supply or administration, everyone that drank, except the duty officer of the day and the staff noncommissioned officer of the day, would head for happy hour at their designated clubs. The officers club at the Ky Ha Airfield consisted of a thatched roof building, previously in use as a church, which was purchased from the civilian town of Ky Ha. Our support squadron marines, who were doing Seabee like work erecting tents, building outhouses and showers, were also tasked with the chore of going into the village and liberating the church building piece by piece and putting it back together again on our designated site.

The sides of the new building were open to the elements but the roof was nearly waterproof and only leaked a little during the monsoon season. The men also dug a three-foot deep trench on two sides of the building for us to dive into in case of mortar attacks. Of course, when it rained the ditch filled up with water so we all joked about drowning during an attack.

The attack never came. The air group commander made our lives a little more uncomfortable by not allowing indigenous personnel to work on the base at Ky Ha as construction employees, maids, kitchen help or other miscellaneous tasks like burning the oil drums from under the outhouses, filling sandbags and building defensive bunkers. We attributed the lack of a mortar attack or infantry infiltration to the restriction of indigenous personnel from our base, thus limiting leakage of the location of our defensive positions to the enemy. Our sister air group, stationed about 60 miles north of Ky Ha at Marble Mountain, near Da Nang, allowed many indigenous workers and was regularly under attack. Most of the attacks included accurate pin-point mortars and very well organized enemy infantry attacks at the weakest links on the perimeter defense positions. However, the Marble Mountain Air Facility was on flat ground which provided excellent visibility to the enemy and our site at Ky Ha was on a slope on the eastern side of a ridge so we were not visible from the western side or from the river on the west and north which made our site essentially protected in defilade.

I didn't know it at the time but there were actually a few Marine Corps pilots in our squadron who did not drink. There were also some pilots who would have one or two drinks and quit. I found out about these nondrinking, or light drinking, misfits one night on our scheduled "stand-down." Those of us who did drink were in the habit of heading straight to the bar around 1700 and loading up.

About 2200 one moonless night, a messenger, a lieutenant, from our squadron Operations Department came running into the bar yelling, "Any pilot who has not had too much to drink, report to the Ready Room."

I knew I'd had too much to drink but I went down the hill to the Ready Room anyway. The squadron executive officer was there and addressed me. "What the hell are you doing here, Pincer? I know you've been at the bar ever since it opened."

"Yes, sir. I just came to see if I can help out?"

"You're not flying tonight, Pincer, but you can get over to the flight line and see if they need any help getting the aircraft ready to go."

"Yes, sir."

I left the Ready Room, which was a hard back tent with the sides rolled up, but I lingered just outside to hear the briefing. It seems a battalion of marines were taking heavy casualties from a large regular North Vietnamese force and were requesting reinforcements or withdrawal. The duty squadrons were already overtasked with resupply and medevacs, and our squadron was being tasked to provide the transport for the reinforcements or to pull out the marines that were in trouble. The decision had not yet been made whether it would be an insertion of reinforcements or an extraction of the troops in danger.

I headed for the flight line as instructed, but as I suspected, help was not needed there or anywhere else for that matter. The regular night maintenance crew of noncommissioned officers, and men had the situation well in hand. All of the aircraft, which were in an "up" flight status, were already checked by their crew-chief—guns and ammo were loaded and the yellow sheets were ready to be signed off by the pilots when they were assigned. The sergeants and corporals, the ones who are really responsible for running the Marine Corps and their men, were well ahead of the game.

The mission, as it was finally determined, was flown as an extraction. Our crews were required to fly on a moonless night into dark zones that were just big enough to accommodate the size of the aircraft, hold the aircraft on the ground under fire, while the marines loaded themselves, their equipment and their wounded and then deliver them to a rear echelon position. It took three trips to get it all done. None of the aircraft, not a single one, sustained any damage other than a few holes in the skin from small arms fire.

Two days later, the marines decided to go back into the same zones and insert twice as many troops. Our squadron was assigned the mission which would be accomplished as a routine insertion, in broad daylight, into the same area of the previous extraction, but which the enemy had now abandoned. The ultimate difference however, in spite of now completely sober pilots and the absence of enemy fire, was that almost all of the aircraft sustained some damage from clipping the trees with the main rotor blades or tail rotor blades, broken tail wheels, over-speeding the rotor head or over-boosting the engine.

The result of the experience eventually led to a joke about the rule concerning drinking, smoking and flying. The actual rule is stated as, "No drinking for 24 hours before flying and no smoking within 50 feet of the aircraft." The joke-enhanced rule for combat became,

"No drinking or smoking within 50 feet of the aircraft." In reality, the flight schedule for the following day usually did not come out until late in the evening but a copy would be delivered to the bar as soon as it was printed. Pilots in the bar would check to see if they were scheduled to fly early, and if so, they would stop drinking and head to bed. We actually monitored each other to make sure this procedure was followed.

Extension To Duty

"What the fuck is this crap? I hear we're gonna have to stay an extra month." I overheard a conversation from some of the lieutenants talking loudly at a table in the bar. The army and air force have 12-month tours, and we have 13, and now we're gonna be extended to 14?

Another said, "Yeah, I guess so. Apparently, the new birds are not coming out of the factory fast enough, or they're not getting combat ready modifications fast enough, to meet the planned relief date."

"So now we're lookin' at October before we can bail outta here?"

"Well, maybe... The XO thinks we might be lookin' at November for some."

"Fuck it. Gimme another drink. I'm gonna get so drunk I'll still be too hungover to fly tomorrow. I don't give a damn if I'm on the flight schedule or not." Their conversation seemed to conclude.

I didn't participate in the complaining. Our original tour of duty in Vietnam was scheduled to be 12 months—September 1965 through August 1966. The three-week Trans Pacific ride on the *Princeton* didn't count. However, in August '66 we were informed we would not start rotating personnel out of Vietnam until October. There was so much bitching from the lieutenants, the CO called a muster to go over the complaints and explain the reason for the delay. All but three of the lieutenants were reserve officers who did not plan on careers in the Marine Corps and were very outspoken about their dissatisfaction.

The problem was a delay in readiness of the new CH-46 helicopters, which were slated to replace our old H-34Ds, but there simply were not enough new airplanes with the appropriate combat modifications to replace us.

Danny and I made up two-thirds of the regular marine officers, and we volunteered to stay even longer, if necessary. Our CO decided to rotate everyone by seniority within his rank. Junior man in each rank would go home first, and then the next most junior would follow. As one of the most junior first lieutenants, I would have gone home at the beginning of the rotation, but Danny and I asked the XO to separate the regular officers and rotate us after all of the reserve lieutenants were gone. The third regular lieutenant was not happy about the suggestion, but he was fairly senior academy grad like Danny and would have gone home toward the end of the lieutenant rotations anyway.

As soon as each individual rotation date was known, most marines made "short-timer" chains of one kind or another. Mine was made of simple linked paperclips from which I could remove one clip each day. By the time I was made aware of my rotation date, there were only 21 days to go, so the chain was only long enough to go around my 18-inch neck for two days. Since we were so busy with daily flights I had little time to think about it. Sometimes it would be three or four days before I would pull the chain off its hook by my rack and remove the clips.

The one-month extension covered the necessary overlap, although the start of the gradual rotation, which started in October, was not complete until sometime in November. Everyone was home before Thanksgiving.

The trip home was long and lonely. We had gone to war together on a magnificent ship as comrades in arms. Warriors of the world banded together to go and do whatever was necessary to protect the people of South Vietnam from the aggressors of the north. We were sent home alone, dead or alive, wounded or whole, one by one, on contracted commercial airliners.

Our squadron commanding officer and the sergeant major were the last to go. As is always the case with marines—take care of the troops first—they will always be heroes of mine.

I flew from Da Nang to Hawaii to San Francisco. I could have waited In San Francisco for another day to catch a flight to the Southern California area, but I was too anxious to get home. I took a cab to the bus station and caught the next available ride to Los Angeles. That was a long ride also. About another eight hours but better than waiting overnight.

I wondered if Jamila would be anxious for me to come home. We had some communication by letter during the tour. Routine stuff about our daughter, the weather and the war news at home. I told her how much I missed her, which was very true, but actually, most of the time, I just tried to keep my mind otherwise occupied. Dwelling on her—the absence of her, the sexiness of her, the idea of her—always brought on a problem in a situation where there was no relief in sight.

I wondered if life would be the same between us, or would the long separation cause a significant change? We had always been so open and honest with each other. I missed her terribly and longed for her company more and more as the miles clicked down on the California freeway at a pace that seemed even slower than the last days that dragged by in Vietnam. The trip would require a bus change in Los Angeles or a cab in order to get to Tustin. I dreamed of our days together in Pensacola and fell asleep in the cramped, uncomfortable and stinky surroundings of the Greyhound bus. My daydreams turned into night dreams, which probably would have been a wet dream, but the bouncing bus finally rumbled to a stop in downtown Los Angeles.

I realized it would definitely have to be a taxi to Tustin because I didn't want to waste another minute getting home to Jamila. Hopefully, she would still be in bed and wanting to take care of what the dreams had caused. *That could be the perfect ending to the tour. Who needs parades, adoring crowds, welcome-home parties and all that crap.*

END

Epilogue

It was the suggestion of my AA sponsor that I write down all of the past or present significant events or circumstances that brought humiliation, anguish, or pain into my life. The original idea included the concept of ridding myself of bad memories by wadding up the written words and throwing them away or burning them to represent the physical act of leaving behind or dismissing the pain, like he suggested with the fifth step, and then forgiving myself for my mistakes or my part in the events. As you can see, most of the time, I was unable to follow his suggestion completely. Sometimes when the deepest sadness or most painful regrets would send me into a black hole of depression, I would follow the directions entirely, but of course, it was still there on the computer memory—or these days, in "cloud" storage—and it remains in the recesses of my mind in a similar manner.

More and more stories are revealed as I peel back the layers of memory, but those are the subject of other books as *Slurred Saga II*, about another airplane, another combat tour in Vietnam, another period of single life and a Caribbean Island adventure; and *Slurred Saga III*, which includes noncombat adventures and setting a world aviation record.

We like that! The brain committee is not always so unanimous. We've found a new way of living a self-examined life, and we're earning the privilege of making intentional, thoughtful, meaningful decisions rather than just existing and muddling through. While life is not perfect, it is not expected to be. The committee has learned that being sober is not just about not drinking. It's an adventure and process through which we travel while learning to live our lives without alcohol or other mind-altering drugs.

Yes, along with several well-qualified and respected leaders, my Higher Power now occupies the chairman's seat on the brain committee and has veto power over proposals by other members. The jerk who used to say, *"Let's go get drunk and be somebody,"* has been long gone for over three decades, and I don't miss him at all.

But if you liked these stories, the next *Slurred Saga* begins at homecoming with exotic Jamila in California next year.

www.ingramcontent.com/pod-product-compliance
Lightning Source LLC
Chambersburg PA
CBHW030513080526
44586CB00011B/171